THE AMERICAN
MEDICAL MONEY MACHINE
THE DESTRUCTION OF HEALTHCARE IN AMERICA
& THE RISE OF MEDICAL TOURISM

JAMES R. GOLDBERG

Published by
Homunculus S.A. de C.V.

Library of Congress Cataloging-in-Publication Data
Goldberg, James R.

The American Medical Money Machine: The Destruction of
Healthcare in America and the Rise of Medical Tourism
James R. Goldberg.

Categories
Healthcare - Political Sciens - Current Affairs

ISBN 978-0-615-31887-5
2 4 6 8 10 9 7 5 3 1
First Edition - Rev. 02-10

Jain Lemos, Editing Consultant
Cover design by Brittany Jackson

ABOUT THE AUTHOR

Dr. JAMES R. GOLDBERG, has served as a senior level executive and CEO with deep experience in running early and mid-stage technologically complex businesses with a major focus in healthcare.

He has been a Principal of one of the world's leading technology/business consultancies, the PA Consulting Group, based in London, England.

He served as Executive Director of the Lawrence Livermore National Laboratories healthcare initiative, a U.S. Defense Research Laboratory program aimed at converting military technology into medical wonders.

Jim has invented over 12 technologies that have received U.S. and International Patents.

Goldberg earned his undergraduate and advanced degrees at Michigan State University, New York University, Stanford University and European study programs including the Sorbonne, France, The University of Mainz, Germany and the University of Madrid, Spain.

www.theamericanmedicalmoneymachine.com

www.bumrungraddeath.com

A telephone call from Bangkok brought the shocking news that the author's only child, Joshua, was dead. He was twenty-three years old.

That call set in motion a cascade of shocking events and discoveries revealed by James R. Goldberg in The American Medical Money Machine: A double murder has occurred—the murder of Joshua and the murder of medical care in the United States.

Recounting the details surrounding the death of his son, Goldberg quickly discovers that terrible forces are at play—forces armed with unlimited money and power—whose only ambition is to cover up and protect the alleged perpetrators in the United States, half a globe away from the scene of the crime in Bangkok.

Goldberg's three-year examination is meticulously documented. The murders his investigation reveals not only the actual causes for the death of his son but also a vast and previously undiscovered ring of corruption in America.

To add even further dimension, plans have been laid for decades by the American insurance cartel to send patients overseas for cheaper care. This foreign care will significantly increase profits for the cartel while providing no assurances of safety or recourse for injured patients.

Frustrated after attempts in Thailand to find justice for his son are disregarded, Goldberg turns to alternative American authorities and organizations for assistance.

Pursuing answers and pleas for assistance, Goldberg runs head on into The Joint Commission (JC), a quasi-governmental U.S. agency charged with accrediting hospitals. The JC actively conceals information, obstructs justice and protects Bumrungrad, one of the hospitals it had accredited and is obligated to monitor and police.

Based on a tip, Goldberg expands his investigation into organ harvesting and trafficking. A frightening new question arises: Were his son's precious young organs the motive behind his murder?

As Goldberg painstakingly traces organ-harvesting practices in South East Asia, mounting evidence points to organ theft as the motive for murder.

The American Medical Money Machine weaves two stories and brings us all to a comprehensive intersection; we are shown the reasons behind the current crisis in the United States health care system as well as the way in which Medical Tourism is being aggressively marketed as a solution to this crisis.

Goldberg makes it clear that understanding the odious intentions of the Money Machine is the first step in making informed decisions about what to do next.

IT IS A MATTER OF LIFE AND DEATH.

CONTENTS

Dedication
For My Son, Joshua

*His Laughter Can be Heard
by Anyone Listening to the Wind.....*

Acknowledgements & Comments

I like books that allow for a quick read. I want to get the big picture and usually do not have time or patience for anything less. Yet, once my attention is captured and if my interest deepens, I want to uncover more.

I imagine that you, my readers, feel the same.

In undertaking the writing of this complex story—really, many stories within one story—I want to extend to you the same courtesy that I wish many authors would extend to me.

I have structured my book so that my narrative and major points are found in the primary text font.

My thoughts, reflections, questions and conclusions are written for a fast read. Secondary and tertiary information, such as reports, excerpts, footnotes, bullet points and charts, are presented in alternate fonts. I've done this in the hope that if a point piques your interest, you can delve deeper, at your own choice.

**Further references may be discovered on:
www.theamericanmedicalmoneymachine.com,
www.bumrungraddeath.com**

I make no pretense that this work is a traditional, academically researched story. However, I have been as robust as possible in supporting each of the claims made. Many of them challenge common wisdom and provide a dramatic counter-view to the prevailing "mindset."

I have endeavored to tell a complex story in the following pages. In order to gain a full understanding of my assertions it is necessary to read the entire book. Like many novels, the story does not become clear until the very end. This is the case with The American Medical Money Machine.

Also, to keep the pace of the book fast, a page turner, if you will, I have placed very important information in the appendix. The information that resides at the end of the book is there to be read and understood. It supplies details and facts which directly support the text. I urge you to read these important notes.

Thanks to the inspiration and courage of Noam Chomsky for his brilliant and insightful analysis of the hegemonic direction that the United States has taken. Michael Moore is applauded for his film, *Sicko*, which highlights snippets of a much larger story, which I have endeavored here to tell in far deeper and broader depth.

Deep thanks are only one small way of expressing my gratitude to Dr. Anna Feldman Vertkin, M.D, Jain Lemos, Andrea Augenblick, Kent Allen, Brittany Jackson, John Joss, Alistair Henderson, Helen Haskell, my anonymous advisers in Bangkok and the millions of visitors to Joshua's website, **www.bunrungraddeath.com.** They have brought me wisdom, direction and at times, comfort.

Thanks also to those who provided their own personal case histories. I extend appreciation to those, who at great risk provided inside information regarding the workings of Bumrungrad Hospital and the Joint Commission.

I am grateful for the many thoughtful conversations I have had with Walt Bogdanich, three time Pulitzer Prize winner of the *New York Times*.

Gratitude is also appropriate for the courtesies shown to me by Emilia DiSanto, assistant to Senator Charles Grassley, Senate Finance Committee.

Leslie June Taylor Randolph has my ever-lasting admiration. She pushed me over the edge to confront my demons and helped me summon the courage to dedicate myself to completing this work. It has not been easy re-living, through writing and countless edits, the death of my son. I made a promise to him, and to you, that I would.

Deep wishes for happiness for the dozens of Josh's friends who rallied to celebrate his life.

INTERNATIONAL FORWARD

Do not be misled by the title of this book: The American Medical Money Machine is concerned with the effects of a vast and worldwide problem.

The birth of the problem was in the United States. The consequences of the problem are international. No country, developed or not, is immune from the ramifications of the insidious greed and contempt found in America as it relates to healthcare.

Corruption is not the only problem afflicting healthcare in the United States and elsewhere. Massive public service departments overwhelm tax payers and deprive patients such as in Great Britain, where, by the year 2007, more than 600,000 non-medical workers swamped its National Health System. In Great Britain there are more bureaucrats than doctors!

Flooded with bureaucrats who supervise and whose supervisors supervise the supervised, the cost of the English system has become staggering and unmanageable. Management structures stand in the way of the sacred relationship between doctor and patient, adding staggering cost to health care. The issue here: what do these management structures add to increasing the quality of care at affordable rates?

The American systems of Medicare and Medicaid have nearly 500,000 employees. This overhead burden, as in the U.K., deprives patients of real care and limits the amount of available money which a doctor and patient, together, decide is in the best interest of optimal treatment. These bureaucrats have no understanding of medicine and drastically interfere with the one and one relationship between patient and physician.

The American Medical Money Machine, is in effect, a cartel operated by formal or informal agreement. The term is roughly defined as a cartel is an (explicit) agreement among firms or producers that agree to coordinate prices and production.

The opportunities for fraud are enormous. American Medicine, instead of being measured by successful outcomes, is measured by hospitals and administrators by "billing events." Billing events are encouraged and are carefully measured. Successful medical outcomes are not.

Certainly, the United States does not have a monopoly on greed and unrestrained avarice. Nor does the United States have a corner on instituting management structures that produce lots of motion and virtually no action.

Where money and power is concerned, the world is populated with government and corporate entities that will seize on any opportunity to scam and scheme, steal and lie. Many will do so claiming good intentions and a warm heart. They will go out of their way to sugar coat their sinister motives. The more money available, the more money stolen.

In the case of the United States, the cost of healthcare is equivalent to the entire French Gross Domestic Product (GDP), or $2.252 trillion in 2007. Yet, the French medical system stands first in worldwide health rankings where the U.S., which was number one in 1965, now hovers around 40th and is dropping rapidly.

Countries who proffer real social concern have exerted controls in the realm of healthcare, recognizing the sacred covenant which a government owes its people to make every attempt, whether successful or not, to formalize sincere efforts to enable the well being of their people.

Many countries have socialized their medical system in the hopes of creating a level playing field and equal access to quality care. The results are mixed, but the effort has, I believe, been made in earnest. The U.S., however, has been riddled with corruption and greed in healthcare ever since Medicare, the U.S. system designed to provide medical care for the poor and elderly, was made law. This wave of corruption started in 1965 when the U.S. began its long downfall in quality and safety of medical care.

Socialized Medicine = Rationing

Consequent to healthcare rationing, which is an unfortunate by product of the socialized medical model, people have found themselves placed on intolerably long waiting lists in order to gain access to care. Many, in desperation and concern, whether justified or not, have sought alternatives.

The main alternative has been to create private systems to stand alongside of public options. This model obviously favors those who can afford to pay the "freight." The result is a multi-class healthcare system; one for those of modest or little means and the other for the wealthy.

The exceptionally high cost of medication in the United States is further exacerbated by the need to have a prescription from a doctor for every RX medication. So, where as a patient in Mexico or India may purchase a generic or brand name drug without a prescription (with the exception of controlled substances) U.S. residents must first make an appointment with a doctor and then pay more for their medications than in any other place on earth. The system in the U.S. did not evolve by accident. Powerful interests have seen to it that every opportunity for profit is realized.

The large U.S. pharmaceutical companies have virtually eliminated competition and have instituted laws which require that a patient cannot self treat with a medication they already know is likely to cure their problem.

Many other issues are at play that explain why the cost of healthcare in the United States often places people in a position where they cannot afford insurance or private payment for a doctor. Nearly 50 million Americans have no form of insurance at all.

Those who do have insurance are often subject to disputes with insurance companies who refuse to pay for benefits or who argue with a doctor's diagnosis and treatment plan. Sadly, the insurance industry has profited enormously by withholding patient benefits and physician payments. The amount of corruption, on top of this atrocious state of affairs has made theft and fraud commonplace in the United States healthcare system.

Few violators are caught and few are prosecuted. The large insurance companies have been given a license, by the Federal Government, to steal at will and although some of these firms are fined or sanctioned, their executives are never held responsible personally for their criminal actions—almost none go to jail.

The situation is getting worse.

Another model, which has been growing rapidly and is about to explode in popularity; to seek health care in other countries whose cost structures are lower, making care, which is unavailable at home, affordable even for those of modest means. This model is called Medical Tourism or, as I prefer to call it Medical Outsourcing.

The phenomenon of Medical Tourism has its roots in the "accidental" tourist seeking care while traveling. This quickly gave way to those who were seeking cosmetic operations that, in most countries, are simply not covered under any public or private insurance plan.

Hence, places like Brazil, Mexico, Thailand and others started to deliberately draw people willing to travel to distant places in search of the appearance of youth.

Surgeries or treatments not yet legal in one country may be conducted, legally, in another. Many countries do not carefully regulate what can and may not be done medically. Surgeries not approved in a given country can be had elsewhere without problem. Medications, not approved for use in one country, are regularly dispensed in another.

It is, therefore, not surprising to discover that many American healthcare companies have been working on the plan of exporting patients overseas for many decades. Many of the facilities to which Americans are beginning to be sent for medical treatment are, indeed, owned and or operated by American interests.

Safety First

In Europe the safety of a drug must be demonstrated. In the United States, both safety and effectiveness must be scientifically demonstrated before the medication can be sold.

In the United States and most parts of Western Europe, doctors are restrained from receiving bribes and kickbacks from pharmaceutical companies for using their drugs. In many other countries, no such restrictions exist and companies who are restricted at home have a field day in pushing medications, like drug dealers, to doctors and patients, whether the drug is suitable for their condition or not.

In Thailand, as an example, it is a well established policy that doctors receive a 20% kick back on medications they prescribe. Pfizer has been a leader in Thailand, bribing doctors to use their drugs.

One Pfizer drug, Neurontin is prescribed in Thailand for all sorts of purposes for which the drug was never formally licensed in the U.S. This is not a trivial drug and has many stunning side effects.

Because it is expensive, Thai doctors often prescribe this drug in very large dosages and for conditions totally unsuitable for its use. The more the Thai physician prescribes, the greater the amount of money he or she pockets. Neurontin is linked directly to an increase in pancreatic and other forms of cancers. Apparently, for money, this is not of concern to Thai doctors, the Thai Government or Pfizer. The patient suffers while others profit.

In addition to the free hand that drug companies have in actually paying doctors to use, or more correctly put, misuse their medications, drug companies are free to provide vacations, cash bonuses, subsidies, luxury dining-all as consideration for the use of medications. The patients are dammed.

Going to Extremes to Avoid the Unavoidable

Those who may be dying of incurable diseases will go anywhere and spend any amount even on the slightest chance that some therapy might save their lives.

Twenty five years ago, Laetrile, which is still thought by many to be a cancer cure, drew thousands of people from the United States to Mexico in hopes that their lives might be spared.

The clinical evidence for Laetrile still shows no difference between Laetrile and a placebo.

Where there is smoke, there is fire. In 1995, UnitedHealthcare Group, an American insurance behemoth, started selling an insurance product for locating organs around the world for those who were not likely to receive lifesaving organ transplants. Reliable news is now becoming available which verifies that a worldwide organ trafficking business is in full swing.

Many countries that engage in the sale or purchase of organs refuse to acknowledge or discuss this dramatic problem.

The Organ Grinders

In my chapter on Organ Trafficking, which has now become a worldwide black market business, I discuss in detail how prisoners in China are often the enlisted "donors" for recipient patients from around the world.

Children in India or other economically desperate countries are often sold or stolen to become donors of kidneys, livers, eyes or even hearts.

The degree to which the black market traffic in organs has evolved is just now becoming understood: from New York, London, and Eastern Europe and to South East Asia.

Left unregulated, all sorts of terrible crimes are committed and the success of the "grafts" (transplants) are usually very poor considering the diseases the donated organs might carry as well as the sub-optimal conditions in which the organs are "harvested."

No world treaties exist that provide protection for recipients or donors. The amounts of money squeezed off are astronomical and have attracted organized crime and quasi-established organizations that benefit with impunity and without responsibility, whether donors or patients live or die.

The lack of regulation in countries such as Thailand, India, Singapore and Malaysia, to name but a few, make preying on relatively rich foreigners a paradise of opportunity.

Too Many Patients, Too Few Doctors

Adding to this complex world wide medical crisis, there is a global shortage of doctors. As a result of declining U.S. reimbursement levels and oppression by the U.S. Government and insurance companies, doctors are fleeing from medicine in droves.

These physicians are either not replaced or their positions are being filled with nurse practitioners or by younger, largely foreign born and trained doctors who are marginally competent, inexperienced and unlicensed! Their schooling and training requirements are far less than in the United States. The U.S. recruitment of medical personnel is big business, yet, even with aggressive effort the shortage remains significant.

Despite active recruitment, the shortage of doctors and nurses in the United States is beginning to crest as the baby boomer population comes of age and healthcare needs increase.

The problems will soon become unmanageable based on the present system of corruption and administrative overload.

A quiet debate in the U.S. Congress has been held for the last several years to accept foreign trained doctors, without re-certification or examination to make up for the current shortfall of U.S. trained physicians.

This debate has not yet been resolved, but it appears to be moving in the direction of relaxation, rather than fortifying credentials.

The problem and solution equation is simple: either bring in less expensive and experienced doctors or send patients to places where care is less expensive. The U.S. government working closely with the insurance industry has spawned a situation in which healthcare in America has declined in quality and expanded in cost. The taxpayers have born the brunt of corruption and are now faced with the alternatives of either not receiving care or seeking it elsewhere. In either event, the insurance industry in America is set to profit.

Properly and competently trained doctors in the United States simply cannot practice medicine as the politically dominated insurance industry has forced on them more and more "cost savings," a metaphor for underpayment. The model is about cost, not cure or correct treatment.

Well trained physicians who have spent a fortune on their education and years of their lives, cannot countenance the absurdity of delivering responsible medicine based on a four minute patient visit and the recipe care demanded of them by both the government and the insurance mafia.

Those doctors or patients who resist face punishment, blacklisting and extradition from their chosen professions. Patients who protest are also black balled and dropped from their healthcare plans or saddled with health premiums, co pays and insurance "deductibles" which are totally out of their reach.

Caregivers and patients suffer financial ruin and indignity while the health insurance industry bags unfathomable amounts of money for their senior executives. This industry systematically looks for ways to disenfranchise quarrelsome doctors and discard sick patients.

Something is going to give. The situation is going to become much, much worse—not just in America, but throughout the world.

Good Story, Bad Story

There are important implications both for the countries who are exporting patients and for those countries who are importing patients. Since the entire Medical Outsourcing phenomenon is relatively new, these implications have not been well researched or considered: it is mandatory that Medical Outsourcing AKA Medical Tourism be thoroughly understood.

The concept of Medical Tourism was born in Thailand and sponsored by the American executives who run Bumrungrad International Hospital.

Bumrungrad is a publicly traded company on the Thai Stock Exchange but evidence exists to show that the company is secretly controlled by one of its original owners, Tenet Healthcare of the United States.

The government of Thailand, anxious to boost their economy by attracting more tourists, signed on, supporting the concept of importing patients from around the world to fill the gaps in healthcare around the world.

They correctly predicted the chaos and pandemonium which was about to settle in on vast portions of the Western World populations who were seeking alternatives.

The Thai government, prodded by Bumrungrad Hospital and their avaricious affiliates, saw the opportunity to build their airlines, hotels, restaurants, tax base and resorts and thought the idea of combining medical care with vacations, hence Medical Tourism, was a good one. These countries (Thailand, India, Singapore, UAE, etc.,) have since spent billions and more than 300 hospitals around the world have sought and obtained the coveted American accreditation of the JCI, a fictitious imprimatur sold to hospitals. This accreditation means that these hospitals would be trusted by the public and could accept American and British insurance policies for a wider range of procedures.

I discuss the fraud wrapped up in this bogus accreditation in many sections of this work.

These countries are no longer interested in attracting a tourist who becomes ill while traveling.

What they really want and are building is an international infrastructure which is an extension of the American medical network!

In other words, they want to become a part of the "network" of providers for which patients, insurance companies and governments will pay, but at far lower rates than on U.S. turf.

European Union medical care which has been socialized is burdened by very heavy overhead costs and prescription of cheap medications which have often been replaced by better, newer and more effective medicines. Cancer rates throughout Europe are significantly higher than in the United States.

European hospitals are largely staffed by foreign trained doctors whose medical experience and competence is questionable. Britain often recruits doctors-from Arab countries.

Recently, approximately 12 Arab doctors, who were also terrorists, were foiled when their plan to kill British patients was discovered. The British jailed the terrorists and then proceeded to hire replacement doctors—from Arab countries!

Medical Outsourcing appears to be good for the exporting countries who benefit by lower costs, even factoring in the cost of transportation. The importing countries are excited because they will be bringing into their countries a whole new generation of travelers who will receive medical treatment and recuperate in a beach-side resort or hotel; places once considered distant and exotic.

On the surface, all of this looks fine. Scratching a bit below, however, the story is very different.

In the event of botched medical procedures performed in Thailand or India, patients return home with infections and other life threatening problems. It then falls on the healthcare systems of the "home" countries to fix what was broken somewhere else.

Unhappy Down Under

The Australians have reported alarming consequences for butchered surgeries abroad and the enormous financial strain the "fixes," when possible, have placed on their medical systems.

Since injured patients are not likely to return to Bangkok to get "fixed," it falls to the governments to pick up the pieces. Australia, in close proximity to South East Asia, has seen an alarming number of problems and their news media and government have voiced outrage.

In addition to trying to glue the broken parts back together again, Australia has taken great umbrage with doctors from foreign lands, particularly Thailand, who arrange for clandestine meetings with Australians. Clandestine meetings in hotels throughout the Australian Continent to consult with Aussie patients destined for treatment in another country are widespread and uncontrollable.

Correctly, Australians are very unhappy with foreign doctors practicing medicine, without a license, on their home land. The Aussie police have attempted to control this problem, but without much success.

Australians have no legal protection or recourse if harmed while being treated abroad. Hence, economic recovery is virtually impossible as most countries who import patients have little or weak malpractice laws and regulations.

No Legal Protection

Countries where Medical Tourism is being actively developed have legal systems which are complex and arcane. Judgment is typically left to a panel of judicial commissioners, who are prone to being "influenced" in one way or the other.

There are no International treaties, as of this writing in 2009, which protect patient rights. This is a serious problem.

Making matters worse, doctors in places like the United States will not touch patients who have been injured overseas. They don't want to assume the liability of attempting to correct some other doctor's mistake.

American physicians and hospitals at times have no experience with the kinds of surgeries that may be performed in a place like Bumrungrad.

Unless these patients want to make yet another trip and incur additional expense, they may well die or live miserably with an injury for which they cannot find any doctor to attend.

Draining Resources and Lower Prices

Importing countries suffer from a drain of their best doctors, lured away to work on foreign patients. These doctors receive much higher compensation and enjoy enhanced prestige. This leaves the native population with fewer well-trained doctors to attend to their care: the phenomenon of Medical Outsourcing expands this problem will become more acute.

In addition, blood supplies donated by locals are withheld from locals. This donated blood supply is held for foreigners who will pay more and will receive priority above the natives.

The costs of medications in overseas countries are far lower than in the U.S. or Europe. This is because they have burgeoning free markets for medications and competition is encouraged, especially with generic equivalents.

As foreigners pay higher prices for these same drugs, the cost to the local population is also likely to increase. This makes access to needed drugs more difficult for natives and spells trouble in the long term.

From the viewpoint of the exporting countries, as patients begin to migrate overseas for cheaper care, further pressure will be exerted on home doctors and hospitals to lower their costs in order to be competitive with foreign health industry suppliers.

The U.S. as with many other countries has already sought to save money by paying doctors less. Doctors are leaving medicine in the U.S. because they have lost their license to practice independent medicine. Doctors have become corporate slaves. They must do as they are told and accept capricious payments from corrupt insurance companies.

U.S. corruption runs so deep that only 24% of the 2007 dollars paid out for healthcare actually reached the patient and the doctor. Insurance companies practice medicine without license and override the decisions of the practicing physician on a daily basis. In essence, medicine does not exist in the United States any longer. Corporate industry administered healthcare has taken over, lock, stock and barrel.

Call the Concierge

As foreign hospitals join what in the U.S. are called "provider networks" patients will be forced by the government and their close ally, the insurance mafia, to choose a lower price option; the overseas "opportunity."

U.S.-based nurse practitioners and far less experienced doctors will receive lower amounts of money for their services and our best doctors will either leave medicine entirely or seek to establish private practices, if the law permits, to establish a client base of the wealthy.

Concierge services have sprung up where one pays a yearly or monthly fee simply to gain access to a doctor. This is on top of the cost of insurance or private payment. Prices for Concierge services typically amount to $25,000 USD a year.

In the United States there is no competition in the healthcare marketplace.

Free market forces in healthcare ended twenty years ago as the insurance cartel set its hooks in the public with the encouragement of the United States Government.

The U.S. Healthcare system is in shambles: patients are treated like numbers or objects. This debacle promises to only become worse as new programs are instituted and controlled by the same insurance and government Mafia which has seen to the downfall of truly excellent medical care in the United States. As patients and doctors have suffered grievously, a select few individuals and corporate entities have become fabulously wealthy.

Despite the promise of the "boom" of tourism to essentially third world countries who are becoming the importers of disenfranchised patients, the new sources of funds that are set to flow into these countries are not likely to be distributed with an even hand.

The medical money machine in the U.S. has been laying the groundwork for this global outreach for years. Many major corporations have invested heavily abroad, entering into partnerships that own, control or manage foreign hospitals. In essence, the problem the insurance Mafia has created at home, which works exclusively to their financial advantage, is being solved by sending patients abroad.

I am not suggesting that free markets should be restricted. However, these markets, especially when it comes to health care, must be tightly controlled with respect to patient care, quality and safety. At present, no such regulations exist and the opportunity for corruption, death and havoc is overwhelming. In the last chapter of this work, I do propose some solutions to deal with the oncoming crisis. This is a major, global crisis which is of concern around the world.

Hardly anyone knows that this is happening. It is happening right in your own backyard.

The March of the Money Machine

Corporate and government interests in the U.S. have rarely operated without a selfish agenda. Perhaps, the Marshall Plan after WWII was an exception. There have been few others.

As the United States medical money machine goes global, the entire world will suffer if the machine is not controlled and regulated by strict international agreements. Patients must be given legal guarantees and protections, that no matter where they go, they can count on a world standard of quality, care and safety. If something does go wrong, which is the nature of health care; there must be mechanisms to seek justice and compensation. Incompetence and greed must be controlled, allowing for a global system of care to arise that provides real assurances and not just promises to people whose lives are being placed in the balance.

I have learned how the American healthcare system can be demolished by the greed and brutality of corporate and government incompetence. I have been personal witness to the rise of Medical Tourism and the plans set to create a new wave of health care around the world.

I learned this after my only child, Joshua, while a patient in a U.S. accredited hospital in Bangkok, Thailand: Bumrungrad International mysteriously died at 23 years of age. This tragedy took place on February 23, 2006 at 9:00 PM. His death changed my life.

I hope that reading this book will change yours.

Never Forget: At One Time or Another, We Are All Patients

I pray that my discoveries will help to create an uproar and demand that this society reorganize its priorities and bestow on its people the highest recognition of their worth, the honor of great healthcare, devoid of greed or deceit, fraud or theft.

The stink of corruption in medical care must be washed out of the fabric of our culture.

This book is not intended to be encyclopedic, as the examination of each of the stories buried within would fill many volumes.

My intention is to set the context and to get to the key points which involve "social engineering," and the imminent danger which this terrible reality holds for all of us.

With luck and perspiration, other works will follow, on paper and on the screen, which will help illuminate the drama of the unbelievable journey on which I have embarked.

About the Structure of the Book

First, we will walk through the news of Josh's death through my meeting with my son's killers. Then, we will step back to look at the larger issues of the history of corruption in the American health care industry, how it got so bad and is about to become even worse with the advent of Medical Tourism.

We will then cycle back to the details of Josh's actual murder and its complex cover up. The motive behind his assination was to harvest his organs. A chapter devoted to Organ Trafficking details the scope of the international problem and the black market—a world in which my son was to become an unwitting participant.

The last chapter provides some practical social and political solutions to the inevitable problem of Medical Outsourcing. Prognostications are provided which outline what is likely to happen in this country and around the world in the next wave of corporate health care and what can be done to regulate it.

A final chapter is devoted to Josh's memory. It is, in fact, his Eulogy.

Subsections in the appendage to the book provide real suggestions for those considering medical care overseas. Additionally, an extensive bibliography have been provided as has an Afterwords describing how the book was written and the impact writing it has had on me.

The interweaving of two inextricably related stories will, in the aggregate, reveal how I learned about the entire picture. The structure, in fact, reflects the reality and the sequence of events and discoveries I actually experienced in reaching a solution to

PRELUDE ~ THE NIGHTMARE

This is the beginning of two interwoven stories. The first is the murder of my son at the internationally "self" acclaimed medical tourist Mecca, Bumrungrad International Hospital in Bangkok, Thailand. The second is the murder of the American healthcare system by covert organizations operating for astronomical self-aggrandizement, largely unrecognized by the public, who have been deliberately misinformed.

The Stinging Words Brought News
I Can Never Forget

From: Daley, Daniel N
Sent: Thursday, February 23, 2006 10:33 PM
To: Jim Goldberg
Cc: Bangkok ACS; Thitithanapak, Pattawish
Subject: Joshua GOLDBERG
Bangkok, Thailand
February 24, 2006

Dear Mr. Goldberg:

It is with deep regret that we must confirm the death on February 24, 2006 of your son, Joshua Goldberg, in Bangkok, Thailand. As I explained in my phone conversation with you, I am sending this message to assist you in making some decisions that must be faced at this time. We are prepared to help you in whatever way we can, and, if you wish, we can serve as your liaison with appropriate local authorities.

Please do not hesitate to contact us in Bangkok at the American Citizen Services unit in the Embassy's Consular Section: The time in Bangkok is 12 hours ahead of Eastern Standard Time.

The Embassy's emergency duty officer can be reached after working hours.

For further information or assistance, you may also contact the Department of State's Office of Overseas Citizen Services.

May I extend on behalf of the United States Government our sincere condolences to you in your bereavement?

Sincerely, Dan Daley
Vice Consul, American Citizens Services.

The letter from the U.S. Embassy's Vice Consul in Bangkok ended one stage of my life and started another.

One ~ NO MISTAKE

The telephone startled me. It was late on the evening of February 24, 2006.

The call was unexpected. My ear pressed to the receiver, I knew that this transmission was from far away. I recognized the hiss and the slight delay. A Dr. Peter Morley announced that he was from Bumrungrad Hospital. He said he was sorry to call with bad news.

What bad news, I thought? That my son's release from Bumrungrad was to be delayed from the next morning? That he had developed a complication? WHAT was the bad news?

Morley said that Josh was found "unresponsive" on the nurse's 6:00 AM rounds.

"What does unresponsive mean?"

Nausea overtook me. My body sank; my knees landed on the hardwood floor; my elbows broke my fall.

"What are you telling me? That my son is dead?"

"I am afraid he is."

"Impossible! Surely you must be mistaken. This MUST be about someone else. Josh is scheduled for discharge in a few hours."

"No, I am afraid it is not a mistake."

"Who are you? Is this a joke? I spoke with Josh just a few hours before. I have done so every day since he had been admitted, sometimes two or three times a day, during the past eleven days! This must be a joke! Who are you, God Damn it!"

Morley asked if someone was there to help me. I was now flat on the floor, dizzy; The river of tears had begun. The river of tears that will never end.

Morley said that Josh had been in good shape but that he might have obtained some "lollypops" while in the hospital. These "Lollys," Morley insinuated, in combination with the other medications my son was taking, could have caused his death.

(I later learned that "Lollys" are a kind of naturally derived Thai street speed.)

BOOM!

The ruse had begun. Morley, Bumrungrad's Chief Medical Officer, had just suggested that Josh was dead by his own hand. Our forensic investigators and the Thai police clearly dismissed this conjecture, but a bell once rung can not be un-rung.

Bumrungrad was to publicly ring this bell again, slandering a dead boy in an attempt to devalue his worth and his life.

I gained enough composure to demand that my son's medical records become immediately available. I told Morley that I would be at his hospital after I had buried my son; that I wanted those records and I wanted to meet with the physicians who treated my son, especially those in attendance at the time of his death.

The records were, to my surprise, produced. The key "actors" in my son's death have always been kept from me, under virtual lock and key. I have come to understand that this was for their protection.

In June of 2007, in filings with the Thai Government and the Bangkok Police, I named Dr. Morley in murder charges.

After three years of going round and about with the police in Bangkok, I realized Morley and his alleged accomplices will never be prosecuted in Thailand for the murder and the subsequent cover-up surrounding Josh's death in Bumrungrad hospital.

Josh had gone to Thailand to be ordained as a Buddhist Monk.

His life is over, but the drum of his swirling music is not still; his story and the doors he opened for me are now open for you.

I could never have guessed where that shrill call in the middle of that night would take me:

> ➤ What I would learn.
> ➤ How I would learn it.
> ➤ Who I would come to teach.
> ➤ What crimes I would uncover.
> ➤ What discoveries I would make.

What the implications of those discoveries would mean to me and, astoundingly, to everyone else.

All things are ultimately connected and one story portends another. The death of my son, tracked with another story, larger and even more terrible: The Destruction of Healthcare in America and The Rise of Medical Tourism. He was killed by people and he was killed by a terrible system.

Joshua's death lit a firestorm. I struck the match.

In the three years after Josh lost his life, I often sharp-jerk awake from a deep dream-swept sleep, rising out of the countless fathoms from the floor of my unconscious to a state of complete alertness, instantly: a frightening ride.

In the early summer of 2009, the Obama Administration is perched on the verge of unwittingly giving birth to a "new" process and system for health care in America. This may well seal a terrible fate for healthcare and forever enrich those who should be in jail. The saga appears destined to continue.

Obama's new system anticipates a socialistic distribution of medical care that promises to make big business even bigger. Their effort is cloaked in a noble robe of care for all.

Behind this image is a naked reality: unimaginable sums of

money will be given to the "insurance cartel" to "manage" in the alleged interest of the people.

It's an insidious and evil plot. It's a shameless fraud.

Before throwing the switch on a program of such social and cultural magnitude, it would be well advised to look into the black hole. This black hole has provided America progressively poorer care for patients and astronomical profits for the medical money machine.

The American Medical Money Machine Goes on Vacation

As brazenly opaque as all of the so-called establishment players have been about the death of my son, I decided to be, conversely, utterly transparent. This is a story written as social and economic changes transit from the state of glacial change to overnight revolution.

I am convinced that the invisible elephant in each of our living rooms must be made visible.

This elephant also rampages in doctor's offices, pharmacies, hospitals and the disparate and far-flung healthcare facilities of the once great American medical landscape.

The American Medical Money Machine is going international. Hold on to your hospital gowns as Medical Outsourcing becomes fully integrated into garden variety U.S. healthcare insurance policies.

The changes planned by the insurance mafia and the United States Government promise to be astounding and will affect us all.

Two ~ Doing The Necessary

The United States Embassy in Bangkok, Thailand

After numerous contacts with the Vice Consul of the United States Embassy, plans were made for Josh's final arrangements.

I was advised that the Buddhist Monastery where Josh was currently prepping for his final ordination rights was set to send seven bare-footed monks over the mountains to Bangkok, to retrieve Josh's body. They were prepared to cremate him and enshrine him in a place of great honor.

The Embassy explained that Josh's body had been taken by the Royal Thai Police to their Morgue for a post-mortem examination.

Instinctively I insisted that the Embassy and Bumrungrad Hospital retrieve and freeze samples of his peri-mortem blood for my independent analysis. This small request seemed perfunctory at the time, but was later to have major significance when both the hospital and the police refused to have the samples released to me.

Gut Wrenching Details and a Broken Heart

The endless trip from New York to Bangkok is now a blur to me. I was overcome with a numbness, yet there was a high–speed, continuous mental movie playing in my mind that recreated all that had happened in Josh's short life, and in mine.

Bangkok is city exploding with people—18 million or more. It is a city sprawling with gigantic towers and a mix of motorcycle put-puts and limousines.

Since his death had occurred over a weekend, an autopsy could not be conducted immediately. The autopsy was scheduled for Monday, February 27, 2006. The Embassy had arranged, thereafter, for Josh to be embalmed.

I felt I was living a hallucination as a Mercedes limo deftly whisked me to my hotel in the heart of Bangkok city.

First, the call in New York and now my battered body in Bangkok, a half a planet away; it was bizarre and felt almost fictitious.

In the early morning, Payson, my driver, fetched me at the Hyatt Regency and drove me to the Police morgue. The facility lay at the back of an enormous university hospital and medical school complex. Winding through a maze of short turns, stops and starts we eventually pulled up to a platform where a hearse with its rear door open stood empty and waiting.

It is without any intention of sensationalism that I must interject the following graphic details of what ensued. I do so in the hope that by adding dimension to the reality I experienced, the gravity of such an affair will be fully appreciated.

Paying to Dress the Body of My Son

I inquired as to whether my son's body was inside the Morgue. I was invited into the inner chambers, accompanied by white uniformed attendants.

Josh's mother (we had been largely estranged for over a decade), had bought burial clothing. I tucked them under my arm, trembling as I turned the corner to see my darling boy, laid out on a metal stretcher, naked.

A small woman, dead, was on a gurney next to Josh's body. I pushed the gurney holding the dead woman gently aside to be able to stand closer to my son.

He did not look dead. His ears and nose were stuffed with cotton pads and his eyes had been glued shut with adhesive. He had a full and unshaped beard. He looked as if he was asleep.

I carefully examined his body and immediately began having premonitions that things simply did not fit. Josh did not look like someone who should be dead. There were no marks on his body, no signs of resuscitation. His gaze was that of someone calmly sleeping, not dead.

My theoretical musings instantly dissolved. I could not awaken Josh, though I tried.

> ➢ Josh was dead. Morley had not lied.
> ➢ Josh did not move when I talked to him. He did not react when I whispered in his ear.
> ➢ He was there, yet he was nowhere.

The attendants were immune to my sobs and chanting; they had other business and they needed to get on with the many other bodies I suddenly noticed were positioned, helter skelter, around the morgue's antechamber.

I handed the attendants Josh's funeral clothing. They pushed the clothing back at me, clearly implying that if I wanted the boy dressed, I would need to do so myself.

The 24-hour trip and sleepless nights before had taken their toll. My knees gave way. I staggered outside until the attendants clothed my son's corpse. I paid the attendants three U.S. dollars to dress my only boy. They thanked me and disappeared.

Doing the Necessary

The head attendant appeared in a few minutes and asked me back in to the morgue. Josh was still on his steel gurney; the gurney had been covered with a muslin sheet. His coffin was beside him. Bright white and gold Buddhist symbols adorned the box.

They hefted the ends of the four ends of sheet, struggling to lift Josh into his casket. The attendants were clearly straining though Josh was not a big person. Without thinking, I pushed away the gurney of another nearby dead woman and grabbed an end of the sheet, joining the attendants in gently laying Josh's body into the box, which was lined with foam rubber. A veil-like shroud was carefully placed over him and the cover of the coffin was nested in place.

Time was money. The morgue workers wheeled Josh's body out into the open air and loaded the coffin into the hearse. I followed, chanting and crying, my mind numb with disbelief. We would never have time to say farewell.

The ride to the monastery, in caravan behind the hearse, took three hours, the blink of an eye.

I remember very little, as I was out of my body. The long road that led to the monastery came to a split.

We slowly drove up a side alley to a pagoda structure with a crematory to one side and a simple temple nearby.

The ceremony lasted three days and nights. One hundred monks filled the air with three hours of daily chanting. Josh's casket was set up on a bier—two sawhorses—and was festooned with blinking Christmas lights and a string that ran from the coffin to a large Buddha statue and then to the seat of the head monk who conducted the ceremonies.

I was presented with my son's monk's robes and was told that Josh's ordained name was Pra Tatawatoe, meaning Teacher. These holy people saw my son as their teacher. They said he had something to teach them and the world.

His Buddhist hymnal and text was presented to me with trembling hands. A Thai monk, who did not speak English, said through an interpreter, that he had much to teach Josh and was sorry that he had not been able to converse in English with him. He also said that Josh had much to teach him.

Digging deep for wisdom, I told this kindly, yet stern-looking man, "Now you can teach each other. The opportunity to converse openly in the realm of pure thought would make language unnecessary."

Plans Never to be Realized

I had learned that the monastery had planned for Josh to become their international marketing spokesperson, spreading the word of the existence and purpose of their monasteries around the globe. Now, this intended mission would have to wait.

The ceremonial site of Josh's crematorium.

It took all night for Josh's body to be transformed into pure ash. The sealed casket was placed on the pyre and family members and friends each tossed a torch into the waiting woodpile below the casket. The iron door was shut and the smoke began to billow skyward.

To protect the body one of the monks to whom Josh was closest—Gordon, an American from Harlem and a former Soldier of Fortune—slept on the steps of the pagoda, stoking the fire during that unforgettable night. He said that my son was his brother.

Monk Gordon, one of Josh's mentors.

In the morning, the ashes were pulled from beneath the funeral pyre and sorted through by hand for bone remnants.

These bits of what was once his body were lovingly placed on a perfect white linen cloth, saturated with liquid essence of rose petals and sprinkled with yellow and red flowers.

I joined the monks in the process of culling through the remains. The embers were still very hot, bearing an acrid yet sweet smell that I will never forget.

I found two small pieces of teeth. I placed them in a ceremonial box, where they remain enshrined in New York in a Spirit House, a traditional place among Thai Buddhists where the living and departed may come together to be joined again.

The monks at Thamkrabok and the mountainside in which Josh is enshrined will now protect him.

I had important business to do in his name: To honor his memory and to find out how the impossibility of his death had become so very real.

Statue of Buddha at Thamkrabok Monastery.

Three~ Meeting Murderers

I had reminded Dr. Morley, Chief of International Medicine at Bumrungrad that I fully anticipated receiving Josh's entire hospital chart.

I wanted to know what had happened to my son in exact detail. I wanted to know everything about his entire hospitalization and death. I also made it clear that I wanted to meet the doctors and nurses who attended him.

I arrived at Bumrungrad Hospital at 10:00 AM to meet Morley. Bumrungrad is an imposing building. The self-proclaimed Mecca of Medical Tourism is a 1,000-bed hospital in the middle of downtown Bangkok. It has a Starbucks in the lobby, several restaurants and all the amenities you would expect of a luxury hotel. Floor to ceiling, marble covers the place. Liveried door attendants are on duty 24/7 The impression is of a resort, not a hospital.

Arabs, Thais, Brits, Americans, Aussies, Japanese . . . an international array of humanity swarms there. It is a busy and strange scene.

I was ushered into a small meeting room. The head of medicine for the hospital was there along with the director of quality control, a young woman, both Thais. They greeted me with forced formal respect.

I immediately made it clear that I had wanted to meet with the doctors who had attended Josh. Their absence was brushed off by Dr. Morley, who explained that they were simply "not available."

I was furious.

I could see that they were nervous, sweating profusely even in our air-conditioned conference room.

My background as a senior executive had trained me to always get close to the persons closest to the "issues."

Two words into the meeting, it was clear that I was to be deprived of the thing that I most wanted: to talk to the people who saw my son die.

It was no accident.

I told the three representatives of Bumrungrad that I was an experienced management consultant and technologist and that I was highly educated. I made it clear to them that they could not fool me—about anything.

Born and raised in New York, being blunt is not difficult for me. "Don't try to deceive me or mislead me—I will catch you—and if I don't, the people I will retain as experts in forensics and pharmacology will."

The expected words of appeasement came, but I did not believe them.

Please refer to www.bumrungraddeath.com: all correspondence with Bumrungrad and the Joint Commission is there in its entirety.

In Their Own Words

My correspondence with Dr. Morley that led up to that first meeting was telling:

From: Jim Goldberg
Sent: Thursday, March 02, 2006 2:04 PM
To: Peter Morley (Dr.)
Subject: Re: RE: RE: Joshua Goldberg

Dr. Morley,
I just spoke with the U.S. Embassy who has received the preliminary forensic report . . . the other, more complete to

follow in 2 months!?

The cause they list is cardio pulmonary failure . . . which is meaningless. I wonder if you might call them or have someone do so who can talk with the pathologist who conducted the autopsy. I want details.

I am expecting that Joshua's charts will be translated by the time we meet. I want to go over them line by line.

Thank You,
Jim Goldberg

There was no death certificate in the hospital chart and the cause of death has never been provided by Bumrungrad.

There was also no death summary filled out in the hospital chart, a mandatory procedure at any hospital in the world.

The hospital also refused to have any person on the hospital staff speak with any member of the U.S. Embassy despite my request that they do so.

The medical charts I received were written in both English and Thai. Both languages were poorly scribbled. I wondered how anyone could read them. I was to learn that it did not matter what the charts said. The charts were for show; they were meant to be self-effacing. However, Dr. Anna Vertkin, M.D., the forensic specialist who joined in the investigation, was able to see through the blur to reveal hideous inconsistencies and outright lies in the charts.

My requests for my son's hospital charts were answered by the International Medical Director with the dictum that if I wanted him to remain helpful, I should be more respectful in how I addressed him. He calls me "mate," an Australian euphemism for "buddy."

My son had just died and this man had the audacity to address me as his mate.

From: Jim Goldberg
Sent: Monday, February 27, 2006 4:41 AM
Subject: Dr. Morley

Dear Dr. Morley,
I would like you to preserve the serum sample drawn from my son at the time of his death.

I am still perplexed as to why you did not run a toxicology screen and other analysis. In any event, please do not destroy this sample.

I have asked Mr. Daley of the U.S. Embassy to arrange for a briefing from you and Josh's attending physician to review his chart. There are questions which I have and would like a detailed briefing as well as copies of his fully translated chart.

I have asked that this meeting take place on the 8th . . . after I return from Thamkrabok and Josh's funeral.

I have also asked that a female neurologist, who was covering for another neurologist at the time of Josh's admission, would be available for me to meet. I had spoken at length with this woman the morning after my son was admitted.

I look forward to seeing you, despite these very devastating times.

Jim Goldberg, New York

The matter of the blood samples first retained by the hospital and then by the Thai police, has been a major issue.

The hospital and the police have both refused to turn over the sample of the blood for independent analysis. Additionally, the FBI in Thailand and in Washington would have no part in taking custody of the samples or in performing an analysis in their laboratories.

One would think that the suspicious death of an American citizen abroad would afford one the resources of the United States Government. Not so.

Dr. Morley tried to dissuade me from involving the U.S. Embassy. Why? I was 8,000 miles away and needed help. The Embassy had offered their assistance. Yet the hospital stone walled their participation. This was another early sign of deep problems.

None of the doctors who attended my son, including individual doctors with whom I had spoken subsequent to my son's admission to Bumrungrad Hospital, were made available to me.

I called one of the doctors listed as an attending physician on Josh's hospital chart, Dr. Sukitti, a heart specialist. He told me that he was not one of Josh's treating physicians, though he was listed as such on the medical charts. He said that Morley, the Chief of International Medicine, was running the case.

In June 2007, I made an unscheduled visit to the hospital and to the clinic of Dr. Sukitti. I was met by guards and Dr. Morley, who instructed them to physically beat me, which they did as Morley fled down the hall at full gallop. Dr. Sukitti sequestered himself behind a locked door in an examination room of his clinic.

What Hath God Wrought?

(See Appendix #1)

Morley, in further email correspondence referenced that Josh had been tested for arsenic shortly after he died.

My son was admitted to Bumrungrad for an unexplained loss of feeling in his left leg and loss of motion: they called this condition drop foot. Josh's condition was never properly diagnosed after 11 days of hospitalization.

It is curious that Dr. Morley referred to a screen for arsenic. Why?

Was he suggesting that my son had taken his own life? I had spoken with Josh a few hours before his death. He was in fine spirits and looking forward to being discharged.

Importantly I was alerted that the hospital had, contrary to my orders, administering addictive opiates or derivatives thereof to my son. I knew that Josh was clean and sober upon entering the hospital and had been for months. I specifically instructed both the admitting nurse and the neurologist on call that he not be given any addictive substances, yet they did. Not only did they ignore me, they gave him IV morphine, very fast acting and highly addictive.

I additionally learned from a confidential source in Bangkok, contacted through my website, that Dr. Morley had six years earlier been fined and convicted of practicing medicine in Thailand without a license. Now, he was Director of International Medicine for the largest hospital in all of South East Asia.

(See Appendix #2)

My initial requirement, upon learning of Josh's death, was for me to personally meet the individuals who attended him and, especially, to talk with the very people who the hospital claimed to have been present at the time of his death.

Instead of producing these key witnesses, Dr. Morley had now interjected his "team." None of the doctors or nurses who directly treated my son was a part of this team. What happened to the people I wanted to meet?

Instead, hospital "officials" attended the meeting. Their absence was incriminating.

Where were these doctors and nurses? Gone with the wind, it would seem.

Facts Start to Focus the Blur

Morley handed over my son's hospital chart, a little over two hundred pages. There were promises made about further explanations forthcoming. There were also explicit assurances that the hospital would get to the root causes of Josh's "Sentinel Event."

The Joint Commission which accredits hospitals in the U.S. and now, overseas, defines a Sentinel Event as follows: A sentinel event is an unexpected occurrence involving death or serious physical or psychological injury, or the risk thereof. Serious injury specifically includes loss of limb or function.

The phrase, "or the risk thereof" includes any process variation for which a recurrence would carry a significant chance of a serious adverse outcome. Such events are referred to as "sentinel," because they signal the need for immediate investigation and response.

The Bumrungrad managers said that they had informed the U.S. Food and Drug Administration and Pfizer, the maker of one of the suspected drugs regarding the events surrounding Josh's death.

Upon returning to the U.S., I called the FDA and Pfizer and found that no communication or notification from Bumrungrad had taken place. This was a ruse-one of dozens to follow.

Although Bumrungrad is encouraged to report Sentinel Events (incidents of great danger, death, injury or patient harm) to the Joint Commission on the Accreditation of Hospitals, they failed to do so in the case of my son. Their lack of concern for the safety of others was evident; instead of sharing potentially life saving information with the world, they secreted it!

June 29, 2006: Bumrungrad Fails to Alert the FDA and Pfizer

One of the six drugs, of the 20 administered to Joshua on the day of his death, was believed by Bumrungrad to be causative in his death. The drug is Zeldox, or, in the U.S., Geodon.

As noted above, I contacted both the FDA and Pfizer who had no record of any such reports.

Consequently, I reported the incidence of my son's death to the Joint Commission calling for their immediate investigation and for the suspension of the accreditation of Bumrungrad from accreditation.

The Joint Commission who has a special committee established to overseas the reporting of Sentinel Events only reported 8 from Jan 2006 through December of 2008. Josh's Sentinel Event or mysterious death was never reported. The Joint Commission accredits 17,500 healthcare organizations and only 8 Sentinel Events were reported, according to the publications of the Joint Commission, for a period of two years!

(See Appendix #3)

Despite numerous communications with Bumrungrad and the agency which accredited them, The Joint Commission never responded to my questions and letters.

Extrapolating the number of accredited institutions (17,500) bearing the Joint Commission imprimatur, delivers an incident rate of .0001142% per average year. Remember, reporting of these Sentinel Events is meant to save lives throughout the world.

Subsequent to Joshua's tragic death, Bumrungrad management told me that they had withdrawn Zeldox from their pharmacy formulary (inventory). Zeldox is known to have a significant QT prolongation effect, i.e., a slowing of the firing of the heart, which has been known to cause sudden death as a side effect.

Based on the hospital charts, I believe that Zeldox was given to Joshua Goldberg along with five other drugs, each with a similar history of QT prolongation. Any one of them, in any dosages, can be lethal.

I was also astonished to discover that, although Joshua was to be discharged for outpatient therapy on February 24, 2006, the night before his intended discharge he was administered 20 medications. This seemed to make no sense for a patient who was yet undiagnosed and medicated so heavily just before he was to leave the hospital. My intuition was later to be validated.

Timeline of a Tragedy

(See Appendix #4)

I was careful to construct a chronology of events from the time Josh first advised me of his medical problem to his death at Bumrungrad. Events were moving at light speed and I was concerned that I not miss any detail—even the most insignificant—in my effort to get to the heart of what I now believed was a terrible crime.

The records they provided were poorly kept and sloppy. They made serious mistakes by not redacting or removing critical pieces of information which would later prove to be extremely damaging to their case.

Perhaps Bumrungrad felt that no one would actually look at a 200 page hospital chart written poorly in two languages. Perhaps it was simply a matter of arrogance. Whatever their intention, or lack thereof, made the job of exposing their crimes relatively easy for trained forensic specialists.

A Demand is Made on the Joint Commission

By mid-April 2006, it was obvious that the Joint Commission (JC) was becoming guarded, verging on non-cooperation. Events had moved rapidly from my first telephone conversation with Maureen Potter at the Joint Commission. I began to see the JC as co-conspirators. This characterization of them turned out to be spot on.

Potter had promised full cooperation.

Yet, I suspect that Ms. Potter had consulted with her superiors who reminded her of the real business of the Joint Commission: protecting their accredited hospitals from public scrutiny.

I made a strong demand of Ms. Potter, then head of the Joint Commission International (JCI). My demand for full disclosure was met with her explicit promise that the JC would be entirely forthcoming. They were anything but!

Though the Joint Commission is a not-for-profit organization that ostensibly is established to serve the people, the JCI did not respond to my request for answers.

Silence, delay or denials are the JC's standard procedure.

The JCI suggests that their silence is the organization's privilege; yet, what authority entitles them to such secrecy? A reasonable person might well ask, "What are they protecting?"

(See Appendix #5)

The demands I made of the JC and Maureen Potter were crystal clear and to the point.

I explicitly informed the JC of the complete lack of cooperation of their accredited hospital, Bumrungrad. The JC was informed in no uncertain terms of the pharmaceutical errors committed by Bumrungrad.

Further, I brought to their attention that a police investigation was underway and the American Embassy was also looking into the matter.

They were asked to provide copies of all reports regarding Bumrungrad hospital. I further demanded to have copies of reports of the 6 Sentinel Events at Bumrungrad about which Maureen Potter informed me had taken place a year prior to Josh's death.

The names of the doctors allegedly present at Josh's Code 3 were provided:

➤ Dr. Opas
➤ Dr. R. Visissak Suksa-ard
➤ Dr. Wongsawan Wongprasert
➤ Dr. Sira Sooparb

- ➢ Dr. Sukitti Panpunnung
- ➢ Dr. Peter Morley
- ➢ Dr. Apichati Sivayathorn

I demanded that these people be interviewed by the Joint Commission and a report be provided to me describing the results of these investigations.

As with all my communications and requests of the Joint Commission, no response was ever received. Their ensuing and persistent silence and non cooperation made it clear that JC is being paid for public protection without any consideration whatsoever to their mission: to assure patient safety and quality care.

In other words, their standards were written as window dressing. What actually goes on behind the closed doors of their accredited hospitals is of no concern to them. In short, they had contrived a way to pretend to the public that safety and quality care was being monitored and that accreditation actually meant something real.

I reminded Potter that this was serious business since the public relied on their endorsement and traveled to their overseas accredited hospitals with the expectation that the JC's accreditation was significant and meaningful.

It is my considered opinion that the Joint Commission authors of medical proclamations are masters of prose. They write expansively about protocols, processes, patient safety and the like. The problem is that this is fluff, a hoax.

Reading their standards and rulebooks is like reading a science fiction book. The JC literature does not mean what it says; the authors of this literature do not seem to feel that they can be held accountable. Categorically, every attempt I made to obtain information from this quasi-official accreditation organization was rebuffed or met with indignation and silence.

The Commission was given responsibility by law of the United States to act as an agent of the people; the Commission has failed miserably in its sworn duty. It has also engaged in a premeditated effort to protect its own interests and those institutions that pay yearly for protection.

Asking for Help

I am an unrelenting sleuth who has learned that it is no shame to ask experts for help. Meticulous preparation and research is mandatory when one wishes to confront wrongs of major magnitude. Subsequently, I retained two world-renowned experts to help in the medical forensics involved in Josh's case.

I am fortunate that one of the forensic examiners, Dr. Anna Vertkin, M.D., a Diplomat and Director of the American College of Forensic Examiners, took on my son's case pro bono.

The great number of medical mistakes and inconsistencies in Josh's case astounded her. She would not simply walk away from what she sensed to be sheer butchery.

In addition, the famed Dr. Henry Cohen, a Board Certified forensic pharmacologist at New York University, examined the drug combination supposedly given to Josh during his hospitalization at Bumrungrad.

The forensic findings are earth shattering.

Summary of Key Expert Medical Forensic Findings

Drs. Cohen and Vertkin provided me with many reports over the next several weeks and months. This included their initial findings based on Josh's medical records and charts, our meetings with Thai Police pathologists and reviews of the autopsy results.

Dr. Vertkin first detailed the proper and recommended standards of care recognized by medical professionals worldwide. For clarity, Dr. Vertkin first listed what is expected as basic standards of care as related to Josh's treatment and condition.

Immediately following the listing of proper standards of care, 16 in number, is a list of 24 explicit failures by Bumrungrad to meet those standards of care.

These failures were brought to the attention of the Joint Commission, Bumrungrad Hospital and the Thai Police. All my entreaties were ignored and I have never received any response by any of these institutions or agencies. Their consistent reluctance to be held accountable for any of their 24 documented mistakes is astounding. It is also, sadly, predictable.

(See Appendix #6)

Initial Medical Conclusions from Dr. Anna Vertkin

Within a reasonable degree of medical probability, the actions of the physicians, pharmacists and nurses involved in care of Mr. Goldberg caused him unnecessary pain, suffering and ultimately death.

In conclusion, within reasonable medical probability it is the actions of Bumrungrad International Hospital and its staff caused Mr. Goldberg unnecessary pain, suffering and ultimately death.

Failures of the standard of care during hospitalization, cardiac arrest and after death are so egregious that a full investigation of Mr. Joshua Goldberg's care and circumstances of his tragic death by the independent third party is mandatory.

My opinions are based on my review of the available medical records, doctors and current medical information indexed by Medline/Plumbed, New England Journal of Medicine, current editions of the medical texts. My opinions may change as further or different information is presented to me for a medical review. Thank you for allowing me to assist in the review.

(See Appendix #7)

Additional Findings of Dr. Anna Vertkin, Subsequent to Meeting with the Thai Government Pathologist

Dr. Vertkin's Conclusions

Subsequent to Dr. Vertkin's initial forensic conclusions, the police pathologist in Bangkok began to hedge, apparently under pressure, to back off from his initial findings.

Dr. Vertkin flew to Bangkok to consult with the Thai Pathologist (there are no forensic investigators in the Thai Police force) and confronted him, point by point, subject by subject. He agreed and confirmed in writing with all of her conclusions.

Although his opinion might have been swayed by the assertion of "influence" by people who wanted Josh's death to look favorable to them, the Thai Pathologist could not deny the solid medical evidence supported by the autopsy, the reports, the hospital charts, the photographs and the face-to-face discussions.

Dr. Vertkin opines as follows:

It is my opinion as confirmed by autopsy findings and photographs that Mr. Joshua Goldberg had rhabdomyolysis with involvement of the heart.

This was of several days duration and may have been resolving pending further studies.

It is my opinion on the basis of the autopsy that death occurred approximately at 8 pm on February 23, 2006, not February 24 at 6:35 am as claimed by Bumrungrad or 5 am, as stated on the official death certificate, due to the following additional clinical data:

> - *Food digestion analysis.*
> - *Significant urine retention of 650 cc. (Involuntary urination would occur in an individual except in a coma at 150 cc of urine.)*
> - *Prolonged duration of the brain edema.*

> *Resolving livido.*
> *Beginning of auto digestion and fermentation in the abdominal cavity as indicated by significant abdominal swelling at 13:30 pm on 24 February 2006.*
> *There is no evidence of ANY resuscitation efforts as confirmed by intact bed clothing, lack of intubation injuries, lack of the chest compression injuries, liver lacerations, and skin and pericardium electrical burns.*
> *The findings uncovered by autopsy require criminal investigation into the sudden death and the subsequent cover up of Mr. Joshua's Goldberg's death at Bumrungrad Hospital. The circumstances of the unexpected death, the cause of death and mode of death remain unknown at this time.*

Pharmacological Findings from Dr. Cohen

Dr. Henry Cohen's findings, from a pharmacological perspective, indicate that the cause of death was due to simultaneous mixture of up to six contra-indicated drugs, each with the potential to cause death.

His report, which is highly technical, concludes, "Neuroleptic malignant syndrome appears to have caused Josh's death—caused by contra-indicated medications."

The entire report can be found on the website www.bumrungraddeath.com in the Medical Documents section.

Note that not one of the failures cited in Dr. Vertkin's reports have been refuted by Bumrungrad or by the Royal Thai Police Pathology Department of Chulalanghorn University (The Royal University of Thailand).

Dr. Cohen, after reviewing the case, conferred with Dr. Vertkin asking, "Have you ever seen anything as horrible as this in your entire life?" She told him no. He replied, "Neither have I."

I did not meet her until several weeks after Josh died. Dr. Vertkin's reports were based on a careful examination of the hospital records and a personal meeting in Bangkok with the Bangkok Police Coroner, who had performed the autopsy on my son.

It is very important to note that someone at the hospital "blew the whistle," reporting that something bad was happening at Bumrungrad and that the police ought to intercede quickly. If it had not been for that person's intervention, the rest of this story would be very different.

My Worst Fears

The consultations with Dr. Vertkin and Cohen confirmed my worst fears.

I was able, through science, to confirm, that officials at Bumrungrad International Hospital had lied to me. The death of my son was neither an accident nor the result of medical malpractice.

To the contrary, the early findings suggested that he was killed and not just by negligence. His death, as the facts were revealed to me, appeared to be the result of a deliberate plan. I could find no other explanation.

But, why? Why kill a kid of twenty three who was trying to find meaning in a complex world?

These revelations have only added salt to the eternally incurable wound of losing Josh.

These precise technical details and expert analyses of the events leading to my son's hospitalization and death emboldened me to relentlessly follow the path that would eventually solve the riddle of my little boy's death.

The journey down that same path would provide an unanticipated ringside view of a medical machine that has victimized American society and is now set to conquer the world.

The Forensics Do Not Lie

Six drugs were said to have been given Josh the day before and on the day of his death. They are known to have serious side effects and should never be mixed.

Subsequent to additional peri-mortem blood analysis, shocking revelations emerged. Only some of the drugs that Bumrungrad's records indicated were "on board" was actually found in Josh's blood.

Upon first hearing this, I was confounded.

Why would Bumrungrad admit to having prescribed medications that they knew to be contra-indicated? These were medications that when mixed could have easily resulted in death, though some appear not to have been administered. Why did the hospital charts and the actual blood analysis not agree?

A mole in Bangkok suggested an answer: to throw investigators off the real path.

By making it appear that Josh had died from a deadly mixture of medications, attention could be distracted from the other possible ways he might have died . . . or, more accurately, killed.

This could mean several things:

Everything in the hospital charts, from his alleged "unresponsive" state to the pronouncement of death, is entirely falsified. Not one word of the hospital record of the alleged Code 3 is true.

The sinister cocktail of medications supposedly administered was also a ruse. What were they trying to cover? Why the extensive smoke screen and diversions?

The following individuals named below appear in Josh's hospital chart as having been present during the Code 3. Despite persistent efforts with the police, none have been interrogated. Yet, they hold the key to confirming what did or did not happen.

Anyone familiar with standard police work knows that the first suspect interviews are with those present at the scene of the crime. They are:

> Dr. Opas, Pathologist;
> R. Visissak Suksa-ard Visissa, B.Sc., Medical Technology;

> Dr. Wongsawan Wongprasert, Nephrologist;
> Dr. Sira Sooparb, General Medicine, Nephrology;
> Dr. Sukitti Panpunnung, Cardiologist;
> Dr. Peter Morley, Director of International Medical Care;
> Dr. Apichati Sivayathorn, Chief Quality Officer.

Remember, the report of Josh's death stated which stated he was "unresponsive" at 6:00 AM on Friday morning, February 24, 2006. It is highly unlikely that any of these people would have been on duty at that time. Especially, since the doctors listed are from Bumrungrad's senior staff roster.

More likely, they were at home, fast asleep. Bumrungrad, despite persistent questions about this, refused to answer any questions or provide explanations or clarifications. It seemed to me then and now, that they were desperately hiding and covering up their mistakes and compound errors.

I believe that Dr. Morley controls the people above. None of them attended at the time of Josh's passing. There never was a Code 3 performed to save my son's life.

It is strange that two nephrologists and one cardiologist were listed as participants in the Code 3. It is unheard of that two nephrologists would have attended a "code blue." Josh had neither cardiac nor renal problems. Despite the fabrication of the Code 3, those whom Bumrungrad chose to list bolsters the argument concerning organ harvesting: heart and kidney doctors were listed as present. My son had no problems with either his heart or his kidneys.

I doubt that anyone at Bumrungrad involved in orchestrating my son's death and its cover-up felt that his body would slip out of their control.

The records indicate that even before he died—as much as two days prior—his attending doctors had scheduled "an appointment" with the hospital pathologist, presumably to prepare to perform an autopsy. The request sheet in the records indicates only that a request for a consult was made, but was never completed.

In fact, had it not been for the whistle blower (presumably someone working at the hospital) who alerted the police that something was amiss with Josh's treatment, the hospital would have already conducted their own post-mortem.

When a foreigner dies in a Thai hospital, Thai law insists that police be immediately notified. The law also states that the body should be transported to a government facility, in the interest of conducting an "objective" examination as to the cause of death.

Bumrungrad's plan to proceed with an independent autopsy is both against Thai law and extremely suspect.

My son's autopsy had been ORDERED, while he was still alive and about to be discharged.

The Smoking Gun: A Mistake Reveals Hard Truth

Josh was absolutely the victim of foul play. His death was badly covered-up.

Idiotic mistakes and document falsification has been revealed through strenuous analysis. However, the blunder which follows is utterly shocking and incriminating.

The portion of the EKG below, dated February 24, 2006, was all that was included in my son's hospital chart. When I complained that the rest of the strip was not there, I was told by Morley that this was all I should expect.

This was odd, given that Morley had explained that the hospital had a 30-minute revival Code Blue protocol. By standard practice, the entire Code 3 procedure should have been continuously monitored.

Several weeks after my first and only meeting with Morley on March 10, 2006 I received a DHL package which contained an EKG strip that was about14 feet long. An accompanying note said that this was provided as the balance of the EKG depicting when Josh finally "flat lined."

Dr. Morley was playing me for a fool.

Have a good look at this, not because it is Josh's chart, but because it isn't.

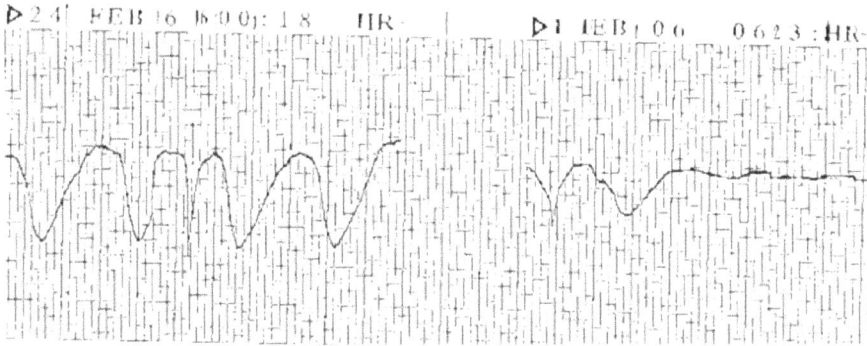

Josh's EKG strip (purportedly), provided by Dr. Morley.

Notice, that the date on the left side of the strip reads 24 Feb at 6:00 AM, the time hospital claims to have started their Code Procedure. On the right side is the additional material supplied after my return to the United States.

While the hospital did modify the date by hand, apparently, to reflect the time of my son's death at 6:35 AM as reported on his chart, in their haste they neglected to modify the automatically stamped date: 1 Feb 2006: ten days before Josh ever set foot in Bumrungrad International Hospital.

This unbelievable fabrication suggests that **neither** of these EKG strips were taken from Joshua Goldberg. They belong to others! Despite my pleas to the Thai Police to obtain the hospital computers and EKG machinery, they were never examined.

Josh's hospital chart is replete with mistakes of this kind. I don't know if this is a blessing or a curse but, for whatever reason, they either were not careful enough or thought that no one would ever take a good look.

They were wrong.

When I finally understood this piece of information I was overcome with paralyzing sadness. These readings were not from Josh's heart. They represent the hearts of others whom I shall never know.

What's more, they were presented to me in a sinister attempt to deceive me, to persuade me to believe that these were the last signs of my son's life.

The cruelty required to conceive such a plot is beyond comprehension. The shocking reality sunk in when these strips of paper finally revealed their true meaning. The people in charge of my son's care were personified demons. They walk in darkness and they walk at Bumrungrad International Hospital.

Forensic Pharmacology

Dr. Cohen provided me with his summary of pharmacological forensic analysis. Prior to presenting his report, my apologies are offered, as the technical nature of this type of reporting makes for tedious reading.

When talking about a murder, the details are vital.

Cohen found no less than 6 contra indicated uses of medication. Any combination of two or more could easily result in death!

(See Appendix #8)

The nagging question of motive was lurking as a fundamental and material part of my investigation. Why would my son, at 23, as harmless as a soul as one could hope to meet, be murdered in by doctors in a hospital? This was not just a murder due to malpractice or incompetence. I was now convinced of that. This was murder for a deliberate but as yet undiscovered reason.

Subsequent to releasing Dr. Cohen's Possible Cause of Death findings via our website **(www.bumrungraddeath.com),** an individual who formerly worked for the company owned by Bumrungrad responsible for setting up the hospital's medical informatics system contacted me.

He told me that this system was not even operative at the time of Josh's death.

Furthermore, despite the hospital's assurances that the system was operative, not one note appears in Josh's extensive hospital chart as to who overrode any contra-indicated medications, medications for which any pharmacist would have provided warnings to physicians before filling.

This division of Bumrungrad has since been sold to Microsoft, according to the Wall Street Journal and Bumrungrad Press Releases. I contacted Microsoft about what had happened: they had no comment.

The facts indicated on Josh's autopsy charts are highly suspect. These appear in the analysis that the hospital and the police performed on my son's blood.

To be clear, the hospital performed its own initial analysis of the Josh's blood. Peter Morley claimed that Josh's blood was negative for arsenic poisoning, but the official results of the hospital's blood analysis has never been released.

At my request, a vial of Josh's blood was stored in Bumrungrad's freezer until transferred to the police, where only a small portion was analyzed.

The police have still refused to turn over the remaining portion, approximately 5-ml of blood, so that I might perform an independent analysis.

The police sent the sample to a local Bangkok laboratory for analysis but the sample was returned without any tests performed. The lab "changed their mind" and said that they were not equipped to perform the required tests. Josh's blood sample is still being held by the Royal Thai Police.

Obviously, neither the Thai Police nor Bumrungrad were anxious to have an independent analysis performed. They, together, worked hard and consistently at making it impossible to find the truth.

By now, I had become accustomed to have obstacles thrown in my way. Although terribly frustrating, I developed a full appreciation that the blank stares and unresponsiveness of the authorities, including those in America, were not accidents.

Four ~ Bumrungrad:
"Bummers" to the Locals

Situated in a bustling part of Bangkok on Sukhumvit Road, Bumrungrad Hospital occupies what appear to be several city blocks. It takes its place, comfortably, with many luxury skyscrapers that in good times are filled with tourists and ex-pats. The place has a carnival-like atmosphere. The area is alluring for the unimaginable abundance of things to buy and deals to be had but frightening for the palpable chaos of its roar and tiny streets.

Bumrungrad Hospital is a city within a city. Its owners call it the epicenter for Medical Tourism. Judging from the Arab clientele milling outside and in the enormous main lobby, it appears more like a Mecca: The floor-to-ceiling marble in the open, three-story atrium gives one the sense that Bumrungrad is more luxury hotel than hospital.

The Birth of an Illusion

Upon deeper discovery, that's just how they want visitors and patients to feel. A vacation—a medical vacation. Circa 1996, a kind of Congress of Interests in Bangkok defined strategies by which tourism could be enhanced by developing a new phenomenon: travel for medical care.

At this Congress, publicists affiliated with Bumrungrad fashioned the catch phrase: Medical Tourism. It seems to have stuck, striking a profound chord in the Western World. The scheme combined the new notion of a vacation in an exotic place with comparatively inexpensive medical care. The Western media machines, hungry to fill air time and print space, gobbled this up like heaps of junk food with the kids on a Saturday afternoon!

I examined Bumrungrad and its behavior from various perspectives. By cross-fertilizing information about this company, the glamour of their pitch, the glow of their media relations and the hype, interwoven with the supposed promise of Medical Tourism/outsourcing, may be offset by understanding Bumrungrad reality: a ruthless money-making machine with Mafia ethics. Their business? Playing hardball with your life.

International biohazard symbol.

Selling it Hard

The aspiration and hope on the part of its champions claims that Medical Tourism will provide an answer to what is broken with medical care in the United States and throughout the world.

There are certainly stresses on the healthcare systems of countries with socialized forms of healthcare that have resulted in declining quality of care, limited access to doctors, restrictions on testing and diagnostics, limitations in choice of medications and higher co-pays and deductibles.

It is my view that Medical Tourism is akin to running from something that is broken to something that is also broken.

Medical Tourism seems a glistening concept that beckons, perhaps because it is exotic and unknown: traveling to a place about which one has only dreamed for a medical procedure, combined with recuperation by the sea, drinking Mai Thais.

This is cannon fodder for people anxiously waiting to sell you a medical adventure in paradise. Imagine a 747, revving engines, winging its way to the lure of an affordable solution to a bad knee, clogged artery or defunct kidney. Who wouldn't be tempted? Romance and healthcare: powerful medicine to sell.

It's Shiny and New

The images focus on what is frustrating and inconvenient about healthcare at home. Gone are the jam-packed Emergency Rooms. Patients will have no more concerns over waiting to see a specialist for another two months. The miracle of quality healthcare comes within financial reach for the uninsured 60 million in the U.S. and the 50 million more in the U.S. who are underinsured.

It even feels like a lullaby with the promise of restful sleep, followed by an awakening to good health.

The staff will greet you with smiling faces, hail and well met. Their probity appears beyond reproach. Let's face it: everyone likes to have their asses kissed!

Here's what a recent visitor to Bumrungrad wrote in an email to me:

I am in Bangkok today and needed to visit a hospital. After my initial consultation,

I felt there was something unusual here. It is like a Vegas casino. Most who attended to me were overly warm, but 1 attendant whose English was not understandable became irate, and the warmness they try to portray suddenly disappeared, I feel lucky to have left unharmed. After previewing your site I've decided to bear my pains until I can return to Canada to see my doctor."

I was amused by this writer's reference to Vegas. Only this time, you are gambling with your life.

At Bumrungrad your backside will be kissed passionately from the moment you walk in to the time you pay your bill. "I enjoyed my open heart surgery so much that I plan on coming back for the face lift and boob job I have always wanted. Hell, I might even consider a sex change which I see is also on the menu!"

HOSPITALS & CLINICS	
Sex change	1,625 us$
Orchiectomy	125 us$
Tummy tuck	1,250 us$
Breast enlargement	1,125 us$
(Mammoplasty with Mentor/ES prostheses included)	
Liposuction	625 us$
Facelift (Rhytidectomy)	875 us$
Browlift (Forehead lift)	625 us$
Eyelids surgery	200 us$
(1 US$ = 40 Bht) Prices vary with daily exchange rate	
All prices include medicine, anesthesia etc.	
Foreigners are charged as same as Thais	

Bangkok newspaper ad with menu of medical services.

Time to wake up and smell the coffee. My grandfather told me that if something seemed too good to be true, it probably is.

For you, this is about your body. For them, it's about your wallet. They will do, say and promise anything to book your business. Anything!

The "Knee Replacement Get Away Package" will quickly turn into extra tests, more medications, a longer hospital stay, complications, infections and the like. Just like in the real world. Hey, we're in the real world?

What You Don't Know Could Kill You

My investigation into Bumrungrad's history and operations is comprehensive.

However, because Bumrungrad operates in a super secret stealth mode, my investigation was restricted by the limited information that is publicly available, some of my conclusions have necessarily been inferential. In cases of inferential conclusions, I have tried to triangulate information to test an idea.

Triangulation is a navigational term, for example, to find the location of an airplane or ship, three points of reference are taken and correlated to determine precise location. Think of your GPS satellite navigation system.

To undertake an investigation this big, I had to dig deeply, often in unobvious places, to find material to substantiate my suspicion that Bumrungrad Hospital and its diverse operations cross the line, time and again, into a world of deception and sinister activities.

"We're the Good Guys!"

"If there's a mistake, we fix it," said Curtis Schroeder, an American who is Group CEO of Bumrungrad Hospital. As with most major institutions, Bumrungrad requires all attending doctors to carry malpractice insurance. "But the idea of suing for multi-millions of dollars for damages is not going to be something you can do outside the U.S."

Schroeder gets to the point quickly: You can't sue us! We're not afraid of you! I am still waiting for Josh's resurrection, Mr. Schroeder!

Schroeder lists his credentials as being Board Certified. Nothing is mentioned as to any certification he holds or where this certification has been issued. The fact is that Mr. Schroeder is a former executive of Tenet Healthcare. Tenet placed Schroeder in position to watch over their Thai interests—that being Bumrungrad Hospital.

After Tenet's supposed departure, Schroeder saw the diamond in the rough. Without the inconveniences of operating a healthcare company in the United States, with its meddlesome government and nosy police, Schroeder apparently stayed in Siam to make hay while the sun shone.

Curtis Schroeder, Group Chief Executive Officer and Director, Bumrungrad Hospital Public Co. Ltd.

His office declined to answer my request that Schroeder provide the certifications claimed in his biographical reference.

Mack Banner, Bumrungrad International's CEO.

Mac (James) Banner, CEO of Bumrungrad, is also a former Tenet Healthcare executive. Banner and Schroeder spring from one of the most horrific business organizations in the history of the United States, Tenet Healthcare. The crimes of this organization are discussed in the chapter *Tenet Healthcare: Masters of Deceit?*

Still Want These People to Operate on You or Your Loved Ones?

Bumrungrad insists the care given to my son was appropriate. If that were so, why would the hospital—and its doctors and various executives—continually do everything possible to delay responding, deny the findings of other professionals and lie about his care?

Why would they not share what they claim is an internal assessment regarding my son's case? Why would the American accreditation agency, the Joint Commission, stonewall my call for information and for full disclosure?

The answer: Money. Mullah, Scratch, Bread, Gold, Coins, Green, Cash. Money. Lots of it! The JC is desperately afraid that their long-held secret will be publicly released.

The secret is that foreign accreditation is for sale and is a sham. Bumrungrad and the Joint Commission are in a co-beneficial business relationship instead of one where objective accreditation is bestowed on a worthy institution.

When informed of Schroeder's remarks that his organization fixes what it breaks, I publicly replied, "What I'm dedicated to doing is to try to alert people to at least do their homework and consider carefully what they're getting into. Why is this such a good deal? You might not walk away.

That's what happened to my son.

Correspondence

My website, www.bumrungraddeath.com, has a Correspondence section. My e-mail exchanges with Bumrungrad and the Joint Commission are posted in their entirety, except for legally restricted documents. I "captured" these dialogues to provide transparency.

My wish for transparency directly opposes the tactics taken by both Bumrungrad and, even more sadly, by the Joint Commission.

It's important to weigh these streams of correspondence. Do you sense Bumrungrad's hostility and recalcitrance in responding to questions about my son's death? Can you see how they clearly don't like being held accountable?

I believe their exact words reveal their real intentions: distract, delay and deny. These are textbook tactics when the goal is to exhaust your opponent in hopes they will eventually disappear. Most do!

A Little History Explains a Lot

National Medical Enterprises and its subsequent embodiment, Tenet Healthcare, are two notorious healthcare companies in the corporate history of the United States. Their dastardly past, which is a matter of open public record, represents, for ordinary folks, treason and mutiny on their fellow citizens. They are also the founders of Bumrungrad Hospital!

Board Certified? For a Day!

Unlicensed!

The nice looking, cordial Oriental doctor claiming U.S.-issued Board Certification is quickly being replaced by the resident confidence man (or woman). Just ask to see their credentials.

After Josh's death, I meticulously read through Bumrungrad's website. They claimed 500 of their then-roster of 750 doctors were Board Certified.

To verify these figures, which I suspected were exaggerated as were other Bumrungrad statistics, I proceeded, helped by my lawyers, to hire a researcher who spent two weeks at the Ministry of Health in Bangkok, checking the credentials of every listed doctor on Bumrungrad's list. Our researcher discovered information that prompted me to publish the following news alert on www.bumrungraddeath.com. Ten doctors appearing on Bumrungrad's rooster of doctors held no license to practice medicine!

(See Appendix #9)

When we asked Bumrungrad and the Joint Commission to verify the 500 Board Certified Doctors claimed on their website, they still did not respond. What they did was to revise the number from 500 to 250.

The guiding principle of Bumrungrad's presentation is to appear to the public in any way that they wish; to hell with reality. This chameleon organization has switched its website facts numerous times in response to being caught in bald faced lies.

What is even more egregious is that the Joint Commission International sees no problem with this behavior: why should they? Bumrungrad is paying for that accreditation, which amounts to the appearance of credibility—that's all that matters.

Avoiding the Law

Bumrungrad International Hospital maintains representative offices in many countries around the world. Their website reports the following:

Following is a list of Bumrungrad International's authorized overseas representative offices. Our representatives will assist you in every way possible to ensure that you receive the information and support that you need.

- ➤ Cambodia
- ➤ Ethiopia
- ➤ Germany
- ➤ Hong Kong
- ➤ Kuwait
- ➤ Macau
- ➤ Mongolia
- ➤ Myanmar
- ➤ Nepal
- ➤ Nigeria
- ➤ New Zealand
- ➤ Oman
- ➤ Portugal
- ➤ Seychelles
- ➤ Taiwan
- ➤ Ukraine
- ➤ Vietnam
- ➤ Yemen

Why is this important? The United States is not part of this list. Nor is Great Britain, Australia or Canada. Yet, Bumrungrad actively promotes their hospital services and medical experts to these countries. Of course significant numbers of patients come from these wealthy nations!

Our website visitor system allows us to track the geographic location of reader. The rough split follows:

- ➤ 1/3 from the United States;
- ➤ 1/3 from British Commonwealth countries;
- ➤ 1/3 from the rest of the world.

Additionally, inquires we receive about Bumrungrad are heavily weighted from those in the U.S. and British Commonwealth states.

Furthermore, our website is listed high in the results of search engine (i.e., Google) searches for "Bumrungrad" or "Bumrungrad Hospital," and usually immediately after Bumrungrad's official site.

A majority of visitors to the Bumrungrad site are also likely to visit our site about Josh's death.

The brunt of Bumrungrad's publicity efforts and insurance company alliances are with U.S. and British-based companies. So, the absence of offices in the U.S. and Britain begs a significant question: why?

Did you guess the answer? That is right: liability!

Shortly after Josh's mysterious death, Bumrungrad's wholly owned subsidiary (Global Care 2000, a medical informatics software company based in Baltimore, Maryland), was abruptly removed from the Bumrungrad website. We tried in 2006 to contact Global Care's headquarters in Baltimore but directory assistance revealed that Global Care was not listed.

A private investigator confirmed that if Global Care had been doing business in Maryland, they had left their office. Why?

A software engineer who formally worked for Global Care 2000 contacted us via our website. He explained that the pharmacy component of their information system was not in operation at the time of Joshua's death. This directly contradicted the representations made by Bumrungrad that Global Care's system was fully operational at the time.

The letter from the software designer is particularly important as it provides a number of details as to the internal workings and misrepresentations provided to me by Bumrungrad with regard to their wrong doings related to medication administration.

(See Appendix #10)

Bumrungrad even supplied bogus charts supposedly generated by the pharmacy system to demonstrate that they were following best practices and that their pharmacy system caught the six contra-indicated drugs that they represented were given to Josh on the day of his death.

Global Care 2000 was purchased by Microsoft in 2007. Microsoft Press Release, 19 October 2007

Based on the knowledge gained from this insider, formerly employed by Global Care 2000, we know that Bumrungrad was attempting to perpetrate yet another brazen fraud on Josh and his family. Why?

Bumrungrad, aware that they were liable for crimes for which they could be held accountable in the United States, rushed to remove any vestige of their U.S. presence. The Baltimore office of Global Care 2000, though listed as a U.S.-based subsidiary, had no telephone, no website and was not listed in any U.S. or Baltimore directory after Bumrungrad became aware that it was in legal jeopardy of being sued in the United States.

Any previous evidence of U.S. offices maintained by Bumrungrad in the U.S. was decimated from their website and printed materials.

Based on this, it was no stretch to surmise that Bumrungrad executives realized they could be subject to litigation in the United States. Despite their aggressive publicity efforts to the American public, including their glowing 60 Minutes debut, Bumrungrad wanted to veil their real activities and promotional campaigns in the U.S. to avoid litigation in a venue bound to be harsh in judging the crimes I allege.

In other words, Bumrungrad wanted it both ways. They wanted to promote in the U.S. but didn't want to be liable, for fear of the power of the U.S. legal system.

Consider again, the statement of Curtis Schroeder, Bumrungrad President and Chief Executive Officer: "But the idea of suing for multimillions of dollars for damages is not going to be something you can do outside the U.S."

Remember his statement well. Schroeder, like the others from

Tenet Healthcare who currently run Bumrungrad, feverishly juggle between putting on a nice face for the public and hiding their real agenda. We do business and promote ourselves as the best, but if we are NOT, you can't touch us!

Yet, they, in fact, can get away with murder.

They are protected by the expanse of great oceans coupled with being beyond the reach of any jurisprudence that would surely deal a swift blow to their illegal and criminal activities. They found this out in the Tenet days, when their former employer was found guilty of heinous crimes and fined billions for their offenses.

But not in Thailand! Not in any other country in which they do business. The U.S. and the British Commonwealth Countries have strong laws that would put Bumrungrad on the ropes. Hence, they avoid it as Dracula avoids the sun.

Are you still interested in getting "serviced" at Bumrungrad? Muse over this next tidbit.

No Bill, No Liability

Josh was admitted to Bumrungrad and received "services" beginning on February 12, 2006 until his death on the night of February 23, 2006. Bumrungrad and World Access reports the date of his death as February 24, 2006 at 6:35 AM. We know from the forensics that this was impossible.

The reports of World Access, the third-party administrator retained by Josh's insurance company, Blue Cross of California, approved his care and assured Bumrungrad of payment.

Further examination about World Access and its role in Josh's demise is provided in our chapter exclusively dedicated to World Access. They deserve their own!

The transcript I obtained from World Access, a wholly owned subsidiary of the world's largest insurance company, Allianz of Germany and Switzerland, revealed constant requests by

Bumrungrad for tests, medications, increased hospital stay and the like. Bumrungrad was set, on what we are informed about and believe, is their normal course: milk the cow for as much milk as possible.

Yet when Joshua died, Bumrungrad did not bill World Access or Blue Cross of California for any of the "services" he received. Not one penny! Why would an organization notorious for pushing services, tests and medications—not to mention increased hospital stays—forego billing for pre-approved charges?

The answer comes down to the second most important word in Bumrungrad's mantra: **Liability. Money** is the first.

The mystery of why Bumrungrad never billed is surprisingly easy to solve. Had Bumrungrad billed for "services" rendered to Joshua, they would have become responsible and liable for producing all of Josh's medical records! By virtue of their contractual understanding with World Access and Blue Cross of California, all their actions and records would have become subject to investigation.

No Bill, No Liability. No Bill, No Investigation

The hospital, by foregoing what we estimate to have been at least $25,000 in Josh's medical care, Bumrungrad's owners quickly determined that it was far safer for them to pick up this small tab, thus avoiding what they most feared: accountability, liability and responsibility.

The fact the hospital did not issue a bill was so eye-popping to me that I dug into this on all fronts, believing that we might be laboring under a mistaken impression. They certainly did not skip their billing as a gesture of condolence. Hospitals always render final charges to insurance companies and individuals, even if the treated patient succumbed under their care.

Josh was fully insured and his "care" at Bumrungrad was just another case. Since the retained third-party administrator for Blue Cross of California, World Access, was to manage foreign-care patients, their bill would have been paid without question.

Five~ Tenet Healthcare: Masters of Deceit?

Tenet Healthcare Has Had Two Comings

Who really owns Bumrungrad International Hospital?

Dr. Michael J. Wynne of Wollongong University in Sydney, Australia, has written extensively about the battle the Aussies have waged and won against U.S.-based National Medical Enterprises (NME.), subsequently known as Tenet Healthcare Corporation.

Their NME moniker had become so thoroughly tarnished after their huge Medicare fraud and criminal abuse of psychiatric patients in the early 1990s that they changed their name: giving rise to the illusion of a "fresh start." It was not.

Tenet Down Under

The Australian experience with Medical Tourism has been profound. Given the close proximity of Australia to South East Asia, many Aussies have sought care in places like Bumrungrad Hospital.

The stresses placed on the Aussie medical system from correcting foreign medical errors, botched surgeries, improper medication regimens, post operative complications and infections, are well reported in the Australian Press.

Based on my research, Australia serves as a unique venue in our ability to understand what impact Medical Tourism/outsourcing has on a society. Given that Australia is relatively isolated and small in population, we can more easily model, given their experience, what is likely to happen, or is happening in other countries. In other words, Australia serves as a microcosm for our analysis.

Dr. Michael Wynne's observations and reporting are searing Here's a bit of what he has to say with regard to NME/Tenet.

During the course of my research, I called Australia several times to speak with Dr. Wynne, but he is either retired or unavailable for unknown reasons.

"In its first incarnation during the 1980s and 1990s the company was called National Medical Enterprises (NME). It was involved in a massive scandal defrauding Medicare by buying patients for up to U.S. $2000 each from anyone who could persuade them to come to hospital. The company had contracts with bounty hunters and even pleaded guilty to kidnaping patients. It bought patients from Canada."

(NME had found a way around Medicare regulations. Patients that could be "recruited" into psychiatric facilities could be held against their will for up to 14 days. During this forced psychiatric hospitalization, patients, without their consent, could be given drugs, electroshock therapy and other "treatments." Some of these patients, which included children, committed suicide while in captivity or shortly thereafter. Heart wrenching books have been written about the agonies inflicted by NME on its captivated patient population, their families and friends!)

"Vast numbers, many of them children did not need hospital admission. The company lied to them and kept them in hospital for the full duration of their insurance all the time providing them with vast amounts of unneeded treatment. All of this was signed for by doctors. The company eventually pleaded guilty to criminal practices in 1994, was forced to sell its specialty hospitals where the fraud occurred, entered into a variety of integrity and compliance agreements and paid in the region of U.S. $1 billion in settlements and compensation to patients."

(Under this plea-bargain; NME was also required to sell all of their foreign interests. The government argued that by shedding themselves of their now infamous psychiatric hospitals and their growing portfolio of foreign assets, including a significant ownership in Bumrungrad (40 percent) at the time of the plea-bargain, they would be better able to concentrate on re-mediating themselves.)

"National Medical now borrowed money and expanded rapidly by a series of takeovers and renamed itself Tenet Healthcare. It claimed to be a kinder and more ethical corporation and many believed them. Its policies were directed to securing regional dominance by buying up not for profit hospitals."

"NME entered Australia in 1991. I was already aware of its business practices in its international operations and had been assisted by the Australian Medical Association, the Federal Government and International Airlines in having some matters addressed. I did not however have proof of most of its practices and was unable to block its entry to Australia. During the subsequent years I collected information and was involved in the steps which eventually led to NME, now renamed Tenet Healthcare leaving Australia in 1995."

"Tenet's second incarnation occurred after the stringent controls lapsed in 1999. It immediately resumed its former business policies and practices. It used its market dominance to rapidly increase its prices while at the same time targeting sicker patients and complex procedures. This allowed it to circumvent the restrictions on profits imposed by Diagnosis Related Groups (DRGs) funding."

"The second scandal broke in October 2002. It is clear that the many allegations had substance and that Tenet's underlying business practices were unchanged from the earlier scandal. It was alleged that it once again gamed Medicare to generate vast profits, and that large numbers of patients were subjected to profitable invasive cardiac procedures and surgery when there was no need for this. There were a host of other allegations and a large number of government agencies investigated."

"Tenet fought bitterly to avoid another criminal conviction. It settled multiple actions from government, community and private entities reaching a final global settlement of U.S. $900 million in 2006. It also accepted a stringent Corporate Integrity Agreement CIA: Though it paid about U.S. $2 billion in relation to all these matters it did not admit guilt in any of them. It insisted that even though some of its practices had been inappropriate they were not illegal."

Tenet: Meet the Press

Substantial citations regarding Tenet and NME have been in the Press for years. An Internet search uncovers thousands of references.

The following are slim yet representative extracts of the Press attention Tenet and NME has received:

Hitting financial targets, a current Tenet executive said, depend upon, " . . . how you were judged, paid and evaluated." (Source: Los Angeles Times, December 12, 2002)

"Tenet has honed everything down to the fine art of making money," said Ralph Bard, a Tennessee surgeon who lost privileges at a Tenet hospital where he fretted about patient care. "Tenet will do anything—anything—to make a profit." (Source: "Hearts Harden as Tenet Faces the Senate," Davis, Melissa, The Street.com, September 7, 2003)

"I think at the end of the day, if you look at over the past 15 to 20 years of the company, you'd have to say the management has been pushing the bottom line, telling doctors to cut corners, basically saying we are going to evaluate you and promote you based on how well you make money, not on how well you take care of the patients." (Source: Corporate Culture, March 2006)

"The evidence suggests that the corporate culture is so pervasive that they may well be incapable until there is a total housecleaning of those in management that are a part that corporate culture," Attorney Garg Cripe (Author of Greed, Scandal and Wrongful Deaths at Tenet Healthcare Corporation) (Source: "New Orleans Hospital Operator has Checkered Past," CNN, March 8, 2006)

"Stephen Klaidman's comments on his book Coronary: "My interest was in systemic flaws in American medicine, not criminal fraud. But the more I thought about it the more obvious it seemed to me that vulnerability to fraud was a major systemic flaw in American medicine." The book has received high marks, and a Business Week review says, "Klaidman never forgets that, at its core, this is a tale of a company that seems to have cracked under

pressure from Wall Street to continually boost profits." Americans are at the mercy, ultimately, of a giant medical machine. Parts have our best interests at heart. Other parts will grind our bones to make their bread. (Source: Book review: "Coronary, Cuts to Heart of Tenet Scandal," Brewer, Kelly. Redding Record, January 21, 2007)"

The resume of Tenet Healthcare, AKA National Medical Enterprises, is replete with fraud and criminality. It is beyond my comprehension to understand why not one of their executives has been held criminally liable.

By failing to prosecute fully, a strong signal is given. Simply put, do whatever you want, pay the piper and go back to business as usual. They have been, and continue to this day to be, a toxic agent what is supposed to be a lawful society.

Tenet is not alone. It and other big players in the insurance and hospital business regularly are held above the law. They pay for the privilege.

Their political lobby is strong, as are their connections. Jeb Bush, former Governor of Florida, is on their Board of Directors, as is former Senator Bob Kerry (D-Nebraska) who is also the New School President (Kerry is listed on University literature as the Hon. J. Robert Kerry!)

Is there any wonder that our society is in freefall?

Tenet Links to Bumrungrad International Hospital

I was astonished when research in Securities and Exchange records revealed that Tenet, having been under U.S. Federal order to divest their foreign holdings, still appears to own Bumrungrad! This excerpt is extracted from the Tenet Healthcare 2002 Annual Report, their 10-K:

The Securities and Exchange History:
Tenet and Bumrungrad in 1994:

List of Subsidiaries of Tenet Healthcare Corporation 2002

10-K Annual Report
Tenet Health System International, Inc.
(a)Bumrungrad Medical Center Limited (Thailand)

The following is taken from Tenet's, aka N.M.E. 1994 Annual Report:
From Tenet/N.M.E. 10-K of 1994, the Subsidiary Section we found the following:
"In June 1996 NME will open and manage another Asian venture--554 beds Bumrungrad Hospital in Bangkok. We own 40% of the project, which will be Thailand's largest private hospital. We plan further expansion . . . .."

NATIONAL MEDICAL ENTERPRISES, INC.
Subsidiary Corporations
Revised August 17, 1994

Note: All subsidiaries are 100% owned by "NME" unless otherwise indicated.
(b) Bumrungrad Medical Center Limited (40%)
Tenet also expects to sell its 40% interest in the Bumrungrad Medical Center in Thailand and to sell to its partner its 30% interest in the Subang Jaya Medical Centre in Malaysia prior to the end of the second quarter of fiscal 1996.

Tenet and Bumrungrad in 1995

According to Tenet's 1995 Annual Report, 10-K, Tenet announced that it will sell its interest in Bumrungrad to Parkway Holdings of Singapore for $17 million.

It is very interesting that the amount invested in Bumrungrad is not specified in any 10-K we have examined. Also curious that the $17 million selling price is in addition to an undisclosed sum that they declare in their Annual Report, allegedly paid to Bumbrung (Bumrungrad Medical Center)

What's Up Doc?

Let's examine the stated sales price that Parkway, a Singapore hospital chain, supposedly paid to NME/Tenet for its 40 percent share in Bumrungrad: $17 million for a 554-bed hospital (later 1,000-bed), that was built and equipped at the time of purchase. This roughly translates into approximately $30,000 per bed.

The average hospital bed cost in the United States in 2007 was approximately $1 million per bed (this includes acquisition cost of major capital equipment such as MRI, CAT, and Operating Room facilities).

We will leave it to the reader whether $30,000 is a reasonable price per bed for a 554-bed hospital, even if one corrects for lower construction costs in Thailand and adjusts to 1995 prices.

For alleged shrewd financial operators like Tenet, selling an asset of the size of Bumrungrad for ten to twenty times below market price appears to be either a mistake made by fools or a bold-faced lie.

The affirmation in Tenet's Annual Report of its sale of Bumrungrad to Parkway Holdings of Singapore confirms the transaction. Or does it? The following is extracted from Tenet's 1995 Annual Report:

RECITALS

This Asia Stock Purchase Agreement is entered into as of May 24, 1995, between Parkway Holdings Limited, a Singapore corporation ("Buyer"), and National Medical Enterprises, Inc., a Nevada corporation ("Seller").

WHEREAS, Seller, directly and indirectly through its subsidiaries and affiliates, owns and operates an international hospital, diagnostic, pathology, radiology and related healthcare services business currently operating in Singapore and Malaysia and holds interests in certain activities in Thailand (such operations and interests, as currently conducted, are hereinafter referred to as the "Business");

WHEREAS, the Business is conducted by Seller through NME Asia Pte Ltd., a Singapore corporation ("NME Asia"), Pacific

Medical Enterprises Sdn. Berhad, a Malaysian corporation ("PME"), Subang Jaya Medical Centre Sdn Bhd, a Malaysian corporation, and Bumrungrad Medical Center Limited, a Thailand corporation, and together with NME Asia, and the Subsidiaries of the Companies;

Allocation of Purchase Price Pacific Medical Enterprises Sdn. Berhad (2 shares) and Subang Jaya Medical Centre Sdn. Bhd. (6,186,000 shares) U.S. $12 million
NME Asia Pte Ltd (29,800,002 shares) U.S. $323 million less the U.S. dollar amount determined in Section 1.2(ii)
Bumrungrad Medical Center Limited (22,695,000 shares) U.S. $17 million plus all amounts lent to Bumrungrad by NME Inc. or its affiliates (other than NME Asia or any of its Subsidiaries) subsequent to February 28, 1995.

It is illegal in the U.S., and in Thailand, for that matter, for publicly traded companies to "park" interests or holdings in the name of another. When this is done, a proxy is found to hold the interest in their name and not in the name of the true owner. It's fraud.

From 1995, when Tenet announced its alleged 40 percent interest in Bumrungrad, all remained quiet. A reading of any of Tenet's Annual Reports or any its SEC filings indicates no remaining ownership in Bumrungrad.

Then something changed. Whether by error, loss of memory, the introduction of a new accountant or some other unexplained slip, Tenet's 2002 Annual Report revealed the following.

Tenet and Bumrungrad in 2002

In 1994, NME/Tenet, by its own word, was to have sold its 40 percent stake in Bumrungrad. As part of their plea bargain with the Federal Government, the U.S. Department of Justice ordered Tenet to sell all foreign interests (of which Bumrungrad was one of many).

In 2002, without having shown any admitted ownership since

1995 and seven years after the announced divestiture to Parkway Holdings of Singapore, they admit the following:

List of Subsidiaries of Tenet Healthcare Corporation (partial):

> - Assured Investors Life Company
> - Broadlane, Inc.
> - H.F.I.C. Management Company, Inc.
> - Tenet Health System International, Inc.
> - **Bumrungrad Medical Center Limited (Thailand)**
> - Burleigh House Properties Limited (Bermuda)
> - Centro Medico Teknon, S.L. (Spain)
> - N.M.E. International (Cayman) Limited (Cayman Islands, B.W.I.)
> - B.V. Hospital Management (Netherlands)
> - Hyacinth Sdn. Bhd. (Malaysia)
> - Medical Staff Services Sdn Bhd (Malaysia)
> - NME Spain, S.A: (Spain)
> - New Teknon, S.A: (Spain)
> - Medicalia International, B.V. (Netherlands)
> - Tenet UK Properties Limited

Additionally, despite an order from the United States to sell its psychiatric holdings in 1994, the ownership of over 75 psychiatric facilities were also claimed by Tenet in its 10-K SEC filing of 2002.

When I called Tenet Healthcare to clarify this entry, the Investor's Desk executive flatly denied that they had any ownership in Bumrungrad.

When asked to explain why the following entry was included in their 2002 10-K the response was a slammed telephone receiver.

I subsequently contacted the SEC and requested an immediate investigation. The SEC declined to accept the complaint.

I also called Wall Street analysts who track hospital and insurance stocks. One, in particular, whose identity I have been asked to protect, studied this by consulting fellow analysts tracking the same companies. No one knew anything.

An analyst who had befriended me contacted and then phoned the Investor's Desk at Tenet. The answer this time was simply that they had no idea how this entry had found its way into their 2002 10-K. Our source was not willing to push this question further.

In subsequent years, no correction to this 2002 claim of ownership has been addressed. Also, from 2002 to August 2009, no further mention of Bumrungrad has appeared.

Fraud and abuse by Tenet of patients in its psychiatric hospitals and treatment centers triggered the U.S. Government to launch massive investigations and levy largely unprecedented, multi-billion-dollar fines and penalties on Tenet in 1994.

If it were not enough that Tenet has resurrected its ownership of Bumrungrad, they go on to admit ownership of 14 other foreign subsidiaries!

The significance of all this: Tenet, along with other major hospital and insurance companies, has been investing in foreign owned healthcare facilities. Either through direct or hidden ownership, management or consulting contracts, they have been quietly laying tracks for the concept of Medical Tourism and outsourcing American patients.

The largest American health insurance provider, United Healthcare Group, for example, has been selling foreign human organ location and transplantation policies since 1995. This is addressed in the chapter, Organ Trafficking.

This is an expected but hideous outcropping of Medical Tourism or Outsourcing, given that total lack of regulation and that "donated" organs often come from unwilling victims. The full extent of current organ traffic is just now becoming understood as rings the world over are being exposed.

Devils at work.

Tenet and Bumrungrad: Post Game Analysis

Large buildings are filled with expensive accountants and lawyers paid billions to figure out how to deceive at will. And they do.

As with any multi-tiered deception, I contend that it is nearly impossible, even for the best, to consistently and comprehensively cover the layers of lies that go along with complex fraud.

Though it is unclear whether Tenet did or did not sell its interest in Bumrungrad, the fact that it still maintains ownership are quite strong. Why did a 2002 Annual Report reveal continuing ownership by Tenet of Bumrungrad Hospital? If it was a mistake, why was that mistake not admitted in a subsequent filing or correction? These kinds of corrections happen as a matter of course.

Why was the attendant at Tenet's Investors Desk so nasty as to slam down the receiver when pushed on this question? They could have easily said thanks for pointing out a mistake and corrected their oversight. By not doing so, they open up the real possibility that there is something, indeed, wrong.

The nefarious history of Tenet in America and their head-on collision with the government of Australia suggests that where there is smoke there is fire. The ownership question of Bumrungrad is an acrid smoke, thickening each time we revisited the question: who owns Bumrungrad?

What's the Point?

Winning the argument of whether a company with a deep history of fraud and criminality owns a hospital in Thailand is, really, aside from a larger point.

Healthcare, where one expects fair dealing and good faith, where one anticipates compassion and understanding, where one should necessarily count on the highest training and professionalism, is not the place where Tenet, National Medical

Enterprise and Bumrungrad spend their time.

Tenet and NME have a history of egregious behavior. The crimes for which they have been and continue to be sanctioned by the United States are heinous: not even 1,000 top corporate lawyers or public relations spinners can whitewash or deny the fact that Tenet, aka National Medical Enterprises, engaged in kidnapping, drugging and molestation, and participated in various ways to maim and kill human beings. Yet they walk free.

Have we lost our societal minds?

Are these really the kind of people to whom you should be entrusting your life? I suggest that even a hint of impropriety would provide sufficient reason for a reasonable person to stay away from any facility in which they are involved.

In the case of Tenet, we have much more than a hint. We have a flood of information that lends material credence to a simple reality: their waters are foul.

Not yet convinced? Read on.

Six~ Chairman Chai

Considering getting a new kidney, a new knee or a cardiac bypass at Bumrungrad? Get ready to meet the man who calls all the shots.

Aside from the cloudy question of ownership of Bumrungrad, understanding the people "on the ground" is vital.

Note that in addition to my correspondence with management of Bumrungrad, I communicated directly with their Chairman, Mr. Chai Sophonpanich. Additionally, I directed correspondence to the entire Board of Directors. None of my correspondence was answered.

Chairman of Bumrungrad, Bangkok Bank and Bangkok Insurance, Chai Sophonpanich.

Having served on Boards of Directors for publicly-traded U.S. companies I am keenly aware of the fiduciary responsibility and exposure that comes with Board membership.

Only an arrogant Board would ignore inquiries and complaints of the nature that I lodged (see www.bumrungraddeath.com for verbatim records of my attempted correspondence with Chai and his Board).

It's fair, I believe, to assume that little oversight is provided by the Thai Government, whose last Premier, Thaksin Shinawatra, is now in exile as a result of his ouster from power over his amassing a stupendous fortune from cellular telephony, illegally earned while in office.

Thailand is run by elite, primarily Chinese-Thai cadre of ruthless businessmen and women who silently muscle a country of some 70 million.

They work in all forms of business, banking, insurance, medicine, police, military, government and in the Thai Royal Monarchy.

One of Bumrungrad's lawyers, Mr. Anon, made it immediately clear to me that he was **not** a Buddhist but rather a member of the privileged Catholic Thai elite.

I believe that this distinction was touted to flaunt power and not religious beliefs. The controlling class of Thailand are Thai Chinese and as they readily and proudly offer, Catholic.

Bumrungrad Hospital, in addition to its nefarious historical roots with Tenet Healthcare and N.M.E., is dominated by one of the most ruthless and feared Thailand moguls, Chai Sophanpanich. His reputation, as reported to me by Bangkok insiders, is not that of a warm, fuzzy little bear.

It is not uncommon for Oriental business to be diversified over dozens of different industries. They do a good job of keeping it in the family and keeping it under control.

Here's a brief look at Mr. Chai Sophanpanich's empire, an empire that has, as one of its crown jewels, Bumrungrad Hospital International.

Chairman Chai Flies Only on Air America

Members of Bangkok's U.S. Diplomatic corps, who have requested anonymity, provided interesting background on Mr. Chai Sophanpanich.

A look at the map of Thailand makes it clear why the U.S. set up massive military installations during the Vietnam conflict. Among them are Thailand's immediate neighbors: Vietnam and Cambodia.

During the Vietnam conflict, the C.I.A. ran the legendary Air America., not an airline with scheduled Disneyland stops. This was a transport system and drug-running operation managed by the U.S. for drugs sold in Western markets to covertly finance secret United States operations.

Legend has it that the Chai family fortune was derived from the relationship with the C.I.A. The observant reader can appreciate why diplomats who provided this information required anonymity.

Mr. Chai is a true mogul in the best tradition of the Oriental magnate; operating silently and out of public view. Among many business interests, Chai is Chairman of:

➤ Bangkok Bank;
➤ Bangkok Insurance Company;
➤ Bumrungrad Hospital International.

Chai sits atop some of the most powerful organizations in South East Asia. The composition of the above Boards of Directors shows that these organizations have closely interwoven activities and ownership interests, all controlled by Chairman Chai.

For example, Bumrungrad Hospital is insured by Bangkok Insurance. Bangkok Bank and Bangkok Insurance each own significant stakes in Bumrungrad.

You Have My Assurances, We Are Insured

Though Bumrungrad says that it is fully insured, how many claims do you think Chairman Chai will pay out of his insurance company for mistakes at Bumrungrad? I asked. They declined to answer.

Recall that Bumrungrad Hospital, Bangkok Bank and Bangkok Insurance share the same Chairman: Chai Sophanpanich. To best appreciate the ethics of Bumrungrad, look at the activities of the other companies under the watchful and—according to Bangkok insiders—ruthless eye of Chairman Chai.

Bangkok Bank is, perhaps, the largest commercial and consumer Bank in South East Asia. Hence, it is important to note the Cease and Desist Order issued by the United States Department of the Treasury naming Bangkok Bank for money laundering:

(See Appendix #11)

I have expounded on Chai to convey that Bumrungrad is just another means to make a killing. Chairman Chai does not play for small stakes. It's the big time or no time.

Make no mistake; Chai has greedy counterparts in the United States, Britain and around the world. But Chai is behind selling you something you should be cautious about buying: healthcare.

I have worked with many of the world's largest corporations, to the Board and Senior Executive levels. Companies tend to assume the character and personality of the person on top.

Proper health care is, of course, a business. But once that business loses compassion and care for the people who entrust them with their care, horrendous things can happen. And they do.

The Medical Tourism phenomenon—really the outsourcing of medical care—has its roots in Thailand.

Medical outsourcing operates with impunity and without regulation. There is no legal recourse when something goes awry. They will tell you anything you want to hear and whatever it takes to get you in the door.

At the end of the day, no matter how much icing and decoration is put on this rancid cake, it tastes like what it is and not what it appears to be: shit.

No one should be deceived by the slick websites, the pretty pictures, the concierge and the doorman at the hospital. The outsourced patient is simple grist for their mill. If something goes awry, they will cover up and toss out your remains as if you were human garbage or, spare parts.

Seven ~ The Star Tangled Banner

The tangled world of healthcare seems like an undecipherable riddle. What's wrong? Who's responsible; the doctors, the insurance **megalopoly**, the pharmaceutical giants, the hospital owners, the government, Medicare? The suspects are seemingly everywhere!

I do not want to espouse a deliberate conspiracy theory about how the pieces of this dizzying puzzle are put together. However, whether deliberate or by happenstance, it is unmistakable that a toxic interaction of interests has congealed and solidified behind the "crisis" of healthcare.

I believe that the picture illuminated in the following pages holds a new perspective on what has gone wrong. I realize that such a bold proclamation may seem presumptuous, but I am willing to go out on that limb!

I beg the reader's patience and forbearance. To understand how I have solved the puzzle, you need background knowledge about the critical Actors you will get to know in this book.

The Bottom Line

The cornerstone of my revelations is that there is a complex fabric of social engineering masterminded by the health insurance cartel that is targeting the well being and the lives of an entire nation.

Mine is a tale about insidious characters with sinister and dark motives. It is an unobvious tale. My intention and hope is to lay bare a stark and frightening reality: that we, as a populace, are being set up for a fall of epic proportions, perpetrated by corporate interests and compelled by unrestrained greed in which no life, anywhere, is sacred.

My journey has led me to Bangkok seven times, to the General of all Police in Thailand, to Interpol and the FBI, to the CIA to the Office of the United States Ambassador in Thailand, to the Senate Committee on Finance and the Sub-Committee on Healthcare, to The Joint Commission in Oakbrook, Illinois.

My career has been devoted to solving complex technical and business problems. Often this has involved working with major corporations, many of them ferocious competitors, a quality fundamental to capitalism.

I have also seen that many corporations go well behind the rules of decency, crossing over into gain at any cost. This is the unfortunate and terrible reality that I have discovered in my journey to find the truth out about who killed my only son.

Most, in America believe evil could never be perpetrated by individuals who seem like decent people. I have always struggled with the idea that the recognition of true evil in others is anathema, an illusion that we imagine. It is not.

Who were these people? What were they doing? Why?

For 36 months, while engaged in a dogged investigation of what happened to Josh on the night of February 23, 2006 around 9:00 PM Bangkok, Thailand time, I struggled with the nightmare and trembling of having lost my son.

The pain is so deep there is no form of expression to describe how this reality has permeated my every moment. I have contemplated how to relate this terrible tale. It is far beyond just the grieving of a devastated father. It is critical and urgent because my investigation has revealed a tacit or explicit conspiracy in the healthcare industry.

Seeing the World as it Is

There is evil in the world, and evil agents. The sooner we confront that the faster we can move to a solution where integrity has a chance and honor can be resurrected to eradicate the forces of suppression.

The investigation into Josh's death revealed things I would have never imagined. I wish I could have constructed the telling of this story by concentrating on him—solely—but his death, his murder, is a key to a much larger door.

The opening of that door has shocked my sensibilities, astounded my logic and contradicted all the assumptions I had acquired in my lifetime.

As is the case in classic propaganda intended for social control, we are sold distortions by media sources, whose powers are now conveniently consolidated in the hands of a very few.

Government and industry—or what Eisenhower called the Military, Industrial Complex—have perversely abused and disemboweled our traditional balance of powers. These powers have become closely interwoven, leaving little opportunity for redress by the ordinary citizen.

The healthcare industry, subsequent to the government's entry into healthcare in 1965 and the formation of Medicare, has seen unbelievable corruption and billions stolen by corporations and individuals who receive slaps on the hand and symbolic fines, which are included in the cost of doing business.

Only individual doctors, pharmacists and small-time players are severely punished. The big corporations are, with a few minor exceptions never subject to criminal prosecution and conviction.

This Can't Wait

This is an urgent story. Among my revelations:

- There is an American Medical Money Machine;
- My son's death needed to be seen in the context of an International Tragedy;
- There are specific causes and responsible parties who have caused The Destruction of Healthcare in America;
- The new movement called Medical Tourism is actually the latest manifestation of same corruption that has destroyed healthcare in the U.S.

Responsible Capitalism

I am not against capitalism. Far from it.

I am, however, for capitalism with responsibility, social good and oversight that protects the weak, the disadvantaged and the unsuspecting.

The healthcare of hundreds of millions is now firmly in the grip of institutions and individuals who care nothing for precious, miraculous life. They grip only for power and gain. They have found that medical care is a good place to tap into deep veins of wealth and they do so with impunity.

Trusting that balance and fairness will be maintained by relying on the integrity of our government institutions has become a tragic folly, now the forgotten musings of our founding fathers.

The U.S. has become a brutal place since the time I sold lemonade for UNICEF as a seven-year-old kid on the street corner of Great Neck, New York circa 1955, before the crashing fall of compassion in Western society and the rise of unbridled greed.

The following list is by no means comprehensive. It represents the "players:" I encountered along my journey-there are dozens more!

Batter Up! The American Medical Money Machine Roster.

Actor #1 Bumrungrad International Hospital

The self-declared leader of the world of Medical Tourism, based in Bangkok Thailand, formerly and still (we believe) owned by Tenet Hospital Corporation, one of the most egregious offenders of Medicare Fraud that have cost the taxpayers of the U.S. billions of dollars.

This hospital has been the lynchpin in creating the marketing illusion of Medical Tourism.

They have been discovered to have grossly misrepresented their organization, quality of care and even the licensure of their doctors.

Bumrungrad has offices around the world, but not in the United States. They avoid the U.S. for fear of liability. They should be afraid.

The question of U.S. jurisdiction will be carefully examined. The lack of American jurisdiction provides complete immunity from any liability.

The two operational leaders of Bumrungrad are former Tenet executives; good old boys schooled by National Medical Enterprises cum Tenet Healthcare—a major offender in the nonstop game of Medicare fraud.

In the early 1990s National Medical Enterprises, as it was then known, was fined hundreds of millions for Medicare fraud and horrific acts conducted at their psychiatric clinics that the government forced them to shut down or sell. Charges against them also included criminal acts, to which they pleaded guilty.

In addition to their psychiatric centers, the U.S. forced them to sell their foreign interests. In the case of Bumrungrad, they did not. It also appears from their most recent annual reports that they are back in the psychiatric hospital business in full force.

Despite Tenet's (aka National Medical Enterprises) lack of adherence to government regulations and court orders, multimillion-dollar fines have rolled off their backs and not one of their executives has even gone to jail. Not one.

Actor #2: The Joint Commission for the Accreditation of Healthcare Organizations

The decline of healthcare in the United States can be traced back to 1965 when the Johnson Administration enacted the Medicare program. Overnight, the United States Government entered the business of healthcare. The act of Congress that legitimized this program was called the Amendment to the Social Security Act of

1935 or The Medicare Act of 1965.

This critical piece of legislation established the parameters and operational procedures by which Medicare was to be run. A vastly overlooked aspect of this legislation dealt with the seemingly innocuous business of who would become responsible for accrediting healthcare organizations to be eligible to receive Medicare reimbursement.

The 1965 legislation designated a little known group called the Joint Commission for the Accreditation of Healthcare Organizations (JC).

The Joint Commission was formed in the 1920s by a group of physicians primarily interested in standardizing healthcare, hospital and surgical procedures, medication regimens etc. Over the years, the JC operated ex officio of the government. They aligned themselves along the way with another group, The American Hospital Association. The Hospital Association appears to have been instrumental in steering the Congress to designate the Joint Commission with the extraordinary powers of deeming hospitals worthy of receiving payment from the Federal Government.

Actors #3 and #4: The American Hospital Association and Health and Human Services

The American Hospital Association (AHA) is made up of owners and operators of hospitals in the United States. Today, the AHA is an extremely powerful and economically deep affiliation.

Often, insurance company interests are commingled with the hospitals, producing a kind of hybrid where hospitals offer participant systems such as health- maintenance organizations (HMOs), preferred-provider organizations (PPOs) and other types of insurance plans.

The JC's own recanting of its history states that the JC did not seek the endorsement of Congress for the job of accreditation. According to their book, Champions of Quality in Health Care: A History of the Joint Commission on Accreditation of Healthcare

Organizations, their partner, the American Hospital Association, sponsored their candidacy for the position of Chief Accreditor.

The United States Enters the Health Insurance Business

The United States Government and the then Department of Health, Education and Welfare (formerly the HEW, currently Health and Human Services or HHS) realized that they lacked expertise and personnel to determine which healthcare organizations were worthy of accreditation. Also, the government realized that setting standards for medical care was outside their scope and knowledge.

The historic legislation that created Medicare (including designating the JC to act as a quasi-government agency in lieu of or in partnership with the HEW/HHS), would determine who could be on the receiving end of money from Washington.

➤ The legislation contains important caveatsThe accrediting agency (the JC) would have "deeming" authority;
➤ The deeming authority, with approval by HEW/HHS, would set standards for the industry;
➤ The "deeming" authority would have the ability to sanction, suspend or revoke healthcare accreditation;
➤ The "deeming" authority would be responsible for policing the organizations that it accredited;
➤ Statistics and reports would be periodically available to the Federal Government;
➤ In the event of a revocation or suspension doled out by the "deeming authority," (i.e., the Joint Commission), the organization receiving a disciplinary action would have the ability to turn to the United States Justice system for adjudication. In effect, the JC would inflict the penalty but the U.S. legal system would intercede in the event of dispute;
➤ Payment for the services the JC provided for "deeming" healthcare organizations would be set and approved by the Secretary of HEW/HHS;
➤ Accreditation activities are limited to the Continental U.S. and its Territories;

> Medicare benefits are made available to U.S. citizens, living or visiting outside of the United States.

Advising the United States Senate

These points have been forgotten with time, even by the advisors to the Senate Finance Committee that oversees the Medicare program. I was dumbfounded that they had been unaware of the critical points of responsibility designated by the Congress some 45 years ago.

I cast no aspersions here. These are underpaid and overworked assistants to our Senators and Congressmen. But it would seem requisite to have mastered an understanding of governing law.

Whether the American Hospital Association (AHA) or the Joint Commission (JC) appreciated the incredible power delivered into their hands in 1965 is a matter of speculation. What is not a matter of speculation is a simple concept: Without accreditation, Medicare will not pay! Following suit, private insurance will also most often not pay.

This critical financial "valve" is systematically overlooked in the current considerations (Summer 2009) of healthcare reform. Additionally disregarded in the current debate being waged is the exclusive financial hold exerted by the corporate insurance administrators of both public and private healthcare plans.

Lawmakers and policy analysts have chosen not to focus too deeply on the stranglehold the health administrators maintain. This "head in the sand" attitude goes to the core of why our inherent infrastructural problems run so deep: political contributions keep the permanent campaign-finance machines greased.

Everything can be disturbed; it appears, except for the real inner workings of the "administrators." Interest groups spend fortunes to make sure that discussions remain silent on just how much money is being stolen from patient care and stuffed into the pockets of a few mega-insurance manipulators.

Without attention to the core problem, everything that follows will be an exercise in futility. The house, no matter how elegant, will not stand if its foundations are corroded with corruption.

This is the world in which we live. It is the world we must change.

Actors #5 through #9: United Healthcare, Blue Shield, Blue Cross, TriCare and Tenet Healthcare

The power accompanying the accreditation concept is beyond measure.

As of 2007, daily Medicare expenditures hit $1.2 billion, rising by the minute.

With President Obama's plan to expand Federal health programs to include virtually the entire population come unprecedented amounts of money for the private insurance administrators to dole out, largely, as they see fit. The other option open to health administrators such as United Healthcare, Blue Shield, Blue Cross and Tenet Healthcare is one that they have taken many, many times: steal!

The record of theft is staggering, measurable in the trillions. Without fear of paying personal penalties, executives have little to fear.

Errant doctors, rehab centers and the like are constantly being investigated for having their hands in the cookie jar. Here, I refer to theft by mega-corporations that have adopted theft as a matter of policy.

This policy is played out in numerous ways: denial of care, shorting payments to doctors, increased deductibles and co-pays, substantial delays in making payments, withholding and disputing payments, losing billings and disconnection from telephone customer-service inquires. You name it, they've done it.

It is not well understood that private insurance companies administer Medicare payments and benefits. Medicare, the U.S. Government and private insurers are now so tightly inter-woven that it is impossible to distinguish one from the other.

Remember: having an insurance plan does not mean that you have real medical coverage!   There is a difference between healthcare insurance and medical care!

Crime Pays: Big, Especially When the Police are Out to Lunch

Medicare fraud is big business. The current cost to the system is approximately $600 billion a year, according to the Department of Justice (DOJ).

For the perpetrators, fraud and theft is the cost of doing business. The DOJ proudly proclaims victory at being able to recapture upwards of $1 billion a year, of which approximately $250 million is attributed to the DOJ's costs.

In other words, a net of $750 million is collected for sanctions and fines for violations calculated by the DOJ to be $600 billion, a conservative estimate!

Translation: less than 1.25 percent of the stolen proceeds from Medicare alone are recovered annually, hardly an incentive for the thieves to go straight.

These sanctions are only those that have been identified; hundreds of billions of dollars slip through the cracks. These numbers are also completely separate from the thievery afoot with private healthcare policies in the form of retroactive cancellation of policies, underpayment of benefits, denial of benefits, refusal to disperse doctor-specified medications, slow pay, no pay and delays of every shape and color.

The Soap Opera

A typical scenario: the FBI investigates a company for Medicare fraud. After the perpetrator is indicted, a long and expensive legal battle ensues between the Justice Department and the battalions of lawyers at the beck and call of the megalopoly.

A trial date is set, the parties settle when the jury is seated and no one goes to jail. The Justice Department requires that the offending company issue an, "I'm sorry and I promise to be a good boy," letter and everyone goes back to business as usual.

The lack of legal tooth encourages these mega companies to commit one massive fraud after another. And they do.

A mind-boggling example of how these offending companies are actually rewarded for being criminals is the 1998 revocation of the Blue Shield of California franchise to administer Medicare benefits. Because of self-admitted fraud against Medicare, Blue Shield of California was fined and banned from administering Medicare benefits.

Millions in fees are raked off the top by the administrators for services rendered. Denial of care, underpayment or nonpayment of benefits leaves untold sums in the corporate coffers. This little game is but one manifestation of the types of fraud in which these folks are expert.

Breaking Up is Hard to Do!

In 2004, Blue Shield of California, long dropped as a Medicare administrator, was awarded one of the greatest prizes of all: administration of TriCare, the active military and retiree insurance plan funded by the Federal Government around the globe for U.S. citizens. That's right. If you call TriCare, the receptionist will answer, "Blue Shield/TriCare, may I help you?"

Getting to Know Your Tenet

Tenet Healthcare, perhaps ranking as the baddest of the bad, was slapped with a $900 million fine for Medicare fraud in 2007 and given four years to pay.

Remember, Tenet is an active member of the AHA. Even more interesting, Tenet's Board consists of such luminaries as former Florida Governor Jeb Bush and former Senator Robert Kerry, now President of the New School University in New York City. The apples do not fall far from the tree.

Immediately after the 2007 fines were levied, Tenet declared that three of their hospitals were a complete loss to Hurricane Katrina: They collected $345 million from their property carriers plus tax write-offs for casualty loss. This payment, in theory, puts Tenet ahead, leaving less than $600 million to be paid down in four installments. In their terms, this is peanuts, an ordinary expense of doing business.

The "follow the money" theory makes an important point. To understand the flow of dollars, ask, "Who benefits?"

No Accreditation, No $$$

Coming full circle to our friends at the JC, it should be clear that many cause-and-effect relationships are in play. Without an accredited hospital, Federal insurance dollars do not flow and usually, neither do private insurance dollars. An unaccredited hospital or medical care facility goes away—quickly.

What would a hospital do to get the coveted prize of Joint Commission Accreditation? How about: pay for it?!

Actors #10, #11 and #12: The Joint Commission Consulting Group, the Senate Finance Committee and the General Accounting Office

Conflicting Interests!

Pay for it they do. The Joint Commission charges fees to healthcare organizations to be accredited. The Joint Commission Consulting Group charges fees to have its "Resources" division "help" hospitals prepare for the very accreditation that their parent division will provide.

Senator Chuck Grassley (R-Iowa) and Senator Max Baucus (D-Montana), Co-Chairs of the Senate Finance Committee, have had the Joint Commission investigated for conflicts of interest, AKA self dealing.

The General Accounting Office (GAO) has published two extensive studies commissioned by the Senate of the United

States. Both of these studies have called for the revocation of the "deeming authority" of the JC. The summer of 2008 produced an historic piece of legislation. For the first time since 1965, the exclusive "deeming" authority held by the Joint Commission was revoked.

David v. Goliath

I am proud to have worked with the United States Congress, Medicare and the Department of Health and Human Services. I provided a detailed discussion of the inner workings of the Joint Commission to the Center for Medicare Services (CMS) and the Congress.

In revealing my detailed case study and interactions with the Joint Commission, the Federal Government ended the monopoly previously held by the Joint Commission for 50 years. This was a small victory, but an important one in David v. Goliath.

Currently, the JC admits to accrediting some 16,000 healthcare institutions and organizations in the U.S., all for fees payable yearly to the Joint Commission.

Since 1965, though the Joint Commission has full authority to revoke or suspend accreditation (which, as we have seen, is good as gold), it has acted to revoke or suspend less than one-tenth of one percent of all the accreditations ever granted.

The only implication from this is that the current and past Secretaries of HHS have not discharged their lawful duties to supervise the financial activities of the Joint Commission. I believe that this no accident.

Numerous government officials jump over into lucrative lobbying and industry positions in consideration for playing softball with the Joint Commission and the "pillars" of industry they represent.

In practice, accredited organizations have nothing to fear. The JC, designated by Congress as the official police of healthcare standards in the United States, is paid to do nothing when it comes to enforcement.

While it is true that the Joint Commission and its divisions proffer high-minded advice, which they do with poetic elegance and self-importance, they do not do what the law requires. They have failed to protect the care and safety of patients.

The Joint Commission has placed their "protection" racket of special interests above the mandate of Congress.

Since no one at the Federal Government seems to be policing the police, as also required by the 1965 legislation, it has been a nearly non-stop bash at the continued expense of the American people.

Unless this organization and those who they represent are properly policed, the party will continue unabated.

The JC's latest foray—deeming organizations outside the United States and making it appear as if their accreditations are the same as at home—is fraud, plain and simple. This is where Medical Tourism gains legitimacy. Since few know the true workings of the Joint Commission, the public blindly accepts JC accreditation abroad.

Prime Actors of Shame

In subsequent chapters, we'll delve into an examination of the significance of this little known organization, the Joint Commission.

This harmful organization, which poses as a helpful friend of patients and doctors, is a happy purveyor of ongoing and under-realized fraud.

The primogenitors behind the JC are the insurance companies, the pharmaceutical companies, the hospital conglomerates and, sad to say, the United States Government.

Since the Commission's activities, decisions and meetings are all held under confidential privilege, none of their activities can be clearly seen except by an examination of their disastrous effects.

When I asked the Commission in 2006, 2007 and 2008 to provide the legal basis on which they claimed confidential privilege, they refused to answer. Instead, I was handed the standard line: "We'll get back to you on that." They never have.

I would have expected more from Harold Bressler, since he is the Chief Legal Counsel for the Joint Commission.

Actor #13: The Joint Commission International

Pack Your Bags!

The scenario being played out by the Joint Commission contemplates that the public will accept the legitimacy of offshore healthcare, since it bears the imprimatur of the Joint Commission INTERNATIONAL (JCI). Yep, the JCI is one of the latest inventions conjured up by the kind folks in Oak Brook, Illinois, headquarters of the Joint Commission.

What You Don't Know Can Kill You

What the public doesn't realize is that foreign accreditation is worth even less than accreditation at home.

The wanton, reckless and criminal disregard for the safety of a whole country is the handiwork of the Joint Commission. Under the JC's watch, the U.S. has declined from first in the world in excellence in healthcare to somewhere near 40th (as of 2002) and falling. Good citizens, we're talking about competing with Estonia!

The infiltration of the Federal and State Governmental infrastructures by lobbyists is so pervasive as to make it impossible to distinguish where one leaves off and the other begins.

Read this and weep: we spend three times more per capita than any other nation on earth to live with a system that is near to Third World status. So where is all this money going?

The money machine does not operate unless the accreditation is in effect. In a sense, the moniker of legitimacy needs to be in place for any person to have enough confidence to hop up on the operating table. This moniker is brought to you by people who don't care if you live or die: the Joint Commission and its secret cabal who meet behind closed doors, hidden completely from public view.

They have been accountable to no one. Their decisions impact trillions of dollars. What's even more amazing is that hardly anyone knows that they exist or what they do.

That's just the way they want it: keep the primal source of power underlying an entire industry out of sight, out of the Press and away from attention.

As Medicare gravitates from its initial platform for insuring the indigent and poor to becoming the basic infrastructure to cover all Federal health insurance, the Joint Commission has held increasing power over a business that is perhaps one of the largest on the planet. The opportunity for corruption has and continues to be enormous.

It is no secret that this has been happening and continues to happen. The JC has seen to it that its A-Team is protected. Completely!

The Joint Commission does not surface in the debate because they have paid for their perceived right to privacy. In the same way, so has the healthcare insurance industry cartel, a term I will use frequently in this work. They pay big bucks to remain hidden in the brush or crouching behind the coattails of apparently do-good organizations like the AARP. There is more on this astonishing "friendship" in chapters to follow.

Playing With a Marked Deck

So, who is on the A-Team? The Joint Commission consists of 29

Commission members. Hence, the Joint Commission! These members include but are not limited to:

> - the sitting CEO of the JC;
> - the American Hospital Association (AHA);
> - the American Medical Association (AMA);
> - the American Nursing Association (ANA);

Theoretically, the balance of powers sitting on the Commission looks good: those with special interests such as the American Hospital Association and the American Nursing Association and those enfranchised to guard social values such as patients advocacy representation.

The Joint Commission should work well. It doesn't.

The seated CEO/President of the JC, the AHA and the AMA can out vote the other 26 Commission members. No equal representation here. These illusion-makers are great at deception: create a Commission that says it's dedicated to the good of all, but secretly, only gives three of its members any real power.

They look legitimate at first glance, but don't plan on staying for dinner!

Sheer Poetry

Reading the prose and edicts of the Joint Commission makes it appear that mankind is receiving word from heavenly forces regarding medical care and patient safety. Think of something like "Medical Scriptures."

Their rhetoric is brilliant. They have also succeeded in wielding enormous force over the entire medical community.

The very mention of a Joint Commission "survey" instills fear in every hospital executive in America. Making this fear even more curious is that the hospitals pay the Joint Commission for Accreditation. Translation: paying to be afraid!

Without the accreditation everything stops: no accreditation, no money, no money, no nothing.

This would not be so onerous if the Joint Commission undertook its mission on a level playing field. They don't. By not policing and enforcing the accreditations they are empowered to "deem", their surveys are merely a show of force and power. The Joint Commission wields fantastic power capriciously and without oversight. They are feared since they can refuse to re-certify a hospital without reason.

At the end of the day, like good mafia captains, the JC collects their protection, um, accreditation, payments, leaving the grateful hospital alone until the next payment becomes due. This is a hard fact.

It's Strictly Confidential

Since the JC's records are claimed confidential, those few who have had their accreditations revoked appear to have been the victims of political agendas. Perhaps this has been motivated for business or political reasons.

The JC have the clout to push down the price of a troubled organization, making it a juicy acquisition target for those friendly to the Joint Commission. Since their records are secret, we have yet to know the depths of their chicanery.

When I queried the JC on which hospitals they sanctioned, they provided a short list of hospitals that had been reprimanded, in different ways, but refused to provide the reasons why.

In the arena of self dealing, we do know that Tenet Healthcare, one of our "bad boys," was represented on the Joint Commission during a time when their Palm Beach hospital was under investigation for Medicare fraud and for performing unnecessary coronary procedures.

The Tenet official sitting on the Joint Commission was not asked to recuse himself from the investigation: a clear conflict of interest. The Joint Commission survey, after a Florida and U.S.

government investigation, re-certified and accredited the very hospital over which the Tenet executive had authority, in his capacity as a representative of the American Hospital Association.

Astronomers cannot see black holes in space. They only know they exist because stars and galaxies sucked into the "event horizon" are never seen or heard from again. They simply disappear.

This is a good analogy for the way in which the Joint Commission, a 501(c) (3) organization, conducts its affairs, enjoying a tax-free ride in the process.

We don't know what goes on inside the event horizon but we can see what happens around it. Instead of the transparency with which they claim to operate, they are as opaque as lead. If the public does not demand change, the secret manipulations of the Joint Commission will remain a well-kept secret. A secret held at the expense of an entire society.

The JC wields enormous power. This power is slung around in virtual secrecy. Absolute power corrupts absolutely.

No minutes of JC Board meetings are publicly available since they are a private company.

Additionally, adding mind-numbing insult to injury, they organize under the aforementioned 501(c) (3) banner: a nonprofit organization operating in the public interest.

They claim confidentiality to protect their vice grip on virtual secrecy and they are doing so under their tax-exempt banner whose codes and statutes mandate complete transparency in the public interest.

Though difficult to discover and prove, the interests of major pharmaceutical ("big pharma") and health-insurance companies operate in lockstep with the Joint Commission. Our society has paid an awesome price for the actions of this elite group of private interests.

By failing to discharge their fiduciary duties as dictated by the legislation of 1965, the Joint Commission has protected the flow of money from the government to hospitals that without accreditation would wither and die in days.

Do You Have 60 Minutes?

The phenomenon commonly referred to as Medical Tourism had been anointed by CBS's *60 Minutes*, along with numerous other mainstream television, magazine and newspaper reports, as being wonderful for Americans seeking cheaper healthcare delivered in luxurious settings, delivered, of course, by the world's leading and most qualified doctors.

Yet my intimate experience in dealing with the daily recalcitrance of the Bumrungrad and the Joint Commission presents a different story.

I knew something was rotten. There was no way for me to reconcile the enormous chasm between the "marketed" perception of credibility and the cold, hard facts that these people had no intention whatsoever of being forthcoming about Josh's death.

It didn't fit. I was not going to accept the thinly-veiled explanations offered by both the hospital and the responses from the Joint Commission.

The actual text of correspondence with both Bumrungrad and the Joint Commission is replete with nonsense and fuzzy catch phrases.

I am an experienced professional accustomed to quickly mastering complex issues and technologies. This is my educational and professional training. I know doubletalk and this was it, in spades.

Outsourcing You!

After wrecking healthcare in America, the corporate medical machine is now on a concerted march to do the unimaginable:

outsource you and your healthcare to the far reaches of the world. By so doing, they are just beginning to enjoy untold new sources of profit, garnished at your safety and expense:

> It is not enough that reimbursement levels to doctors are at an all time low, forcing doctors out of medicine by the droves;
> It is not enough that co-pays and deductibles are at all time highs, making it impossible for all but the well-heeled to afford medical care.

Even if one is insured, there is a reasonable chance your insurance plan will balk at the diagnostics, therapy and medications your doctor recommends. The insurance cartel operates from a "playbook" designed to deny benefits in order to increase profits. As a matter of fact, insurance companies bonus their staff for successfully frustrating a doctor's plan for how best to care for a patient!

Exporting Patients Hurts Healthcare At Home

Physicians and medical professionals who argue with insurance companies can expect to have their careers smashed. Blacklisting assures that doctors will never work again because they dared to question "authority." These companies override the medical professional and, in effect, practice medicine without a license.

Health insurers want more and they have found a new way to get it at your expense and safety: Medical Tourism. I believe that a more appropriate nomenclature would be Medical Outsourcing.

God help you if anything goes wrong! You are in the jurisdiction of another country.

One can have no legal recourse from those who sent you away (employers and insurance companies) or from those who have hurt you (foreign resources enlisted to render treatment without any oversight!).

It's a double bind.

Second and Third World countries with sporadic medical training and experience have become willing participants in the Medical Tourism phenomenon.

Medical Outsourcing cum Medical Tourism is a concept now heartily embraced by health plans and insurance interests . . . a far cry from a sick tourist seeking the best local care where they happen to be. This phenomenon of Medical Tourism is going mainstream and is being institutionalized and incorporated into the very fabric of the way medical care will soon be generally delivered.

At home, the healthcare insurance mavens have made billions but have suffered only modest, painful obstruction posed by regulation. Abroad, these industries can operate with absolute impunity.

In places such as Thailand, Singapore, China, India and Cambodia, regulations are thin to non–existent.

Virtually everything is available and for sale. This prefaces what promises to be a global shift in the delivery of healthcare. Don't take your eyes off this for a second. This is not an abstraction. You could find yourself on the next plane. You think this is crazy? You're not crazy.

Conspiracy? What Does This Mean, RICO?

The historic meaning of the word conspiracy means with intention or with spirit. Conspiracy has come to mean, in modern terms, with common and illegal agreement.

Conspiracy can come in many flavors from activities that are deliberate and coordinated to events that are synchronic and emerge from a common zeitgeist (C. Jung). The results, however, are similar: a common series of actions designed to achieve an intended result.

I will not quibble as to whether the conspiracy in this matter is one flavor or the other. But the result, whatever definition is applied, appears to be bluntly Fascistic, with a common

Eight~ The U.S. Wins at Losing

The context in which Medical Tourism took root is important to understand. Medical Outsourcing aka Medical Tourism did not appear spontaneously. Many catalyzing forces combined, in the United States and other major countries, to the detriment and viability of health care "at home."

Fantastic sums of money are involved in U.S. health care, nearing 20 percent of the Gross National Product and escalating rapidly, according to the Office of Management and Budget (OMB) in 2009.

Yet everything seems to be broken except for the insurance companies, the hospital companies who also offer insurance plans and the pharmaceutical industry. The industry, broadly defined, beats the SP; especially in "down" markets.

Chart comparing Relative Strength of Healthcare Sector vs. S&P 500. (Source John Kosar, Asbury Research, LLC.)

Big and Getting Bigger

This excerpt from an Internet posting on the Rocky Mountain News is nicely concise:

Rocky Mountain News (Excerpts)
Michele Swenson
Published June 9, 2008 at midnight
The U.S. averages twice as much spending on healthcare, with worse outcomes, than any other industrialized nation.

Our country is unique in its dependence on over 1200 for-profit health insurances that function as gatekeepers to healthcare. Shareholder and CEO profits trump access to quality healthcare.

No healthcare reform proposal by any presidential candidate addresses the failure of the private health insurance industry, characterized principally by rising premiums and decreasing benefits. Premium increases of 87 percent over 6 years outpace both cost-of-living and median family income increases.

Commercial health insurance is the 800-pound gorilla, responsible for 20 to 30% of healthcare dollars siphoned to excessive administrative costs, lobbying, marketing, CEO salaries and profit-taking - $1.4 billion stock options to former UnitedHealth CEO William McGuire; $30 billion annual after-tax health insurance profits, plus $32 billion insurance underwriting and marketing costs, revealed by the McKinsey Group Report of 2007.

Profit is a perverse incentive for quality healthcare: imagine for-profit fire or police protection. Underwriting is the art of evaluating and avoiding risk, insuring profits by covering the healthy and rejecting everyone else as a "pre-existing condition."

"Market-driven" healthcare treats health as a commodity, to be negotiated like a car or a house. Free-market healthcare has also spawned "designer hospitals," built to offer only the most profitable specialty services, e.g., cardiac procedures, eliminating less profitable care, such as emergency room and mental health.

The Wall Street Journal (2/14/07) report that gaming the system for profit has given rise to the $20 billion annual business of "denial management" - health insurance middlemen employed solely to search claims for excuses to delay, deny or renege on reimbursements. Thirty percent of provider claims are initially denied, requiring multiple re-submittals.

To protect their bottom line, commercial insurers write policies with reduced benefits, shifting more out-of-pocket costs and risks to consumers, and in turn subjecting more to underinsurance, unpaid medical bills and personal bankruptcies.

Despite cyclic fluctuations and expected exceptions to the rule, the insurance behemoths have shown a steady increase in profitability.

While the giant insurance players have been hoarding billions, a systematic squeeze play has been put on the medical consumer via ballooning premiums, expanding co-pays, inflating deductibles and steady increases in the cost of medications. Co-laterally, as the costs continue to bulge, we are experiencing:

> diminishing quality of care;
> long waits in obtaining medical appointments;
> shorter doctor visits;
> difficult access to specialists;
> long visits to the emergency room;
> medications that conform with insurance company formularies;
> denial of benefits;
> slow pay;
> no pay;
> disputed pay;
> retroactive cancellation of insurance policies;
> unrealistic COBRA payments;
> exclusion of prior conditions;
> denial of psychiatric and psychological care;
> recalcitrant customer service centers;
> interminable waiting times for telephone inquires;
> shortened hospital stays;
> exposure to deadly hospital infections;
> HMOs paying employees not to deliver care;
> dizzying paperwork;
> decreased competition in healthcare insurance.

And Then, Medicare

In 1965, when Medicare was enacted by President Lyndon Johnson under the umbrella of his Great Society, Medicare was intended for those who could not afford health care and people who had reached an age of certain maturity.

In 1965 the United States was, unarguably, the world's epicenter for medical excellence. The well-heeled, when they required healing well, came to the United States for health care. Heads of State, celebrities, the business and social power elite all sought care in the major health care centers of the United States. They were smart to have done so.

The United States was certainly, on a global basis, a distant first in the quality of care, technology, pharmaceutical development and lower rates of morbidity and mortality measured on just about any scale. Then the United States of America got into the healthcare and insurance business.

The Heist of the Century

In the nearly fifty years since, health care in America has been on a cataclysmic dive into a frightening abyss. Every assumption about health care has been up ended.

Progressively, while the cartel indulged in an unprecedented binge, those who deliver health care and those who receive it have been humiliated, subjugated and victimized. Patients and doctors, who have suffered mightily, have sought alternatives. Without exception, all have resulted in a culminating medical and social disaster. Why?

The insurance mob descended on Washington when Hillary Clinton, then First Lady, tried to make things right. Whatever her intentions, the affair turned nasty.

Dear President Obama

In the 2008 Presidential election, along came Obama. The insurance gang was all smiles, captured standing, hands piously crossed, behind the future President of the United States—they all came together for a love fest, proclaiming vows of cooperation and dedication to fixing our terribly broken medical system.

The problem is that most of Obama's advisors are the very criminals who created, voted for and are now lobbying for the status quo. What this means is that the money interests are likely to continue to control whatever reform is result is bound to be even more theft and corruption and patients and the health care system will continue to sink until implosion.

Aside from being astounded by Obama's naiveté, even the remote idea that the insurance cartel executives have Seen the Light and Found God is utterly ridiculous.

The Machiavellian tactics of what I will now refer to as the health care insurance cartel has covered their bases and hedged their bets. This was evidenced a month after the "historic" Obama health care White House love fest. The insurance cartel, according to the AFL-CIO, launched a cloaked anti-government campaign.

Playing Both Sides

Americans for Prosperity (AFP), a front for the cartel, launched a $1.7- million advertising campaign. The ads evoke a ghoulish picture of a government-run healthcare system. Scare tactics, plain and simple.

No matter what the outcome, the cartel will prevail. While publicly fawning over the President, the cartel is secretly pushing chump-change into shill organizations to take an opposing view. In effect, the insurance cartel has rigged the game. By funding both sides of the argument, to their advantage, they win regardless. They are classic double agents.

Having read John Grisham's 2008 book, *The Appeal*, I can't help but think about how many judgeship campaigns are funded, on either side of the debate. These are not the sort of people to go softly into "that good night."

The United States Government announced in mid-2009 that it would use the existing infrastructure of insurance administration and distribution (i.e., the entire insurance industry machine) to dole out monies that are simply beyond imagination. This is no longer $1.2 billion per day ($400 billion a year). Now we are talking about trillions of dollars per annum, according to the Office of Management and Budget.

On this news, the cartel elite quickly revved their jets and flew into Washington to make sure that they would be the ones controlling the flow from the fire hose.

Over the last half-century, their spadework has churned the dirt to give credence to the rise of Medical Tourism/Outsourcing. Efforts have intensified in the last ten years to a degree where the health-insurance establishment profitability is completely out-of-whack with the delivery of health care, the economy and without any sense of economic or legal balance for society.

What we have is an absolute monopoly and a stranglehold on anything representing fairness or competition.

In early 2009 The National Coalition on Healthcare published a devastating report (Source: National Coalition Internet Newsletter) on just how egregiously bloated the insurance industry has become:

Spending for healthcare forces families and businesses to cut back on operations and household costs... $2.4 Trillion... were spent in 2007 or twice the rate of inflation. In 2017, costs for healthcare are expected to be $4.3 Trillion or over 20% of the Gross Domestic Product.

According to a recent report, the United States has $480 billion in excess spending each year in comparison to Western European nations that have universal health insurance coverage. The costs are mainly associated with excess administrative costs and poorer quality of care... 1.5 million families lose their houses to foreclosures each year due to healthcare expenditures and calamities.

Premiums for healthcare coverage have swollen to an 87% increase, on average, in the last 6 years.

Juxtaposed is this report from the AFL-CIO. I include excerpts of text from Mike Hall's AFL-CIO article to aid readers' in their comprehension and to provide additional background context. I consider this study profound:

Health Insurance Profits Soar as Industry Mergers Create Near-Monopoly

By Mike Hall, May 27, 2009 AFL-CIO
Profits at ten of the country's largest publicly traded health insurance companies rose 428 percent from 2000 to 2007, while consumers paid more for less coverage . . . . The report says such conditions warrant a Justice Department investigation . . . . Schumer says the report from Health Care for America Now!

(HCAN) is the starkest evidence yet that the private healthcare insurance market is in bad need of some healthy competition.

According to the recently released HCAN report, "Premiums Soaring in Consolidated Health Insurance Market" . . . In the past 13 years, more than 400 corporate mergers have involved health insurers . . . and insurers are thriving in the anti-competitive marketplace, raking in enormous profits and paying out huge CEO salaries.

These mergers and consolidations have created a marketplace where a small number of larger companies use their power to raise premiums—an average of 87 percent over the past six years—restrict and reduce benefit packages and control and cut provider payments . . .. There were no actions taken against anticompetitive conduct by health insurers in the last administration, in spite of the fact that cases by state attorneys general have secured massive fines against these insurers.

A lack of antitrust enforcement has enabled insurers to acquire dominant positions in almost every metropolitan market . . .. The DOJ should investigate tools used to stifle competition such as physician gag clauses, most favored nations provisions, all-products clauses, and silent networks, which prevent providers and consumers from having the full range of competitive alternatives.

Devolution

Initially, before Medicare took hold, health care dollars were spread proportionately among insurers, hospitals, caregivers, pharmaceutical companies, drug dispensaries and the like.

After Medicare's formation in 1965, there has been a steady evolution in the disproportionate amount of money being corralled into the coffers of the insurers.

Not only are the insurance-cartel executives grabbing fantastic salaries, benefits and parachutes, the burden of bearing costs for healthcare administration has placed an artificial tax on every health care dollar spent. This model has become distorted and bloated beyond recognition.

The amount of money retained by the insurance cartel far outweighs the amount that they reluctantly spend on actually care.

While the system has deteriorated, the insurance cartel has gloated. With the promised onset of socialized medicine in America, they are ready for an historic killing, literally and figuratively.

No wonder the public is seeking alternatives to what the cartel has broken (what do you mean by "broken"?). Free marketplace forces would predict that new products and services will be sought, when the old ones simply don't work. Yet, the cartel broke what they now promise to fix, here and abroad.

The cartel has sidled up to Obama to "help" administer the "new, fair system of healthcare for all in the United States."

Make no mistake: the very cartel that broke the system in the U.S. hedged their bets by creating offshore alternative, Medical Tourism. Medical Tourism is big business for the health care insurance cartel.

A clarification: the overlapping interests of healthcare insurance providers, administrators, HMO's such as Kaiser and hospital corporations are convoluted and intertwined. My chapter, "The Cartel Kings," examines these inter-relations more closely. In the aggregate, these concerns have trillions of dollars in market valuation. Their influence on the economy is immense. They pay their people NOT to deliver care.

The distractions and ruses that the insurance thugs have set up have succeeded in diverting attention away from them, the perpetrators.

Confusion exists as to the source of the healthcare conundrum. Who's to blame? Greedy doctors, hospital management companies, ambulance services, emergency room care for uninsured and illegal alien patients, drug store chains, or pharmaceutical firms? The more confounded the public, the better the cartel likes it.

I do not lay all responsibility on the insurance cartel. What I claim is that, as a percentage, the contribution of the insurance players to this ongoing crime—a form of treason in my view—is so phenomenal, so massive, and so unconscionable that their behavior should be excoriated. They should suffer special punishment for crippling an entire society.

Consider the words of David Balto, former Policy Director for the Federal Trade Commission, July 15, 2009:

"The HCAN (Health Care for America Now) *report provides a much needed spotlight on health insurance markets, and what it found is a toxic marketplace where competition and consumers suffer," said Balto. "Unfortunately, antitrust enforcers have been asleep at the switch for the past several years and have permitted health insurers to acquire monopolies in dozens of markets. Consumers have paid a steep price for this merger mania in higher prices, deceptive and fraudulent practices, and ultimately assembly line healthcare."*

Four hundred mergers involving health-insurance interests in the past thirteen years have consolidated and concentrated the power of insurance in the hands of a few, dominant insurance behemoths.

President Theodore Roosevelt dealt with the Robber Barons of his day (~1900) swiftly and decisively. Cartels were broken and the biggest of the big players, such as J.P. Morgan, Rockefeller and Carnegie were held at bay.

A bolt of lightning from the skies over Washington is what's needed to clear the house of these people. The U.S. has strong anti-trust laws. In the case of the health-insurance industry, none are enforced.

Breaking the will and authority of doctors throughout America has been a key component of the cartel's master plan. Doctors had to be stripped of the once significant role they played in one-on-one patient care, care for which they were, and still are, ultimately responsible.

The healthcare insurance cartel has taken over the practice of medicine and left highly-trained physicians hoping that they will get paid, if ever.

NINE ~ The 50-Year Racket
of the Joint Commission

Pop Quiz

Let's begin with a short examination. All of those who fail this examination will be forced to reread this entire book. (These are all trademarks of the Joint Commission.)

The Joint Commission
HELPING HEALTH CARE ORGANIZATIONS HELP PATIENTS

Joint Commission
International

Joint Commission
Resources

Q: Which of the logos above represent the organization enfranchised by the United States Government in 1965 to accredit healthcare organizations in order that they might receive Medicare payments?
A: The Joint Commission: Helping Health, etc.

Q: Which of the logos above operates without the charter of the United States Government?
A: Joint Commission Resources and Joint Commission International.

Q: Which of the logos above sells accreditation to healthcare organizations?
A: The Joint Commission and the Joint Commission International.

Q: Which of the logos above sells consulting services to hospitals to pass muster to receive Accreditation?
A: Joint Commission Resources.

Q: Which of the logos above represent organizations investigated by the United States Senate for conflict of interest?
A: The Joint Commission International and the Joint Commission Resources.

Q: Which organization had its exclusive "deeming" authority

revoked by Congress in 2008?
A: The Joint Commission.

Q: Which of the logos above represent organizations that have not had their exclusive deeming authority revoked by Congress in 2008?
A: Unknown

Q: Which of the logos above is the parent company?
A: The Joint Commission.

Q: Which organization do U.S. Citizens believe is accrediting healthcare organizations internationally?
A: The Joint Commission.

Q: Which of the logos represent the organization that accredits healthcare organizations internationally, without U.S. Government franchise?
A: Joint Commission International.

Q: Which logo represents the highest profitability of the three?
A: The Joint Commission International.

Q: Which logo represents the organization that employs 1,100 people?
A: The Joint Commission.

Q: Which organization is represented by the logo that employs 54 people?
A: The Joint Commission International.

Q: Have you ever seen these logos before?
A: Probably not.

Q: Did you know that without accreditation by the Joint Commission or the Joint Commission International, U.S. Medicare and private insurance companies will not make payment for any medical services rendered?
A: Probably not.

Q: What is a good definition of unbridled power?
A: The Joint Commission, The Joint Commission Resources and The Joint Commission International.

Confused? You should be. The Joint Commissions wants you to be.

Medicare's Birth: The Beginning of the Fall

In 1965, the year Medicare was enacted by the United States Congress under the Johnson Administration, hospital ownership was not consolidated, widespread and reasonably competitive. Insurance companies paid for services to both public and private hospitals and doctor's fees were not widely disputed. In other words, reasonably self regulated by market forces.

Of course the uninsured and under classes of the poor or working poor had not yet coalesced their political and cultural power and they did not or could not speak with any sort of unified voice.

This is not to say that the uninsured or underprivileged now speak with a strong voice. They don't. It takes money and power to exercise Constitutional rights. They have neither.

The corporate consolidation of the media has led to very careful and controlled reporting of news. Often the stories which are broadcast misinform, under inform or fail to inform. Tight budgets and severe staff cut backs make in-depth reporting, in America, a thing of the past.

The Medical, Congressional and Industrial Complex

Welcome to Washington's seedy game of politics and big business. If not for the last-minute intervention of Eisenhower's handlers on the night of J.F.K.'s inauguration, his now famous speech, which he penned, was to have read: ". . . the military, industrial and Congressional complex."

The Republican bigwigs prevailed on the outgoing President and General to exclude the word Congressional. But that is exactly what Eisenhower meant, and understood. Without the big funds of a government with bottomless pockets, industry, military or not, would not find the funds necessary to make the machine run.

This is the same machine that I call, in the spirit of Ike, the American Medical Machine. The machine uses tax dollars or debt dollars to make the Machine run. And run it does.

The Joint Commission: Kissing the Papal Ring

We all love a deal.

We all also believe that bad things only happen to other people.

Since beginning my investigative journey, my respect for the American judicial system and the Federal and State government has declined.

Voilà, Medical Tourism

With the endorsement and approval of the Joint Commission, all accredited hospitals, deserving or not, carry the imprimatur of safety, legitimacy, and the implicit promise that a patient will receive quality care. After all, the Joint Commission accreditation appears to carry the weight of law. It does not.

The U.S. Government first empowered the private, not-for-profit Joint Commission in 1965 to create and enforce medical standards so that healthcare organizations would be eligible to receive Medicare benefits.

The accreditation logo became the "Good Housekeeping" Seal of

Approval or "Underwriters Laboratories" (UL). Without it, hospitals are barred from receiving payment.

Most people know nothing about the Joint Commission. The same ignorance is even more so regarding the true meaning of the Joint Commission of healthcare organizations. It's a logo, meaningless in the public eye. In actuality, it means the world!

The decline of health care in America is a complex and multi-faceted phenomenon. Understanding health care is far more difficult than comprehending the origins of soaring gasoline prices, where the principal purveyors of price hikes can be easily identified.

The current debacle in American health care did not arise from the mist nor was it conjured by accident. Our medical malaise happened for many reasons. Allow me to offer the following simplification; my attempt at taking a hot knife to cold butter.

To become intimately familiar with the accrediting standards, processes and guidelines, I undertook a deep study of everything about the Joint Commission and this "thing" called the Joint Commission International.

Plumbing the Depths

Adding to my earlier background concerning the Joint Commission, we need to further plumb the depths in which these creatures of the night scurry in secret silence.

The standards for accreditation stipulated by the Joint Commission on International Accreditation (JCI) makes specific recommendations as to how their accredited, internationally-credentialed hospitals should handle situations such as the terrible one I faced. (These standards are provided in full on the website www.theamericanmedicalmoneymachine.com.)

In short, gross violations of the JCI by Bumrungrad are not at question. Though these violations of JCI standards have been brought to the attention of Bumrungrad and the Joint Commission neither seems to care. The Joint Commission International's Maureen Potter quickly pointed out that their standards are voluntary and need not be followed for accreditation to continue. Translation: they are meaningless for patients.

The JCI is a highly profitable arm of the Joint Commission and foreign hospitals accredited by them pay dearly since the U.S. accreditation appears to legitimize and validate these offshore institutions. This validation of perceived value is a fraud and a sham.

Please also note that as of the summer 2009, the Joint Commission International had removed standards from their website. So anyone seeking to understand what they are or mean will be left in complete darkness.

I was fortunate to capture the once-published standards before they were removed from the JCI website.

I can say is that hospitals in foreign lands are staffed by personnel with non-standardized training, where language differences can be significant and where entirely different legal and jurisprudence structures make legal redress impossible.

No matter what these hospitals may profess, any patient cannot discover the qualifications of the physicians. Most of these offshore organizations will refuse to share the qualifications of their physicians. Even if they do, one would be well advised to check, since contriving these kinds of documents is a trivial exercise.

To evidence how little concern the Joint Commission have for their own standards, I include here a stream of correspondence between me and the Joint Commission in Oakbrook, Illinois. This correspondence is available in its entirety on our website www.theamericanmedicalmoneymachine.com.

In the Words of the Joint Commission: #1

Here's what the Commission says about themselves. The following is taken verbatim from their website during the summer of 2009:

The Joint Commission, a nonprofit organization founded in 1951, was created to provide voluntary healthcare accreditation for Hospitals. All but one of the Joint Commissions's founding members continued to serve on its Board of Commissioners as of October 2006, including the American Hospital Association and the American College of Surgeons.

The standards established by the Joint Commission address a facility's level of performance in areas such as patient rights, patient treatment, and infection control. To determine whether a facility is in compliance with those standards, the Joint Commission conducts on-site evaluations of facilities, called accreditation surveys.

The Joint Commission recognizes a facility's compliance with its standards by issuing a certificate of accreditation, which is valid for a 3-year period.

In 2004, the Joint Commission implemented a new accreditation process in an effort to encourage Hospitals to focus on continuous quality improvement, rather than survey preparation.

Previously, facilities were told in advance when Joint Commission surveyors would conduct their evaluations. As a part of the new process, the Joint Commission began conducting unannounced surveys.

The Joint Commission employs over 900 staff members, including approximately 200 Hospital surveyors from a range of disciplines—such as physicians, nurses, and Hospital administrators—who conduct the accreditation surveys. In 2005, the Joint Commission accredited approximately 4,300 Hospitals.

The Joint Commission established JCR to provide consultative technical assistance to healthcare organizations seeking Joint Commission accreditation. JCR is governed by a Board of Directors and employs approximately 180 staff members, including consultants located throughout the country.

In 2000, the Joint Commission expanded JCR's role beyond consulting to include all educational services, such as seminars and audio conferences, which the Joint Commission previously provided. (See app. II for a timeline of key developments in the Joint Commission and JCR relationship.)

JCR also became the official publisher of the Joint Commission's accreditation manuals and support materials. JCR offers consulting services either independently to healthcare facilities or through a subscription-based service called the Continuous.

Service Readiness (CSR) program, which is typically offered in partnership with state Hospital associations. 12 The CSR program provides ongoing technical assistance and education to subscribers through a variety of means, including meetings, e-mails, telephone calls, and conferences.

The Amendment to the Social Security Act of 1965: The Joint Commission Is Empowered

In the government's 1965 words:
b) Duties of accrediting entities
The duties described in this subsection are the following:

(1) Accreditation and approval
Accreditation of agencies and approval of persons, to provide adoption services in the United States in cases subject to the Convention.

(2) Oversight
Ongoing monitoring of the compliance of accredited agencies and approved persons with applicable requirements, including review of complaints against such agencies and persons in accordance with procedures established by the accrediting entity and approved by the Secretary.

(3) Enforcement
Taking of adverse actions (including requiring corrective action, imposing sanctions, and refusing to renew, suspending, or canceling accreditation or approval) for noncompliance with applicable requirements, and notifying the agency or person against whom adverse actions are taken of

the deficiencies necessitating the adverse action.

(4) Data, records, and reports
Collection of data, maintenance of records, and reporting to the Secretary, the United States central authority, State courts, and other entities (including on persons and agencies granted or denied approval or accreditation), to the extent and in the manner that the Secretary requires.

(c) Remedies for adverse action by accrediting entity
(1) Correction of deficiency
An agency or person who is the subject of an adverse action by an accrediting entity may re-apply for accreditation or approval (or petition for termination of the adverse action) on demonstrating to the satisfaction of the accrediting entity that the deficiencies necessitating the adverse action have been corrected.

(2) No other administrative review.

An adverse action by an accrediting entity shall not be subject to administrative review.

(3) Judicial review
An agency or person who is the subject of an adverse action by an accrediting entity may petition the United States district court in the judicial district in which the agency is located or the person resides to set aside the adverse action. The court shall review the adverse action in accordance with section 706 of title 5, and for purposes of such review the accrediting entity shall be considered an agency within the meaning of section 701 of such title.

(d) Fees
The amount of fees assessed by accrediting entities for the costs of accreditation shall be subject to approval by the Secretary. Such fees may not exceed the costs of accreditation. In reviewing the level of such fees, the Secretary shall consider the relative size of, the geographic location of, and the number of Convention adoption cases managed by the agencies or persons subject to accreditation or approval by the accrediting entity.

This is mandatory and should be required reading for every lawmaker.

Read through this aspect of Lyndon Johnson's legislation, which described and enabled Medicare, a key program to his perspicacious vision of the Great Society which was enacted into law in 1965.

What cascades from this seemingly innocuous passage in a lengthy legislative document is profound. In essence, near absolute power is invested in The Joint Commission and The Joint Commission International. This power carries the power of the purse. Although little known, the Joint Commission has unbridled control over the entire healthcare system. In my view, no group should hold such sway: especially the arrogant and secret Joint Commission.

In the Words of the Joint Commission: #2

Mr. Harold Bressler, Corporate Counsel to the Joint Commission, admitted to me in a phone conversation in the summer of 2006: of the 40,000 institutions accredited in the U.S. since 1965, less than one-tenth of one percent has had their accreditation revoked.

Essentially, this directly violates the law, which calls for the Joint Commission to oversee the implementation of standards that they and HHS jointly decide. They do not.

Once given accreditation, it is rarely revoked! If not for the intervention of State Medical Boards in the U.S., hospitals mishaps would go without attention or adjudication. This wanton abuse of fiduciary responsibility flies in the face of the law which requires the Joint Commission to enforce the standards they proffer.

No Resources

Mr. Bressler, his organization's chief legal counsel for the Joint Commission, simply dismissed their obligation under law: "We don't have the resources for policing activities." Please, re-read the legislation that empowered the Joint Commission and draw your own conclusion.

Further adding to this mess, the JC International accreditation has a separate set of standards that makes no promise of oversight. Unlike the United States, however, other countries' medical boards are largely political bodies and fail to become involved with overseeing their hospitals. Translation: the political implications are too hot for them to handle. So, it is hands-off when it comes to countries such as Thailand policing their own.

In India, the country's infrastructure is so anemic that vigorous regulation is not to be expected. India's tax base is less than what American's spend to care for their home lawns and gardens annually!

Joint Commission International (JCI) standards are sold as being on par with the U.S. standards of the Joint Commission (JC). They are not.

Even if they were, careful study of the two would soon reveal that the JC has reneged on its fiduciary obligations to the United States Government. They go further in breaking the law by fostering an illusion that the laws of the United States are being applied to the accreditation of healthcare facilities abroad. The JC was never vested with accrediting powers overseas.

The JC usurped this power and has fraudulently made it appear that the good faith and backing of the U.S. goes along with their international accreditations. Nothing could be further from the truth.

The JC needs to be held accountable for their outrageous conduct, now and in the past.

Additionally, countries like Thailand have virtually no medical malpractice laws on the books. If mishaps occur, there is no local jurisdiction of means for redress. This is a matter of fact.
The no-liability factor makes doing business abroad attractive for medical healthcare insurers who wish only to reduce their costs and avoid liability of any kind.

Add to this the fact that currently, U.S. citizens, if injured abroad, have no rights for redress under our laws. The United States does not and cannot assert jurisdiction over crimes or other torts committed outside of the United States and its territories.

The Racket: The Joint Commission

My first phone call with Maureen Potter, then President of the JCI, was encouraging. She was sympathetic and promised an immediate investigation. She mitigated my concerns by extending reassurances that JCI would look into this terrible tragedy and report back to me quickly.

In 1965, Congress designated the Joint Commission to act in lieu of the U.S. Government in assuring that hospitals that were to receive newly created Medicare benefits would do so because they complied with standards set by the JC (blessed by HHS). The Amendment to the Social Security Act of 1965, actually an Amendment to the Social Security Act of 1935, required that standards be enforced, not simply issued.

If accreditation were withdrawn, the devastation would be immediate.

No money, no hospitals. No accreditation, no hospital.

The power vested in them was awesome. It was the combination to the safe of the United States Government, who today, dispenses more than $1.4 billion a day in Medicare benefits according to Science Daily in 2007, annualized for 2011.

Private insurers who, under contract with the government, act as administrators and dispense Medicare benefits on behalf of the American people.

Much of this money is provided in advance, on a monthly capitated basis per person. In short, the JC was given awesome power and authority. This is aside from Medicaid and other public programs.

The graft and theft is stupendous with fewer and fewer dollars reaching the patient and their doctors.

Coma Chameleon

When Maureen Potter and I spoke again, a month after my initial and seemingly sympathetic conversation, it became clear that neither she nor the JCI had any plan forthcoming. They had no wish to share with me what they had learned about my son's death. At first I was shocked.

The section, Joint Commission Correspondence, found on the website www.theamericanmedicalmoneymachine.com,will provide you with an archive of all email correspondence between me and the Joint Commission, its departments, officers and wholly owned subsidiaries. Readers: judge for yourselves.

Instead of finding solace, I found another enemy. I decided at that moment that I would make investigating and exposing this flavor of evil doing my life's work, in my son's memory.

Solving the Riddle

I intuited that there were disconnected pieces of information about health care, which, for me, began to synergistically fit together.

My son had taught me a lesson, a solution to a giant and terrible riddle. I was seeing for the first time a buried truth that would reveal the reasons behind the crisis and crash of health care in America.

I had wondered about this riddle for a long time, as many of us have. But a clear direction or picture of how it all fit together eluded me. I saw a cacophony of factors at play. But I could not decipher how or even if, they might fit together.

Suddenly I found myself constantly thinking, what the hell is this? Who are these people?

Heretofore, I only vaguely knew that these players existed. Now they were standing on the road, working to block my way as I tried to find out how in the world my boy could have died. It was as if Josh had opened the door for me. The door was his death. What lay beyond was a scene out of Hieronymus Bosch of hell, the Armageddon of American health care.

Gustav Dore, "The Gates of Hell" circa 1850.

Maureen Potter has since been removed from Presidency of the JCI. One can only speculate why. In her place are new players who use circumlocution to confound and confuse. They make up their mission as they go along. Not surprising. This is the same game their parent has played as to their mission in the U.S.

How could every fact I uncovered fit perfectly with all the other pieces of information I had validated?

All the information discovered through my investigations and all the correspondence with Bumrungrad Hospital was provided to the Joint Commission and the Joint Commission International. Why would they both ignore my entreaties?

On the surface this made no sense. But I was ignorant of who these people were or their real agenda. I was about to learn a 50 year old, well kept secret!

Above the Law

Other examples of the callous treatment and non-responsiveness of the JC are evidenced in the communications that follow.

In **(Appendix #12)** I reveal a letter to the Chief Counsel of the Joint Commission from my Bangkok based counsel, Alistair Henderson. This correspondence asks for a reconciliation of their legal charter with the real activities of the Joint Commission and all its divisions.

As the informed reader might have guessed, this important communication never received a response. Arrogance, stupidity, isolation—call it what you may—but the Joint Commission deserves its well earned reputation for being unresponsive to everyone with any ax to grind.

The JC has trampled on human life and its Congressional charter. They are selling standards abroad with absolutely no provisions for enforcement. They are worthless. The situation with the JC's accreditations in the U.S. is not much better. However, State oversight picks up where the JC has legally dropped the ball.

Dr. Voodoo's Hospital is Accredited

For those fostering foreign health care, the imprimatur from the Joint Commission International is a mandatory pre-condition to attract American patients. Without such accreditation, no U.S. citizens would put themselves in the care of Dr. Voodoo from Mango Pango!

The Joint Commission International accreditation is well-contrived and complete hoax. It is a specialized commodity, for sale to the highest bidder.

There are dozens of hospitals in Bangkok, yet Bumrungrad had exclusive accreditation in Thailand for five years before any other hospital was given accreditation by the Joint Commission. One can only speculate as to how much money changed hands as consideration for this exclusive arrangement.

End Game

In July 2008, the JC's exclusive authority was revoked by Congress. The Joint Commission's errant ways have been subjected to multiple Government Accounting Organization (GAO) Reports and investigations by Senators Grassley and Baucus.

My personal efforts in working with Medicare and Health and

Human Services influenced the decision of Congress to repudiate the nearly sacrosanct and exclusive deeming authority of the Joint Commission.

Now, work needs to be undertaken to put the JC completely out of business, their executives investigated and punished according to findings. In addition, the organization needs to be fined for violating the public trust and for their wanton abuse of their tax-exempt status.

The HHS is entrusted to police the JC's activities. This will not happen when high government officials leave public office and take lucrative positions in the private sector.

In the Cross Hairs of the GAO

To be fair, not everyone in government has been sitting on their hands when it comes to the Joint Commission. The Senate Finance Committee and Senators Chuck Grassley (R-Iowa) and Max Baucus (D-Montana) have had the Commission on their radar for years. At the behest of the Senate, the Government Accounting Office (GAO) has been commissioned to investigate the JC on two separate occasions.

Both GAO studies, in 2004 and 2007, revealed what they considered to be irreconcilable problems at the JC. They called for Congress to revoke the 50-year lock the JC has held on healthcare in the United States.

If not for partisan politics, at that time Republican dominated as well as the constant pressure of lobbyists, perhaps the Congress would have acted. Each time the subject was raised on the Hill, it was killed.

Lobbyists do not just pressure Congress, they buy Congress. Having spent countless days as a private citizen advising members of the Congress and Senate, I can tell you that unless these lobbying denizens are removed from Washington little hope remains for true governmental reformation.

Elections need to be financed equally and by the public, not sold to the highest bidder. The sickness of "corporate government" can only be cured by evicting the bastards. A free society cannot survive unless they are. I have witnessed and "felt" this first hand. It's nauseating.

Throw the Bums Out

My research uncovered a GAO report issued in July 2004 titled: Medicare/CMS Needs Additional Authority to Adequately Oversee Patient Safety in Hospitals (GAO 04-850).

This document calls for revocation of the Joint Commission's authority due to negligence, dereliction of duty and other questionable activities.

In a Republican-dominated Congress, this report was never translated into approved legislation. Each time a vote on legislation regarding the JC was raised, it died a quiet, ignominious death in Committee.

It was only until W.Bush was on his last legs and the Republicans were coming undone in summer 2008 that minor legislation was passed to curtail the JC. This was the legislation for which I had supplied testimony. I can hardly take credit for the passage of the bill that finally trimmed the JC's sails but I believe I nudged it over the goal line.

Simply Put

Any person who thinks that JCI accreditation of hospitals has meaningful value or affords protection should think again. It does not.

Only corporate interests are satisfied by the scam of the Jc's providing assurances of safety and quality. As PT Barnum is well known to have said, "A sucker is born every day."

The Medical Tourist money machine is counting on that.

International accreditation by the Joint Commission does not carry the force of U.S. law. It is a marketing gimmick conjured up by the Joint Commission in cooperation with the mega U.S. insurance interests.

We know that the American medical money machine has been investing in foreign care facilities for over twenty years. To reap the seeds they have sewn, accreditation with a quasi-official cast is critical to the next wave of care: overseas.

Ten~ United States
of Healthcare Fraud

Rotten at the Core

I believe that the Joint Commission is among the primary co-dependents in the medical-industry cabal. They enable the machine to work as it does.

Resulting from its preferential relationships with the medical cartel, cloaked cleverly in the guise of a do-good, not-for-profit entity, it has been able to operate with deadly and destructive stealth.

Without their accreditation, the biggest rip-off in American corporate history would not have been possible. The seal of accreditation is the key to Fort Knox. With it, the gold flows out the door into the hands of the Medical Machine. Without it, nada.

Since the flow of government money is enormous and Medicare sets the pace for private insurance, the accreditation of institutions is mandatory for the cascade of wealth that flows from Washington into the hands of the medical establishment: insurance companies and benefit administrators.

Willie Sutton, famous bank robber, was asked why he robbed banks. His answer: "That's where they keep the money!"

Willie Sutton, infamous bank robber.

The insurance and healthcare cartel does not have to rob

Washington; Washington shovels the money into the cartels waiting hands with the following instructions: OK, boys and girls. Be good now and make sure you pass on our billions to pay for the care of our citizens. Don't be too greedy. Keep something for yourselves but remember that this is not your money. It is the money of the people.

The proposal to the United States Senate **(See Appendix #12)** captures the essence of my recommendations about actions needed to be taken pertaining to Medical Tourism and the investigative and disciplinary actions that should be set in motion concerning the Joint Commission.

President George W. Bush was still in Office when this proposal was made. Given the partisan conflicts then (and still) afoot in Washington, little hope was held out that any of these suggestions would be adopted.

With Obama now in office, it is hard to say whether the special-interest groups will still hold sway or whether the Congress will finally fix what is broken in the Joint Commission. It appears as if nothing will change.

The summer of 2009 has seen near riots at town hall meetings where the American public has let the Washington elite know of their profound dissatisfaction with the health care insurance cartel.

Reuters reported on August 15, 2009 that Obama "Keeps Heat on Insurance Firms." We'll see. Neither Democrats nor Republicans are likely to bite the hand that feeds. However, should pending legislation include a tightening of the reins on the health care cartel, the vested interests will find a way around whatever obstacles get in their way.

Since administrations change but Washington bureaucrats do not, the translation of any law into real action depends on the people entrusted with enforcement.

Little Guys Can Make a Difference!

Happily, working with the Senate and CMS and HHS, I was able to supply enough information and rationale to get a bill passed, which finally revoked the 50 year old exclusive "deeming" authority of the Joint Commission. The bill does not go far enough in that it leaves the door open for the Joint Commission to reapply in about one year from the summer of 2009.

Leading up to the Congressional vote in the summer of 2008, I began receiving frantic calls from Medicare investigators. Public comments for hearings had been cut off due to time limits. However, they made an exception and solicited my report.

The stream of self-effacing press releases from the Joint Commission has been constant ever since. They are not about to give up their franchise. It's worth trillions of dollars.

See Appendix #13 for a copy of my correspondence with the staff of the Senate Sub Committee on Healthcare. It is a comprehensive briefing a list of suggestions as to how the Congress should deal with the Joint Commission and how the United States of America should plan for the upcoming wave of patient exportation by the insurance cartel.

It is worth a careful read since it provides not just the identification of problems but concrete and specific suggestions regarding policies which should be developed and made into law to protect American patients, wherever they may seek care.

Part of the insidious problem with which we are dealing is that many past Congressional staff members have gone on to very lucrative positions in industry. They are caught in a double bind: discharging their appointed duties or jeopardize their future fortunes. Most decide to see no evil, hear no evil and speak no evil.

The proverbial principle: See no evil, hear no evil, and speak no evil.

(See Appendix #13)

The actions taken by the Senate and the Congress are influenced by fears of jeopardizing funding for their "permanent campaigns" that most of what they know about wrongdoing rarely makes its way into proposed legislation.

Hence, a good deal of the policies which are proposed, are careful not to step on the rich toes of Congressional and Senatorial supporters—aka—the Lobby. By openly side-stepping the true corruption of healthcare in America, they, in effect, see, hear and speak no evil! This is contrived ignorance for which we all paying a dear price.

This is a profound symptom of a society in free fall. One only has to look at Wall Street corruption, rigged government bailouts of banks, profits realized from war, disintegration of the infrastructure, degradation of the educational system and erosion of the justice system, to name but a few, to know that the American way of life is coming undone.

Eleven~ The Cartel Kings: A History of the Dammed

Health care is ever-present in the daily lives of the entire population. Nearly everyone has had private experiences with the insurance cartel; declining access to care, eroding quality of care, crowded emergency rooms and doctor visits that typically last four minutes.

Where Have All the Trust Busters Gone?

Wikipedia's definition of a cartel provides us with a common basis for discussion:

A cartel is a formal (explicit) agreement among firms. It is a formal organization of producers that agree to coordinate prices and production.

Cartels usually occur in an oligopolistic industry, where there are a small number of sellers and usually involve homogeneous products.

Cartel members may agree on such matters as price fixing, total industry output, market shares, allocation of customers, allocation of territories, bid rigging, establishment of common sales agencies, and the division of profits or combination of these. The aim of such collusion is to increase individual members' profits by reducing competition.

Competition laws forbid cartels.

Identifying and breaking up cartels is an important part of the competition policy in most countries, though proving the existence of a cartel is rarely easy, as firms are usually not so careless as to put agreements to collude on paper.

Private international cartels (those with participants from two or more nations) had an average price increase of 28%, whereas domestic cartels averaged 18%. Less than 10% of all cartels in the sample failed to raise market prices.

Deals Made in the Dark

The American Medical Money Machine appears to operate through explicit agreements to control and normalize prices. The consequence of this is high premiums and low reimbursement rates; there is surprisingly little, if any, price elasticity in U.S. major markets.

Competition is often nonexistent as the big fish swallow up the small. Only the biggest barracudas are surviving; they have ironclad control over advertising, marketing, government lobbying and information sharing.

All Rolled Up

Only the biggest of the big can buy unilaterally retained legal representation. Like UnitedHealthcare Group, the other remaining big players such as WellPoint, Blue Shield-Blue Cross, Kaiser, Aetna and Cigna, pay lavish yearly retainers to America's most aggressive and largest law firms to tie up and squash any who dare tread on their freewheeling activities.

The Protection Racket: Justice for Sale

The importance of buying access to the legal system should not be underestimated; the insurance cartel retains the nation's largest defense law firms with millions in yearly "wait in the dugout" fees.

Aggressive plaintiff law firms exist, but unless a case is outstanding on its merits and the plaintiff firm can afford to take a case on a contingency, only a Rockefeller or Kennedy can afford a team of lawyers at an average of $500 an hour per head to fight an open-ended battle with insurance companies who regard their legal costs as donut money.

Maintaining a lobby presence in Washington can involve costs up to $200,000 a month per company. This, too, is pocket money for the insurance heavyweights. It is a fortune for a wronged patient or doctor.

So much for the concept of "And justice for all." Justice "for all who can pay" would be far more precise.

The Cartel All Stars: A Deep Bench and No Umpires

Because the lines between health insurance, hospital corporations and other financial modalities that distinguish the healthcare Mafia (The American Medical Money Machine) Fortune magazine's May 4, 2009 roster of All Stars serves as a good point of reference. **(See Appendix #14)**

One thing is clear. The lines of demarcation between the various flavors of healthcare players are completely fuzzy! Consider the jumbled offerings of these products and services: health-insurance providers, managed-care programs, medical facilities, life-insurance companies, medical mutual funds and stock indexes, and so on.

What is not jumbled, however, is that the companies in these businesses rake in colossal bucks. The rankings represent what place a given company occupies in Fortune's list of the 1,000 Largest Corporations in the United States. Revenues, in billions, are for 2008.

Appendix #14 lists are grouped by financial categories established by SIC Codes and there are many overlaps and interrelations.

Insurance and Health Care Industries:
Fortune 1000 Rank Company Industry Revenues—
The Biggest Pieces of the Pie

These companies combined have yearly revenues over 1 trillion dollars. Their market capitalization could easily exceed 20 trillion dollars. These figures suggest the enormity of the stakeholders in the health-insurance game. Not included here are derivative financial products, or monetary instruments, which leverage these companies such as mutual funds or stock indices. The numbers are beyond comprehension.

Roughly, Insurers and HMO's, Pharmaceutical Companies, Financial Insurance Firms and Life and Health Insurance make up over $1 trillion in yearly gross receipts. This figure constitutes approximately 1/5th of the American Gross Domestic Product.

Many other elements of cost and expense are not included. If one includes deductibles, co-pays, write-offs for non-payment, over the counter pharmaceuticals, home nursing care, rehabilitation services and the like, I estimate, easily, that another $trillion dollars can be attributed to yearly healthcare costs. This makes healthcare, by far, the largest component of the United States economy and at least 5 times the amount of the entire Pentagon budget!

Fraud is not included in Fortune's figures. The DOJ estimates that at least $600 billion a year is stolen by the health insurance "establishment" from Medicare and Medicaid alone. If one subscribes to these calculations, at least ½ of the entire economy of the United States is dedicated to healthcare in one form or another.

The pharmaceutical companies seem to stand alone, not overtly commingled with insurance and hospital interests. This is misleading.

Pharmceutical companies maintain Pharmacy Benefit Providers (medication-insurance providers) and finance billions of dollars of research. Hospitals and universities receive untold billions in clinical trials, grants and the like. So big pharma needs to be seen as sharing a similar agenda with the rest of the Money Machine members.

Gobbling Bigger Pieces of the National Pie

Forget whatever the Obama-result may be in this attempt to restructure health care; unless the king fish have their hands permanently removed from the country's cookie jar, nothing will change for the better; in fact, it will get much worse.

Nowhere in the recent gun-slinging debate fought on the D.C. streets over healthcare reform is there serious mention that the cartel will not be participating and controlling whatever form the new "program" takes. It must be understood that Medicare, or government-sponsored health insurance, is administered by and for the cartel as well.

When a Medicare payment is made, the recipient does not get a check from the U.S.; they get it from the members of the cartel acting as government-appointed administrators of your tax dollars to pay for your medical care.

What is the problem with the bargain the cartel has struck with the government? They are in business—the cartel wants to keep as much for themselves as possible and give back only what they are forced to. This is the sad reality we must all face before positive change is possible.

Straight Talk from a Family Doctor

The grotesque influence of the cartel is exerted intimately, not abstractly. A well-published medical activist from San Diego, Jeoffry B. Gordon, M.D., M.P.H., issued this statement in his blog "paradocs." His article eloquently recounts the pain inflicted daily on every doctor-cum- provider who winces under the whip of the cartel. This may sound like dramatic language. It isn't.

As a family doctor I have been fighting for universal medical care since 1965 when Medicare was enacted to save our (impoverished) seniors from medical neglect.

Both Clinton and Obama are taking the wrong path. The main barrier to universal medical care is the private, corporate, for profit health insurance industry. It is remarkably expensive, taking $500 billion yearly in expenses (equal to the basic Pentagon budget) off the top and away from medical services. Its functioning promotes maldistribution of care—both geographically and by specialty—because it has an unfettered profit incentive not impacted by social concerns. Practicing medical professionals must deal with a huge and time consuming bureaucracy [sic] to get prior authorizations for needed procedures and pharmaceuticals . . . and so on.

Progress at Any Price

The suicide rate of doctors in recent years, according to the AMA, is substantially above any of the other professions. Doctors who decide not to take the noose option are leaving medicine in droves.

They simply can't make ends meet. If any of Obama's promises are kept, the reimbursement rates for doctors will continue to plummet to record low levels.

The quality of care is taking a dive while younger and more inexperienced residents are left to experiment, in many hospitals, on the poor and on the minorities.

This dirty little secret is well concealed by sealed court records and by $3,000-suited lawyers who crush any plaintiff, often with the willing help of judges who are, shall we say, brought to see the "light." These folks learned their lessons well from notorious characters like Al Capone who owned judges and DAs in Chicago.

Al Capone smiles for the police in 1935.

Doctor Gordon, in another of his "paradocs" blog posts, writes:

Most people are unaware how similar the major health insurers are to our failed Wall Street firms. They are corporate cash cows and have virtually no fiduciary responsibility and few activities for protecting or improving health or the healthcare system. They will devote their vast resources to prevent any meaningful health reform. They have controlled Congress and the mainstream media. The only cure is vigorous popular support for a single payer, Medicare for All reform.

The individual insurance companies are out for profit and must work to maximize their value on the stock market and are not our friends. They treat patients like widgets or cost centers. This is not a culture of trust, caring, compassion, and fiduciary responsibility. If you were dumb enough to hope that Countrywide Mortgage would preserve your home and Lehman Brothers would preserve your retirement fund, then you will be stupid enough to expect Anthem Blue Cross and the other insurance companies to be there to protect your health. Yet it seems all Washington continues under this delusion.

The Hospital Lineup

The top five for-profit hospital operators in the country in 2009, according to *Fortune* magazine, are:

1. Hospital Corporation of America
2. Tenet Healthcare
3. Triad Hospitals
4. Universal Health Services
5. Kindred Healthcare

Remember Tenet? Bumrungrad Progenitor

Did you notice that Tenet Healthcare is second on the list? Remember them, as they are the Bumrungrad backers and still owners, according to their 2003 and 2004 Annual Reports filed with the SEC. Regardless, Curtis Schroeder and Mack Banner are at the helm of Bumrungrad, employing all the skills they garnered while serving as key executives to one of the most odious corporations in U.S. history.

The Schroeder Credo and the Bumrungrad National Anthem:

"If there's a mistake, we fix it but the idea of suing for multimillions of dollars for damages is not going to be something you can do outside the U.S."

I am still waiting for Schroeder to resurrect my son.

Dr. Frist and Foremost: The HCA Dynasty

Before moving on, look at who's on top: HCA. Former Senator Dr. Bill Frist (R–Tennessee) and his son Thomas III serve on HCA's Board. Bill doesn't need Washington anymore, especially after selling his HCA stock and all of the HCA stock held by his immediately family members just before it took a monumental plunge. Bill and all the other little Frists somehow timed their sale just right.

US Probes Sen. Frist's HCA Stock Sale
Posted on: Friday, 23 September 2005, 14:22 CDT
By Jeremy Pelofsky and Richard Cowan

WASHINGTON (Reuters) - A federal investigation into Senate

Majority Leader Bill Frist's sale of HCA Inc. stock widened on Friday when the largest U.S. hospital chain said federal prosecutors had subpoenaed the company for related documents.

Frist, a Tennessee Republican and a potential 2008 presidential candidate, has come under fire for the sale of his stock in the company shortly before Nashville-based HCA warned that earnings would miss expectations.

The lawmaker on June 13 requested the sale of all of his remaining stock in HCA, which was held in blind trusts, Frist's spokeswoman Amy Call said. By July 8, the shares held for himself, his wife, and children were sold by trustees, the spokeswoman added.

HCA Performance Faltered

On July 13, days after the Frist family stock sales were completed; HCA warned that second-quarter operating earnings were likely to fall short of analysts estimates, sending its shares tumbling 8.85 percent.

The company and other hospital operators have been hurt by high levels of unpaid patient bills, rising bad debt and higher admissions of uninsured patients. HCA shares had hit a 52-week high on June 22, reaching $58.60.

HCA, which Frist's father and brother helped found, said in brief statement that it had received a subpoena from the U.S. Attorney for the Southern District of New York for the production of documents.

What makes the Frist menagerie even more of a salient example is that Bill is a heart surgeon. He may be able to fix your heart but has learned that it is probably easier simply to rip it out: the effective consequence of an insider taking the plunder and leaving the stockholders to pick through the scraps.

Bill Frist was on the Senate Finance Committee for Healthcare, the elected officials who oversee Medicare!

Pass Go to Park Avenue

Bill Frist is free and lounging at his Tennessee estate.

The Senate Ethics Committee decided that Bill was not so bad. They let him take his loot. The Senate Ethics crew took two years to decide the case. Bill was long gone from Washington and the Senate no longer had jurisdiction over the good doctor. Ever the watchful elected officials; these are the same boys and girls currently authoring the fix to the nation's healthcare problem.

Profit is a perverse incentive for quality health care. Imagine for-profit fire or police protection.

The cartel is very, very good at what they do. They pay big money to get top talent and most people have a hard time walking away from fat paychecks even if it means selling their soul to the Big Boss.

Administration costs of health care benefits now equal the entire budget of the combined military forces of the United States of America, and they plan on financing a good war every now and then.

Dr. William McGuire, former Chairman of United Healthcare.

William McGuire, UnitedHealthcare Group Former Chairman, walked out of the door, similarly to Senator Frist, with a billion greenbacks, after being investigated the SEC. He was not charged with committing crimes involving stock manipulation and backdating stock options.

Yet, it's now UnitedHealthcare Group and AARP, their front, who are advising the Administration and Senate Committees—as well as the public—on how they propose going about shaving dollars from the broken health care system.

Assuredly, they are not in the least talking about shaving any of their dollars. And we don't see Wellpoint, Blue Shield, Aetna, Cigna or any of the other mega players stepping up to the sacrificial altar. What they are "advising" is shaving dollars out of the dollars that go to patient care and to physicians and medical professionals.

They are talking about shaving dollars out of the system and transferring the cost burden to you in the form of higher deductibles, larger co-pays, elimination of approved medications, restricted diagnostics, limited access to healthcare providers, vastly increased waiting times, declining quality of care by declining payment to professionals and squeezing medical professionals until they cry "Uncle."

But don't, if you know what's good for you, even think about touching their billions.

Give Me a Ticket to an Aeroplane

The cartel's international strategy has been afoot for nearly three decades.

Regardless of how they fare at home—and they will fare well—they have salted the brine offshore and are actively selling the notion that care abroad is equivalent to care at home, except that it is less expensive. They've bought big time into ownership of foreign medical organizations. They have arranged with their buddies in Oakbrook, the Joint Commission and its entire tentacle-like subsidiaries, to expand American insurance coverage to cover care abroad.

The brilliant drama being written by the cartel is to leave the battered shores of medical care at home and depart on a glorious, inspired journey over the seas to Siam and Singapore where gorgeous nurses and Board-certified doctors will work their wonders on your body while you lie, resplendent in 1,000 thread-count sheets and down comforters, your slippers neatly arranged and your Turkish towel bathrobe poised for your trip to the MRI, or—as in the case of my son—the morgue.

These so-called medical vacations will be covered by your insurance. The key: **covered by insurance.** Currently this requires accreditation by the Joint Commission. Don't worry, if the Joint Commission is put out of business as Congress and the GAO have proposed, UnitedHealthcare Group and others are well on their way to establishing their own accreditation standards.

UnitedHealthcare Group probably got this brilliant idea from their British buddies, The British United Provident Association Limited (BUPA), who "accredit" foreign hospitals for their international plans.

Though British accreditation agencies exist, BUPA has taken no chances: they certify their own.

Just like a scene from the film "The Godfather", where one of the Don's most trusted lieutenants sells out to the competing Don, United—who has been allied with their friends the Joint Commission—is preparing to sell the Commission down the river if the Commission's fortunes go south.

Picture This!

Try to imagine a world in which the insurance cartel and the American Medical Money Machine provide their own certifications and accreditations.

Strain, for a moment, to consider that they will sell you on their standards of quality care and patient safety and that they will do whatever is necessary to persuade you to relax because accreditation creates the illusion of reliability!

Without oversight from objective and concerned sources, the meat supply will become tainted, the booze will be watered down, the generic drugs will become placebos and your goose and mine will be cooked.

The Joint Commission, the handmaiden of the industry, has broken the law since 1965. This is well known and must be stopped. Political payoffs and the dirt which has become Washington must be washed clean: now.

Hatched in Illinois:
With a Little Help From Their Friends

The Joint Commission hatched the idea of the Joint Commission International to accredit hospitals offshore.

Few knew who or what the hell the Joint Commission is, even fewer know that the Joint Commission has grievously abdicated its duties at home. Almost no one, outside the medical world and the medical machinery, know that the Joint Commission holds fantastic power and sway.

I relied on the Joint Commission when I did a quick scan of possible hospitals in Bangkok while my son waited on the phone with my instructions as to where he should go for medical help.

The Joint Commission actively and deliberately withheld information regarding the death of my son. They conspired to cover the tracks of Bumrungrad. I will not forget them. I hope you will also not forget them.

I curse the day I was snookered by their fraud. I curse the day I told my son to go the ER at Bumrungrad for care. Instead of competent care, he was put to death for the financial gain of a group of monsters I have taken meticulous care to profile for your examination.

These are the same people who are waiting, now, to greet you at the pearly gates of the Bumrungrad lobby.

Twelve~ Data Control
and Mind Control=Total Control

Information as Artillery

Data can be a weapon: excluding patients from care and pinpointing troublesome providers/doctors. As was discovered in a series of recent cases in New York, the data management system controlled by a wholly owned subsidary of UnitedHealthcare Group was "managed" to provide the industry with pricing standards, the lowest pricing standards. Some call this price fixing. I agree.

Since the insurance industry is immune from HIPPA secrecy laws: data about you and me can be acquired and shared, available to all willing to pay and who are not HIPPA restricted. This shared information is hardly happy talk. It is the way to make billions and to control millions.

While a person with an adult child is required to obtain consent from his or her kid to talk with the doctors and to call in to check on the medical status of their offspring, the insurance companies can log in the data and make it available through their databases, anywhere in the world to anyone.

While a patient needs to give permission to one doctor to talk to another about his or her case, the insurance company can collect and distribute your data at will. Essentially, this is unconstitutional because it creates laws which are unevenly applied. How did this happen? The insurance industry lawyers wrote the HIPPA legislation.

Consider also, as a case in point, the MIB, or Medical Information Bureau, of Braintree, Mass., founded in 1902. According to Wikipedia, MIB Group, Inc. (MIB) is:

A membership corporation (sometimes described as an "industry trade association") owned by approximately 470 member insurance companies, its primary mission detecting and deterring fraud that may occur in the course of obtaining life, health, disability income, critical illness, and long-term care insurance.

MIB's fraud detection and deterrence saves its member companies, on an annual basis, an estimated $1 billion by allowing them to avoid fraudulent insurance applications and early claims.

These savings may be passed on to insurance buying consumers in the form of lower premiums (and higher dividends payable by mutual companies), which may allow them to buy more insurance at affordable premiums.

Dig deeper into the Wikipedia citation and you will find additional interesting details. Check out the article by Bob Littell, in The National Underwriter, titled "The Mysterious MIB—Not Any More." Anyone who has applied for life or health insurance is in their computer database. This data is derived from the same HIPPA exempt data compiled by the health insurance cartel. The next and inevitable step is combining this information with Federal data, providing those with access a complete picture of anyone in the United States of America!

The cartel appears to understand that they will get caught again, fined and sanctioned again, slapped on the hand again, and go back to work again with a fresh shirt and a clean suit the next morning. No one ever seems to go up the river for a nice long, well-deserved vacation. Since personal responsibility is never put to issue and executives appear to enjoy complete immunity, what, pray tell, is the motivation to straighten up and fly right?

Taking a Cue: From Joseph Goebbels

If you want to achieve mastery, study a master: Joseph Goebbels, Professor of Modern Mind Control and Propaganda.

Joseph Goebbels, circa 1935.

To float a fully inflated cartel, it is necessary to have a consummate ability to distribute propaganda, to influence thinking and to establish common mindsets.

History Lessons on Mind Control:
IBM and the Holocaust

Historically the subject of mind and technology requires a bit more attention. A short history lesson concerning a little known and completely underappreciated aspect of the 20th Century record for mind and population control is key to our background in fully understanding what the cartel is currently cooking.

A small precision manufacturing company, The Hollerith Company, caught the eye of legendary Thomas J. Watson, the Founder of International Business Machine Corporation (IBM).

Herman Hollerith, a German American born in Buffalo, New York. His invention enabled great and terrible things.

Wikipedia conveniently summarizes Hollerith's genius:

Hollerith had left teaching and begun working for the United States Census Office in the year he filed his first patent application. Titled "Art of Compiling Statistics," it was filed on September 23, 1884; U.S. Patent No. 395782 was granted on January 8, 1889.

Hollerith built machines under contract for the Census Office, which used them to tabulate the 1890 census in only one year. The 1880 census had taken eight years. Hollerith then started his own business in 1896, founding the Tabulating Machine Company. Most of the major census bureaus around the world leased his equipment and purchased his cards, as did major insurance companies.

To make his system work, he invented the first automatic card-feed mechanism and the first key punch (i.e. a punch that was operated from a keyboard), which allowed a skilled operator to punch 200–300 cards per hour. He also invented a tabulator. The 1890 Tabulator was hardwired to operate only on 1890 Census cards. A control panel in his 1906 Type I Tabulator allowed it to do different jobs without having to be rebuilt (the first step towards programming).These inventions were the foundation of the modern information processing industry.

In 1911, four corporations, including Hollerith's firm, merged to form the Computing Tabulating Recording Corporation (CTR). Into International Business Machines Corporation (IBM), by Thomas Watson in 1924

Thomas Watson knew a good thing when he saw it. As the Nazis rapidly rose to power beginning with Hitler's ascension to absolute dictatorship beginning in 1931, Watson found a dream customer for the Hollerith machines: Adolph Hitler.

The founding tenet of the Nazis was the absolute and minute control of entire populations of people, beginning with the Germans and, afterwards, with the onslaught well underway, most of Europe.

Technology: Tracking Human Prey

The Hollerith machines, which were among the first computers, were used by the New Deal under Franklin Roosevelt to keep census records and shortly thereafter as the administrative foundation for The Social Security program that emerged to salve the great social wounds of the Great Depression.

A special section of the Satanic SS was created especially to collect detailed information about every living and dead person in Germany, using Watson's Hollerith machine.

Hitler wanted to know the ancestry of all to determine whether any person had Jewish blood and if so, how much! Hollerith's punched-card technology was the key. One of the first things the Nazis did was to conduct a probing census, memorialized with punched-card technology that gave way to magnetic tape and now disk.

IBM provided instruction and supervision for the SS and an elite guard emerged, expert in consolidating the terrible data that the Nazis amassed. When the time came, Hitler was literally able to press a button and pluck out, with pinpoint accuracy, everyone he had slotted first for concentrated detention and then, as history tragically records, death.

This effort was so successful that IBM strained to keep up with Hitler's demands for Hollerith machines and the people to operate them.

Absolute Power Corrupts: Absolutely

Fortified with ultra-granular information, the Nazis put millions to death. IBM was there to meet and exceed the Feuhrer's expectations. Invoking technology as a means of population and mind control became a well-established and valued tactic as the world slowly revealed the gruesome efficiency of hunting prey with eagle-eyed accuracy.

Genocide H.Q. WWII: Madison Avenue

Watson, of course, supervised all the goings-on with the Nazis during the entire war from his offices on Madison Avenue in New York City. He wanted to make sure that one of his best clients got great customer service. He wanted to exceed their expectations and do everything he could to assist: in genocide. Not even the lives of millions were going to get in Watson's way.

Edwin Black brilliantly details all this in his work, "IBM and the Holocaust." But while researching and writing his book he discovered that IBM had refused all cooperation with scholars and investigators who have wanted to access IBM's archives. I am informed and believe that IBM has continued to keep the door shut. Not to worry, however, Edwin Black nailed it all in his book. This is not reading for the meek or those prone to nausea.

The diversion into telling the story of IBM and the Nazis is necessary to understanding what our fellow man is capable of, especially when blinded by the color green.

Ingenious, Ingenix!

Enter stage left, United's Ingenix, a wholly owned subsidiary of UnitedHealthcare Group. Thanks to the Attorney General of the State of New York, Andrew Cuomo and others, UnitedHealth Group had their hand slapped with a $350 million fine—pocket change for these mobsters. The following is taken from a publication of the United States Department of Justice. This little paragraph speaks big time to confirm our conjecture concerning the mind control mechanisms of the cartel:

UnitedHealth Group, the nation's largest health insurer, agreed to pay $350 million to resolve a class action lawsuit with the American Medical Association and the Medical Society, the State of New York and the Missouri State Medical Association in January. The suit alleged that UnitedHealth's wholly-owned subsidiary, Ingenix, rigged the databases that health insurers rely upon to set the "reasonable and customary" rates they charge for out-of-network physician fees so that providers and health plan member were underpaid for these services.

The company also settled a separate investigation into these practices by the New York Attorney General for $50 million in January. UnitedHealth admitted no wrongdoing in conjunction with either investigation. (DOJ)

Simply translated, United sells a database through its subsidiary, Ingenix, to whomever will pay and who, presumably is not HIPPA constrained, namely Federal and State government agencies and other insurance companies. By "adjusting" the data it sells, United covertly was able to manipulate the standards by which the "industry" reimburses for "standard and customary" out of network charges. Obviously the lower the reimbursement rate, the higher the profit margin the insurance payer will enjoy. The equation is straightforward: the amount of profit retained is in direct relationship with how little is paid out.

United unquestionably relies on this data for its own purposes and billing policies. But it also sells this information to the "industry," which follows suit and is happy to take the lead set by Big Brother United. Why not? They're making money by following the advice of Ingenix.

Everybody Walks: Everybody Talks

Nobody went to jail. United settled without wrongdoing for pocket change of $400 million and, I have little doubt, went back to business as usual. This is the now well-established pattern: when it finally intercedes to slap the wrists of the titans, the government picks up some nice cash in fines and sanctions, obtains a flaccid promise from the insurance companies not to do it again and its back to, "Nellie, bar the door!"

Crime and No Punishment

In every case we have examined this same pattern of crime and no punishment can be observed: shocking but true. There may be cases where a bigwig goes to the work farm for a while, but this is by far and away, the exception, not the rule.

Aside from the criminal aspects of fixing a database—and this is only one case where they were caught—we are witnessing the mind control and policy control of a cartel at work.

Since United and all the insurance providers have such an intertwined agenda, it behooves them to tow a common party line and policy. UnitedHealthcare products are sold by dozens of other insurance companies.

These are not competitors, they are comrades. So the more all conform to common pricing structures, the less likely the chance for real free-market competition, which is exactly the desired result.

How could this happen in the good old U.S.A.? The answer is simple: there is no difference between the cops and the robbers. The public blindly pays for this rigged game in which the house always wins and the public always loses.

Other Ways the Cartel Sucks Your Blood

February 4, 2009: the Texas Medical Association reports that a recent survey of doctors in Texas revealed that 93 percent of those interviewed believe that insurance companies take too much of their time and attention away from patient care.

Government payers, such as Medicaid, Medicare and TRICARE also rob patients of their doctor's time, according to 87 percent of those interviewed. Texas, the Lone Star State, is not alone.

Denial of care is integral to the ways insurers instruct their employees to rebuff requests for care. Effectively the cartel makes far more money by denying care, not by providing it. It appears to be far cheaper for the cartel players to hire legions of nurse administrators to deny care than to pay to provide it.

Do Not Go Softly Into That Good Night

A recent example brought to our attention captures how the process often works. A patient calls Wellpoint for a medication approval. The patient calls Wellpoint nineteen times. Each time they are distracted or diverted with requests for this or that. The patient asks the doctor for help but the doctor simply doesn't have the time. On the 20th call, the Wellpoint computer tracking system recognizes that this patient is not going away. Wellpoint approves the medication.

How many people have the time to engage in a 20-call marathon with associated disconnections and waiting times? Not many. For all those who give up after a few tries, the cartel mints money.

The Not So Supreme Court

Expect recourse in the courts? Think again. The cases of Davila and Calad of Texas went to the Supreme Court. Both were denied care, respectively, by Aetna Health and Cigna. The lower courts found in favor of the plaintiffs who suffered serious consequences from denial of doctor recommended care but denied by the insurance companies.

These two cases are not unlike the one-in-four of all insurance claims in the U.S. that are disputed or denied. Other techniques for restricting care involve nonpayment, slow payment, review delays and so on.

The lower courts decided, in these two cases, that insurers, who practice medicine, effectively, without a license, are responsible for their actions: that they have a fiduciary responsibility to purchase care for their subscribers.

The Supreme Court of the United States overturned all the lower court rulings, saying that it was the patient's responsibility, regardless of what the insurance contract provided. The Supreme Court, under ERISA law, found that though the insurance company did indeed make medical decisions, they couldn't be held liable for their actions: What a deal! In short, a patient assumes full responsibility for their own care, but has no authority whatsoever in deciding what care will be covered under their insurance coverage! This is an impossible double bind: a situation which cannot be resolved!

ERISA and the United States Supreme Court

Though the Justices were unhappy about the way ERISA law was structured, they disregarded their ability to rule on its constitution and instead sent the plaintiffs packing and dismissed the cases with prejudice. Translation: they and others are barred from presenting similar cases to the Supreme Court. The cartel struck gold—authority without responsibility and profit without recourse.

The Best Laws Money Can Buy

The Justices said that Congress was a better place to fix the inequities in the ERISA law. Given that lobby-influenced Congress passed the law written by the cartel, in the first place, it is highly unlikely that Congress would fix what they deliberately had broken. Broken for the public but fixed, big time, for the cartel.

Litigation is very expensive and time consuming, particularly when it involves taking a case to the Supreme Court. For the insurance cartel, the money is a pittance, but for a typical plaintiff the expense is totally out of reach.

We have come to a point where the public doesn't have much more to lose. I predict a revolution, the nature of which is still unclear to me. However, national strikes, non payment of taxes and rioting of the kind we saw in the 60s in Newark, Los Angeles and Detroit are not out of the question. I predict a significant increase in violence and attacks on institutional buildings such as banks and government facilities. I shutter to even suggest that this kind of revolt might happen, but history teaches us that there IS a boiling point. In the early Winter of 2010, the combination of the bank "bailout" coupled with the obvious corruptive influence of industry on healthcare legislation, spells, in my beliefs, a catastrophe about to happen. I hope I am wrong.

Cry Uncle!

The cartel pretends to cry uncle. Don't be fooled. It's just an act. They are anything but on the mat, pinned for the count. They are happy little beavers building their next dams at home and abroad. There is no end, I believe, to the avarice and decadence to which they aspire. They will conveniently justify their economic formulas.

Widgets are we all. Some savants of this area refer to this as the commoditization of healthcare. For the cartel it is no longer a game of money for its own sake. This is a quest for basic power and control. The money is only a way to keep score. There is no conscience, no compassion and no care whatsoever for their walking prey.

A heist is being played out in doctors' offices, hospitals and homes across a once great land. The traveling show is also on tour at such venues as Bangkok and Bangalore, Singapore and Seoul, Buenos Aires and Brunei.

Revisiting Ingenix and UnitedHealth

Rapidly rolling ahead our imaginary historical movie, the reader is asked to revisit the activities of United's Ingenix.

Massive compilations of data and the manipulation of that data to enable price fixing and total market control is an essential to any cartel seeking to systematically control its markets and territories.

I am informed and believe that UnitedHealthcare Group uses the tools it has at its disposal to do much more than control out-of-network provider reimbursement levels, as was the instant case in New York.

UnitedHealthcare Group and other cartel members already use technology to manipulate markets, set pricing and enable their numerous policies for care denial, sexual discrimination and similar abuses. They have already been fined over $300 million for misuse of their collected data. Often the FBI ceases their investigations when they think that they've earned their pay. Billions are left on the table.

The refinement and extension of databases such as the current $45 million investment by the Blues (Cross, Shield) provides ever-deeper tools to control and manipulate markets; and people. I provided the Nazi and IBM example as a means of illustrating what has happened and what can go wrong by concentrating data and placing it at the disposal of greedy hands.

I am not suggesting that Ingenix, Blue Cross or Blue Shield are Nazi or even Nazi-like organizations. I will, however, go this far: the Nazis used information to pluck people from their beds and businesses and to slaughter them in public and private. The collected data of the insurance cartel is used to kill hundreds of thousands and to inflict unimaginable pain and suffering on the American people and its once great medical system.

Denial of care is big business, an enterprise that involves withholding care, surgeries and medications from people who die as a result. I am informed and believe that these deaths are wrongful and could be avoided. The cartel members like United and the Blues use technology a million times more powerful than Hollerith. Corporate killing is nothing new. Unfortunately, it does not appear to be an artifact of the past.

Scaling the Consequences

Let us say that there are fifty million people in the United States who are privately insured. Let us say that 1 in 4 claims are disputed. Let us further assume that ten percent of those disputed claims involve life-threatening cases.

If we project, conservatively, that only one percent of those ten percent die as a result of confrontations with insurance, the resulting figure is still an alarming 1.5 million people. If we impose even more conservative conditions on this calculation and say that only ten percent of those die as a result of insurance denial of care, we are still talking about well over 100,000 people who die as a result of care disputes.

Whatever calculator one uses, one is still too many, especially when money is placed before life.

Obsession Justifies the Means

Given the cartel's propensity for big bucks, it is not hard to imagine the possibility that cartel members and their subscribing cohorts use all the information at their disposal for economic advantage.

Troublesome doctors who do not toe the line are targets for retribution and castigation. Patients, who actually expect to be covered for their care as contractually promised, can also be singled out and handled appropriately by having the policies canceled and their care denied.

In short, because the cartel's compiled information is sold and shared with other HIPPA-exempt organizations, if you have a hangnail in Fresno, the results will be available for broadcast from Philadelphia to Frankfurt. As soon as your doctor enters your information, the waiting world will know all about your hang nail, your hemorrhoids or your HIV.

The insurance industry has bought very special protections for itself. I believe that the special concessions afforded to the insurance industry are completely without Constitutional basis. But it takes millions of dollars to take cases up to the Supreme Court, who for the last many years has been dominated by justices who will not interfere with insurance-related litigation, unless of course, it is to protect the cartel.

Technological ways to track and control vast populations are here. Granular specificity is possible.

Where you are, what you do, where you shop, who your doctor is, what kinds of medicines you take, where you went to school, what kinds of diseases or genetic proclivities run in your family are only a small sample of data, which is being compiled about every single person in the United States.

Combining private-industry databases (e.g. those established by all the Blue Cross and Blue Shield organizations and UnitedHealth Group), with government databases provides an unprecedented opportunity for oppression and control.

The healthcare reforms contemplated as of summer 2009 refer to the IRS as the most likely administrator for payment collection for government- available health insurance. Since the administration of these policies will almost certainly be done in concert with private industry, the data from these master databases will be shared between government and industry. The consequences are frightening and staggering.

It is no secret or surprise that the data accumulated by private health insurance has already been manipulated to the detriment of Constitutional liberties. When super-sensitive information collected by the government falls into the hands of private players, I shudder.

The Constitution and the Bill of Rights are already so frayed that only a short distance needs to be traveled to achieve a corporate-government totalitarianism enabled by precision data on each soul in the United States and beyond.

Consider for a moment that the National Security Agency and the U.S. Military have been designated by the Obama administration to have ultimate oversight over all cyber systems in the United States. This, of course, is carefully packaged under the banner of national security.

While I have no argument that national security is an issue, the lines between private-citizen protection and national security have been completely erased. At any time the government can suspend the rule of law, arrest and detain anyone they wish should they be characterized, at their sole discretion, as a national security risk.

As recently as August 2009, the Executive branch has declared that if they, at their sole discretion, feel that any lawsuit brought in the United States, lodged by anyone for any reason, is against the national interest, the suit can be struck down and stopped dead.

The business of healthcare currently makes up about one-fifth of the U.S. economy. Special exceptions are already made for insurance companies who, among other ways, are exempted from respecting HIPPA privacy laws.

Since the decision of national security lies solely with the Executive branch, contradictory to 250 years of checks and balances, any given administration can capriciously decide what it deems to be in the national interest.

Should anyone, for example, object to the healthcare policies of the country, it is not inconceivable that they could be arrested and detained indefinitely without legal representation of any kind. In essence, we can all be classified as terrorists of one kind of another, terrorists who are only seeking to exercise their Constitutional prerogatives.

At no time in American history, perhaps with the exception of properly declared states of war, has there been anything close to what we are now observing in the dramatic and fundamental changes being made to the historic rule of law.

Since healthcare is such a dominant theme in our culture and a major component of our economy, growing increasingly significant with our aging population, it is not inconceivable that the corporate government cooperative could swoop down and chill any opposition and do so in the name of national security.

No recourse is or will be available to object to such actions. This holds, for us all, the real and immediate threat of totalitarianism and military/industrial dictatorship. Personal privacy is an artifact of history along with the Constitutional guarantees so carefully contemplated by the Founding Fathers.

Thirteen ~ The Crucifixion
of Doctors in America

Setting the stage for expanded discussion about the insurance cartel, its time to dig deeper into understanding how badly American doctors have been disenfranchised. Their emasculation is a primary reason why people are now—astonishingly—willing to consider putting themselves in the hands of Medical Tourist doctors thousands of miles away.

To control the previous paradigm of physician/patient-centered healthcare, the insurance cartel had to cripple the medical establishment. The genocidal zeal with which their "take no prisoners" strategy has been accomplished, left behind a burned landscape, littered with heaps of destroyed medical professionals.

Doctors, have literally and legally, are gagged by the insurance tyrants from discussing many subjects with patients, including criticisms the doctors may have about healthcare plans.

Somehow, the First Amendment of the U.S. Constitution seems to have been disregarded and discarded, as insurance companies have had the audacity to muzzle freedom of speech. Even more stupendous is that they get away with it.

The Cartel Has its Own Laws!

Insurance companies sell secret lists of blacklisted doctors and patients to each other. Insurance industry players are exempt from HIPPA secrecy laws!

Their successful assaults have created a sad legacy.

The Hippocratic Oath, the sworn code on which doctors stake their careers, is gone. Doctors in the U.S. who accept insurance (the vast majority) are subject to constant intimidation by insurance-company employees who are paid to deny patients coverage for treatment.

In essence, insurance companies practice medicine daily, without license, for millions of unseen patients, making life-and-death decisions that supplant the will of doctors and health care professionals on the front lines.

Should a doctor see fit to sue, they will lose even if they win. The insurance cartel simply blacklists them, drops them from their plans and thirty years of schooling is flushed down the drain.

Don't Call Me Doctor, I'm Your Provider

Keep in mind that in the fifty years since Medicare was enacted, the semantics of the insurer-doctor-patient relationship has been changed. Doctors are now "Providers."

This may seem inconsequential at first, but I believe that it reveals the international disempowerment of the medical-professional community by literally choosing a label that fundamentally eliminates the respect, which ought to be shown to those who have devoted their lives to becoming doctors and practitioners.

"Honey, I'll be home a little late today, I have an appointment with my Provider." It's absurd!

"Provider" implies a kind of servitude to the mega-powerful corporations who play the tune to which nearly every doctor in American dances. Failing to do so can cost doctors their careers. Doctors have become medical hand-maidens and troublesome employees who must be dealt with firmly and often harshly.

While the individual earnings of physicians decline, the profits for the major insurance companies, hospital owners and pharmaceutical companies soar. The balance of power has shifted significantly and it's easy to trace it back to 1965 and the enactment of Medicare.

Doctors are forced into signing plans with ever-decreasing reimbursement rates and fee structures. This institutionalized underpayment ploy makes it impossible for independent practices in most States to be economically viable.

Doctors, consequently, left with little choice, join practices controlled by members of the powerful American Hospital Association, or insurance-provider networks and HMO's.

The consequences for doctors who choose to take a firm stance against their declining reimbursement rates can be dire. If a doctor is terminated from participating in an insurance plan, all other plans that access this termination information, may also terminate these doctors, effectively blacklisting the wronged doctor across the country.

The result of being "terminated" (often without cause or due process, as afforded by various State and Federal laws), is that the doctor will never be able to work again. A doctor who does not take insurance won't have patients or hospital affiliations. Without those essentials, the doctor has no practice. It's called being blackballed. This should properly be named "corporate extermination!" To push my Nazi German analogy a bit further, the Nazi's answered to no one: the insurance cartel operates with complete impunity and answers only to themselves since the Federal Government acts in lock step with the insurance cartel.

It is not surprising that according to the AMA, Psychiatry News 17 July 2009, Vol 44, #14, Page 8, suicide among doctors in the United States is at an all-time high.

Doctors who complain risk their livelihoods; it's possible for them to be barred from practicing medicine. The insurance companies play hardball and have no problem violating due process or the constitutional rights of physicians and patients.

Those who speak up are sure to be castrated and held up as examples of what happens to those who dare to complain. Short of seeking expensive court injunctions, most doctors seek to meekly hide and say nothing, protecting themselves and their families from the tyranny of the American Medical Money Machine.

Your doctor has really become a provider, a supplicant to the cartel's interests. Doctors know this and live with it daily, bravely continuing to practice. They have accepted the ever-declining reimbursement rates for their services. They realize that it is practically impossible to survive unless they

compromise the quality and scope of their medical services.
The system devised by the insurance cartel assures that doctors
in practice in America today are breaking the Hippocratic Oath:
do no harm.

As early as 2001, publications and reports indicated an office
visit with a physician averages less than five minutes per
patient. Many are in the realm of two-to-three minutes.

The briskness of these visits reveals the need for doctors to cram
in as much as possible, rushing through their day, to
compensate for declining insurance reimbursement rates.
Thus, the quality of healthcare on a patient-by-patient basis has
broken down in favor of quantity. Providers have a grossly
limited idea of what is actually going on with their patients.

How Would You Like a Two-Minute Diagnosis?

To illuminate the absurdity of this, try describing your current
occupation or weekly routine to someone in two minutes.
Physicians are also forced into performing unnecessary
procedures or tests just to increase their bottom line.

Of course, there are unscrupulous doctors we know as Quacks,
but many respected physicians, faced with the tyranny of
McCarthy-like cartel oversight, will be compelled to err on the
side of self protection and money generation; engaging methods
of operation that further tap the system and drain unnecessary
money from those with real medical needs.

Doctors who protest the enormous paperwork required by the
insurers to justify their diagnosis or request for diagnostics and
medications (the cost of the paperwork is without compensation
to the doctors) are knowingly endangering their careers. Most,
except for the rare crusader, will not stand up to the insurers
who dominate with impunity.

Fear of being sued is so high that doctors practice self protection
against patients. Hospital corporations and insurance
companies are rarely sued. Ty have, through political power,
seen to it that awards to doctors who sue them are capped at
very low rates for pain and suffering. The insurance interests are
largely immune from prosecution.

Doctors and nurses work on the front lines, serving as sacrificial and expendable decoys. The real power, the money behind these institutions, is well sheltered, out of reach and invisible. Doctors and nurses take the brunt of the litigation, pay enormous malpractice premiums and are directly attacked by the public while hospitals and insurers sit, smirking on the sidelines.

Affordable malpractice insurance for doctors requires huge deductibles and is, even then, often simply unaffordable. The same insurance companies that cover individuals or companies for patient policies own the companies that sell these medical malpractice policies. In many states, malpractice coverage is simply out of sight and doctors go naked and legally exposed. It gets worse.

According to an article in the October 1, 2007 issue of American Medical News, Massachusetts Health Reform Builds Momentum, insurers are now adding personality tests to the application process for medical-malpractice insurance. These companies want to decide whether physicians are risk takers, what others think of their behavior, what is the bedside manner of doctors? Will it lead to higher claims for malpractice?

This same piece says that Iowa-based United Medical Liability Insurance Company, is among the "latest to require that physicians take a communication-skills assessment, akin to a personality test, before issuing a malpractice policy." This humiliation is not designed in the interest of patients. It is brazen control and represents an outright effort to intimidate physicians. These are Gestapo tactics imposed by those who know nothing of medicine-yet have complete control of who lives and who does not.

United of Iowa is a subsidiary of UnitedHealthcare. UnitedHealthcare Group appears to be working overtime to control not only the finances of healthcare, but the behaviors of highly trained doctors and practitioners. They do this overtly and surreptitiously. Every time one reads anything published by AARP, you are being sold the UnitedHealthcare Group party line. I hope the 40 million members of AARP will come to terms with the reality that they are being used and abused by an organization who squeezes every nickle and time from the retired population. My strong belief is that UnitedHealthcare looks at the AARP is the marketing coup of the century; and, in many ways IT IS.

Fourteen ~ The Mediated State

In The Pit of My Stomach

My experiences with the media have left me in a semi-catatonic state.

To be sure, pockets of truth and responsibility in journalism exist, mostly offshore in the British, French and German Press.

Domestically, the Press has been so emasculated through corporate intrusion that there are only a few voices left calling out from the barren landscape.

Journalistic sources offering counterviews to the prevailing message have been labeled by the mainstream as left wing, counter-culture and fanatical.

National Public Radio moves with extreme caution. They have Congress and their subscribers to answer to. They are not in a position to take chances.

Great publications like *The New York Times* and *The Washington Post* have had their editorial budgets slashed and hundreds of journalists in their once-formidable newsrooms have been laid off.

168 Channels and Nothing to Watch

Those journalists who remain seem reluctant to take on sensitive topics, especially when they involve domestic bad boys. The media moguls of the mass media must keep their eye on advertisers, many of whom come from the very ranks of those most deserving investigation.

The major broadcast networks have long since given in to the dominance of their owners. Though there are some exceptions to the money-ruled editorial policies of these organizations, journalism, like medicine, is controlled by an economic model. No wonder flipping from station to station at news time produces little difference in what comes out of the mouths of the talking heads.

It is deeply troubling that our society has become stultified by the constriction of free exchange of ideas via a free Press, historically a hallmark of our democratic society. The concept was pivotal to the Founding Fathers. They embodied their concern in the First Amendment.

With a free Press muzzled—or worse, a Press implicitly or explicitly trumpeting the deliberate viewpoints of particular powerful vested interests—vast numbers of people can be lulled into a hypnotic mindset.

This has been the case with the unilateral party line about Medical Tourism. Sadly, the same anesthetizing effect can be observed in a thousand other places where one channel becomes indistinguishable from another. This is sad; it is also very serious.

I was not surprised when a confidant, personally acquainted with the news-media talking heads in New York, explained that the marketing department determines what will be aired and, more importantly, what will not.

None but the largest and wealthiest players can ante up for the mainstream media game. They benefit and we lose.

The media has become consolidated in the hands of a very few, mighty corporations. Whether directly or indirectly, editorial policy is imposed and influenced by advertisers and the interlocking nature of the Boards of Directors. This is a silent, but deadly consequence of consolidation-an implicit penalty we all pay by sacrificing our guaranteed First Amendment rights.

(See Appendix #14)

This appendix contains a comprehensive list of the consolidated media entities. I make no aspersions as to the intention of these companies to withhold or moderate the news. I understand, the need to assure that corporate profits are no jeopardized by the publication of material which might anger potential advertisers. This is an unfortunate artifact of the capitalist system-reasonable but sad.

Good Evening: Walter Cronkite No Longer Works Here

My attempts to engage a major news provider to report my findings, print or television, met with delays and turndowns. I thought that CBS 60 Minutes would jump at the chance to air a piece counter to their Bumrungrad siren. I was badly mistaken.

Other major "investigative" news programs were the same; they weren't interested in my story.

Two major newspapers (who shall remain anonymous) were interested in my discoveries and asked for my entire files, which I provided. Yet, after a year of playing footsie, their interest fell by the wayside for vague reasons.

Word had been handed down from the two publishers that Josh's story would jeopardize advertising revenue. Already in a state of free-fall advertising dollar losses by 2008, publishers understandably don't wish toruffle their advertisers.

Not So Hot: Down Under

Not all countries have restricted media. Australia, particularly, has been vocal in its outrage over the consequences of Aussie patients seeking medical care abroad.

Australia, with its close proximity to South East Asia, has been particularly vulnerable to the onslaught of avaricious medical interests from Thailand. Australians, faced with delays in receiving care from their own health care system, have been a major component that has sought care abroad.

Beauty procedures abroad (elective, not paid for by national health insurance) are of major interest to Aussies. Bumrungrad regularly sends doctors to Australia to meet prospective patients in clandestine hotel suites to discuss their prospective surgeries. The Australians have not been happy about this, since Bumrungrad's doctors are in Australia, essentially practicing medicine without license. It's hard to stop the practice, though the Aussie police continue their efforts.

The fallout for these foreign procedures has resulted in serious economic consequences for the Australian public health system. Australia has been in the direct firing line of the negative consequence of medical Tourism.

They have not been squeamish in speaking up:

Sydney Herald Horror Story, 01.October.2007
The ugly facts behind beauty Tourism boom
Eamonn Duff and Louise Hall
September 30, 2007 (Excerpts)

COSMETIC Tourism operators are resorting to illegal practices to recruit patients for surgery such as breast implants as concerns grow over botched operations.

The NSW Medical Board is cracking down on operators who are paying Thai and Malaysian doctors to conduct illegal consultations in Australian hotels, a practice banned under the NSW Medical Practice Act.

Operators fly the surgeons to Australia to counteract the growing publicity over botched surgery that leads to infections, hair loss, scarring, paralysis and failed implants.

A NSW Medical Board spokeswoman said the board was made aware in May of an offer advertised by Gorgeous Getaways on its website for free consultations in Australia with overseas doctors before surgery.
Under section 105 of the Medical Practice Act, "it is an offence for a person who is not a registered medical practitioner [in NSW] to advertise or hold themselves out to be qualified & or to give surgical advice and service."

The NSW Medical Board wrote to the company threatening action. However, Gorgeous Getaways was still promoting the service last week, stating, "We have consultation tours in Australia, UK, USA and other countries."

Another medical Tourism company is run by a carpet cleaner and former Transfield technician who says he runs an "enhancement team."

A carpet cleaner! Hello!

Another example from the Aussie Press regarding Medical Mistakes:

AUSTRALIA PAYS THE PRICE
New South Wales Feels Impact of Medical Tourism, 26.August.2006
Risky scalpel tours cut into taxpayers' pockets
Louise Hall and Connie Levett
August 27, 2006 (Excerpts)

AUSTRALIANS suffering from botched cosmetic surgery overseas are costing taxpayers thousands of dollars when they undergo remedial and reconstructive surgery in NSW public Hospitals.

Plastic surgeons are reporting dozens of cases of complications including infections, hair loss, "hideous" scarring, paralysis and failed implants from cut-price "scalpel Tourism" packages.

Dr Anand Deva said he treated one patient every six to eight weeks who had been abandoned by their overseas surgeon once complications arose. The Australians are not covered by that country's local health system.

"Over there, you are a tourist and you are on your own and there is no backup if something goes wrong, whereas in Australia if something goes wrong, we have the Medicare system," he said.
"It is not easy to salvage these cases, [so] is it really fair for Australian taxpayers to foot the bill when something goes wrong overseas?"

The Federal Government is so concerned about the risk of complications from discount or uncertified medical establishments that it has a special travel advisory warning for "medical Tourism" in Thailand.

Parliamentary Secretary to the Minister for Foreign Affairs, Teresa Gambaro, said there had been an increasing burden on embassy staff helping Australians suffering complications, primarily in Bangkok but also in the Philippines, Indonesia, Argentina, Iran and Ukraine.

Chairman of NSW Health's surgical services taskforce, Dr Patrick Cregan, said people opting for cheap overseas surgery risked having unqualified surgeons and non-Accredited facilities.

Suffice to say that the Australians are talking about Medical Tourism because they have experienced it first hand. Since the country has a relatively small population, 22 million, the backlash of Medical Tourism is, for them, palpable. They write about it because it is real, and costly.

Stick to Your Knitting

The United States Press is geared to report about what a great and cost-effective thing Medical Tourism is. Following are representative comments from Steve Forbes, whose eponymous magazine reports that Medical Tourism is a logical next link in the free market chain.

Fox News, in 2006, ran the following:

Overseas Health Care Offers Cost Savings, Risks

Thursday, November 02, 2006, Associated Press

Arnold Milstein, MD, a consultant favoring patient exportation said, "It's just one of the many ways in which our world is flattening," said Arnold Milstein, chief physician at New York-based Mercer Health & Benefits, who's researching the feasibility of outsourcing medical care for three Fortune 500 corporations. "Many companies see it as a natural extension of the competition they've faced in other aspects of their business."

Milstein is making a living prepping the corporate establishment for medical outsourcing when Medical Tourism graduates to a full-blown state of institutionalization. This is where Medical Tourism, as a concept, really becomes dangerous and also becomes very big business: when it becomes part and parcel of your insurance policy.

The AP article goes on to say that Blue Ridge, a company set to be the first to send an employee offshore, was stopped by the United Steel Workers Union. Blue Ridge scrapped its plan for union members to be outsourced but several other U.S. businesses and insurance companies are working with UnitedHealthcare and others to see that this "cost savings" scheme becomes daily reality.

United with Bumrungrad

United Group Programs is already offering a plan that sends patients to Bumrungrad hospital in Bangkok. United sells foreign health plans on the basis that it will save employers more than 50 percent on major medical costs and slash employees' out-of-pocket expenses. Accept their lowest cost provider and you and your company save money. Reject medical exportation and premiums, co-pays and deductibles will increase substantially. This constitutes a kind of financial blackmail.

Under ERISA laws, employers cannot be sued for offering this kind of coverage by their employees. Even more jaw dropping is that the insurance administrator, UnitedHealthcare, is also not liable for anything that goes wrong.

The Supreme Court of the United States, making law instead of enforcing it, has found that insurance companies are not liable in the event of suit, something never contemplated by ERISA law, The Employee Retirement Income Security Act.

The AP article of November 2, 2006 describes how Blue Cross and Blue Shield of South Carolina went to Bangkok to explore how they could get the most bang for their buck! As you might have guessed, Bumrungrad set their hooks into the 1.5 million memberships of Blue Cross and Blue Shield of South Carolina. The Blues of South Carolina are now partnered with Bumrungrad.

Blue Shield is on track to roll out its international program, with follow-up care centers being contracted in South Carolina in case something goes wrong.

West Virginia Proposes to Pay Patients!

In addition, West Virginia lawmakers plan to propose legislation that would give government employees the option of traveling abroad for necessary procedures, which could save the state up to $2 million annually. Incentives are also contemplated by the home state of Senator Jay Rockefeller, including extra sick leave and 20 percent of the cash saved by going abroad—letting workers actually make money on the deal.

While Fox and AP give some weight to risks, they mostly discuss culture shock, expressing repulsion at Third World pollution. They unilaterally evade the question of quality care and recourse in the event of a screw up.

Sadly, this cookie-cutter story is repeated time and again. The hundreds of copy-cat stories about Medical Tourism always seem to get around to the one case that has reached public awareness: Joshua Goldberg, my son.

"If there's a mistake, we fix it," said Curtis Schroeder, an American who is Group CEO of Bumrungrad hospital. I am waiting, Mr. Schroeder, for you to resurrect my only child!

In February, Joshua Goldberg, a 23-year-old American who was traveling in Thailand, died at Bumrungrad after seeking care for a leg injury. His father, James Goldberg, has set up a Web site alleging the hospital administered a deadly drug cocktail to a patient with a history of substance abuse.

Bumrungrad insists the care given was appropriate. Thai

authorities are investigating the case, as is standard with all unexpected hospital deaths. No conclusions have been reached.

The story, planted by Ruben Toral, Bumrungrad, UnitedHealthcare and the AARP, finds its way back into the lexicon adopted to rebut those who would cast doubt on the sinister game of Medical Tourism.

Would you want to have your medical histories published in the press: alcoholism, prescription-drug abuse, sexually-transmitted diseases, psychiatric problems, colostomies or cosmetic surgeries?

The 2006 AP article includes the usual travel-benefit statement hooked onto most of the Medical Tourist propaganda: travel and lodging for two and a tour of the Taj Mahal.

Of course, the Press tracks those patients who have nice things to say post operatively. The American Press, almost without exception, does not report on maimed or infected patients or those sent home in a body bag.

Setting the Record Straight

The personal price I have paid at the hands of the AARP and their watchful parent, UnitedHealthcare has been immeasurably high. The 2007 AARP Newsletter regarding Josh's death at Bumrungrad has become a mainstay in the lore of Medical Tourism.

The mistakes incorporated in the AARP excoriation of my son have been repeated globally. Not one reporter or author of any of these articles has contacted me to verify any of the information that they vamp with unashamed enthusiasm.

I realized, upon embarking on this journey, that there would be sticks and stones. To have thousands of self interested, careless and often outright evil people attack a dead young man, my only son, is an unfair fight.

As I wade through only some of the two million postings on

Google for "Medical Tourism" (as of June 2009), I am struck by how much mental weight and energy has been expended in shooting down the only widely reported case of Medical Tourism crime (Josh is far from being the only case but his is the only case that has reached the top of the debate).

Yes, I put Josh's life up for examination. I did it after clear deliberation. I would never be content to let his murder be swept aside and forgotten when so many others risk the same terrible fate.

Blame the Victim

The Eulogy, the last chapter of this work, touches on who and what Josh was, did and what causes and values he embraced. I urge you to read it.

The powers that be invalidate Josh. They must nullify anything resembling their culpability.

Their future depends on it. Powers like the AARP and UnitedHealthcare use tactics well understood in the caliginous, foul world of professional mind manipulators: blame and discredit the victim.

Josh was blamed for his death by a completely oblique and irrelevant reference to a problem millions share worldwide: he had a prior drug-abuse problem. The AARP and the Press picked this from our website. I purposefully disclosed all of this on www.bumrungraddeath.com and in exchanges with Bumrungrad concerning what medications they should and should not use in treating Josh for anything.

Taking these exchanges out of context, the AARP and the thousands who have followed their suit have greatly wronged the memory of a brilliant and terrific kid.

To set the record straight and silence people and organizations that have maligned and defamed my son, here are the two pivotal correspondences that embody the reality that has been intentionally distorted with squalid, filthy and unclean forethought:

From: Jim Goldberg
Sent: Thursday, March 16, 2006 9:22 AM
To: 'Peter Morley (Dr.)'
Subject: Joshua Goldberg

Hello Peter,

Please look at the EKG taken as attempts were made to revive Joshua. He was alive when discovered . . . .his heart with in arrhythmia . . . perhaps ventricular tachycardia and or Torsade de pointes. This occurred as the EKG clearly shows before he went flat line. If I am reading this incorrectly or if the physicians who are studying his chart are, please let me know. I think the graph speaks for itself and this is NOT a matter of speculation.

Josh was given at least 2 drugs simultaneously which prolong the QT interval . . . .Zeldox and Amitriptyline . . . ..additionally Josh was being given methadone and morphine . . . which decrease blood pressure and depress the CNS.

The mixture of Zeldox and Amitriptyline, I have been advised by a leading psycho pharmacologist, is absolutely counter indicated . . . .and even under the best circumstances requires that a baseline EKG be given before administration. I see no evidence in the chart that such a baseline EKG was given. Zeldox has, perhaps, the longest QT delay of any of the antipsychotics . . . 15-35 ms.

The prescription of Ziprasidone was completely inappropriate . . . Josh was undergoing morphine withdrawal . . . he was not schizophrenic, not delusional or hallucinating . . . which are the primary indications for Zeldox. Why your "psychopharma" person prescribed such a dangerous drug for a patient going through withdrawal symptoms . . . caused by Bumrungrad's administration of morphine to a known drug abuser . . . is beyond my imagination. Why your "psychopharma" person would also couple this drug with others which are known to have a QT prolonging effect and without establishing a baseline EKG is simply, to be blunt, malpractice.

Aside from the debate about Josh's state of mind and why after a cursory and superficial analysis by your "psychopharma" person, it was decided that such an exotic and dangerous drug(s) be prescribed, still leaves unexplained why the drugs he was given were mixed in the first place.

Why your pharmacy did not issue drug drug warnings and cautions regarding the potential lethal effects of the drugs given to Josh the day before and the day of his death is either malpractice on their part of a defect in the alert system you are using.

Why Josh was not on a cardiac monitor given the cocktail of drugs and their risks is, again, malpractice.

Why my extensive conversation with the attending neurologist never found its way into Josh's chart is amazing. Why there is no mention in the chart of my conversation with the floor nurse on the night of his admission is also amazing . . . and clearly negligent.

I have been advised that what Bumrungrad did goes against all standard practice . . . .how this happened in what appears to be your sophisticated technical environment is something I would like to know and the Joint Commission should know. You need to know how these mistakes happened so that they are not repeated again.

I would speculate that your psycho pharma person has little or no experience in treating previously addicted patients for drug withdrawal.

Bumrungrad knowingly created a full blown addiction in a recovering addict.

Upon realizing the mistake of this . . . you folks changed your mind . . . and introduced a cocktail of drugs to achieve a step down and withdrawal . . . a protocol which I am not yet sure was appropriate . . . .In addition, your "psychopharma" person threw in drugs into this mix which are known to have potential explosive and lethal interactions. Pfizer suffered a significant delay with FDA approval on Zeldox/Geodon over this very reason. The literature is replete with references and papers on this. The specifications which accompany the both Amitriptyline and Zeldox warn of these interactions. The specs which accompany morphine and methadone also mention the potentially fatal drug drug interactions.

With all of this known . . . or knowable . . . an apparently capricious decision was made that it was OK not to have Josh on a cardiac monitor . . . Especially in the absence of a baseline EKG.

I am continuing my consultations with world class experts in this field . . . and am continuing to gather data. I suggest you do the same. And I also suggest that you look into how these compounded mistakes happened in your institution . . . .and whether those who administered to my son were qualified. I also suggest that you find out and send to me what your pharma alert system, in use at the time of Josh's death, says about the interaction of the drugs given. Did this information . . . whatever it maybe, make it to the nursing floor?

My son is dead and I am suffering the agony of a parent who loved his kid beyond words. I have to spend the rest of my life . . . as does his mother . . . without our son. I also owe it to Josh, in whose name a foundation is being established to help the poor and needy, had his life unnecessarily ended through what is becoming crystal clear is the apparent negligence and malpractice of Bumrungrad.

I have every intention, Peter, of shining a very bright light on this . . . I have connections in the media in New York and Los Angeles . . . I have access to world leading experts . . . lawyers etc. I will not hesitate for a millisecond to utilize my powers to see that this is made right. I owe this to others . . . and I owe it to the memory of my son.

True, the final Forensic report is important . . . and I am anxiously awaiting its completion. I have arranged for an immediate translation with the U.S. Vice Counsel. In the meanwhile, all I can do is go through what I have been told and what the record reveals to date. What I have thus far discovered s agonizing and disturbing . . . .it is to me . . . and it should be to all of you.

As a first gesture and demonstration of good will, I ask that Bumrungrad provide gratis medical care to the Monks of

Thambrabok Monastery for an extended period of time. As they only travel by car under emergency circumstances, I believe that this care would be infrequent. I ask that this care be provided for a period of at least 10 years and that it be initiated immediately.

I will, of course, want a written contract that these services will be provided. Kindly let me know the disposition of the hospital regarding this request. I think it's a good opportunity for you to help others . . . and to begin the process of purifying the negative karma Bumrungrad has had imprinted in this terrible episode. This will start the kind of win win relationship to which I had aspired when I first met with you and your colleagues.

Does your hospital carry medical malpractice and liability insurance? If so, can you provide specifics?

We have an expression in some parts of the US . . . perhaps also in your country of birth . . . "Don't piss on my shoes and tell me that it's raining." I will not tolerate any bullshit . . . I'm too smart for that . . . and the people whose help I am soliciting to make sense of this are even smarter. Kindly don't presume for a second that any variation of the truth or distortion will not be caught.

I called Mr. Schroeder and I expect that he will have the courtesy of returning my call.

Sincerely,
James Goldberg
From: Jim Goldberg
Sent: Saturday, March 25, 2006 1:34 AM
To: 'Peter Morley (Dr.)'
Cc: 'Mack Banner'; 'Maureen Potter'; 'Daley, Daniel N'
Subject: More Information Regarding My Son
Peter,

In further examination of the Chart you provided, I find no record of any interview with your psycho pharmacologist or psychiatrist and my son which led to his or her tragic decision to prescribe Geodon to my son. Was there such an interview ever conducted? Where are the notes of the Dr. which led him or her to prescribe perhaps the most dangerous of all atypical anti-psychotics available ANYWHERE?!

What made him decide that my son was psychotic in the first place? Where is the DSM analysis which led him or her to the conclusion that this drug was necessary at all?

I spoke with my son every day . . . sometimes twice a day during his entire stay at Bumrungrad . . . including the night of the 23rd of Feb 06 and did not find him to be incoherent, hallucinating or delusional in any way whatsoever . . . the primary indications for the prescription of Zeldox (U.S.name, Geodon), if such a record does exist, please provide it or inform me that no such record exists.

If my son became boisterous or abusive of your staff, you have yourselves to thank.

You administered morphine, strictly against my wishes, to a known and self admitted recovering drug addict, addicted him to that morphine and then realized, as you yourself admitted, that you had made a mistake; and then sought, without apparent experience, to withdraw him by step-down procedure which somehow included the introduction of the deadliest and most dangerous of the tricyclics available; and all of this, without monitoring his vital signs with a cardiac monitor, a blood oxygen monitor or ANY device whatsoever.

Your suggestion that such monitoring was unnecessary reveals a serious lapse in either your understanding or experience or that of your staff as to the potential, published, known and readily understood consequences of mixing the medications you did the day before and the day and night of Joshua's death.

To suggest that there was "no reason" to monitor him is sheer lunacy, insanity and gross malpractice, negligence of the highest order . . . if not outright murderous.

Also, how is it that your pharmacy system, Global Solutions, which shows obvious contraindications information about the cocktail of prescribed drugs never made it into Joshua's chart? Is your IT system or protocols that provincial that information of this magnitude would not be communicated to the nursing floor or to the doctors prescribing such legal drugs with such apparent abandon and capriciousness?

Do you indeed have a protocol for assuring that your pharmacy's information is transmitted accurately and comprehensively BEFORE it is given to those who are giving it? Or has life become that cheap in your part of the world?

Why was his own admission of having been a recovering drug abuser, which you yourself mentioned during our personal interview, never recorded in his chart? You knew about, but the chart, at least according to my read, makes no mention this.

Did my son ever agree, in writing to be given these drugs? Did he ever agree to be treated, in writing, at all? Did you attempt to obtain my consent?

(You certainly knew where to call me to inform me of his death!)

Did you, Bumrungrad, seek to contact his doctors in the US or me, to obtain that person's name?

As per my previous request, I again ask you to name each and every person who attended to my son's care for the entire duration of his stay at the hospital, and inform the police of who they are and to provide them and me with their credentials. I ask that they ALL be placed on immediately leave until this matter is adjudicated.

I ask that you inform the Thai Police of who these individuals are and that you provide them with their credentials.

I call particular attention to the separate matter of what appears to be a highly irregular code procedure. Physicians in this country have informed me that an ECG during the entire procedure is standard . . . .yet the report page in his chart is filled with critical blanks . . . and little information about what was done to revive him. You provide and ECG trace which is 3 minutes long . . . and the ECG machine is turned off only second after a flat line. What protocol are you using for your Code 3 procedures? Please provide it to me, the JCA and the police.

Your code team should be separately itemized; their credentials made known to me and the police and all of its members should be placed on immediate leave. Aside from the lethal cocktail of drugs which appears to have killed my son, their efforts to revive him indicate an even higher level of negligence . . . ...and incompetence. and might well be criminal.

Have you evaluated whether anyone at your institution held any grudge against my son? Have you advised the police of who might have? Do you have security procedures to protect your patients from unwanted intruders?

I further request that you verify to me that these actions have been taken. I fear that the lives of others could be at risk . . . by virtue of your Institution's apparent gaps in protocol and with the blatant negligence, as it appears to date, of those who are involved in the practice of medicine at your institution. I appreciate the immediate delivery of the information I have requested.

Pending the police report and other evidence yet to be uncovered, I am wrathful . . . .yes . . . because I care deeply that others do not die or suffer from the kind of systemic errors that Bumrungrad has made. Depending on the final findings, I also intend that one level or another of significant restitution will be made in his honor in order to fund a foundation which is being established in his name and memory ...

We will get to that part soon enough.

I look pretty good on television . . . I'll bet you and your colleagues will not be nearly as photogenic.

Sincerely,
James Goldberg

I never received answers to either of these emails.

Ready?

These correspondences occurred while I still believed that Josh had been poisoned by Bumrungrad's administration of medications. I no longer believe this. Most of the medications indicated on Josh's hospital charts were not found in his peri-mortem blood. As I have come to learn, his death through improper medication administration was a ruse intended to throw me off the real path.

The hospital records clearly show that Josh had been deliberately characterized as psychotic to justify Bumrungrad's use of additional medications to straightjacket and exert control over my son. No psychiatric consultation was ever conducted; there was absolutely no justification for the supposed use of these medications.

For those unfamiliar with cardiac function, the reference to QT prolongation is important. The QT wave is an autonomic electrical impulse to the heart that involuntarily keeps the heart beating—for a lifetime.

Certain medications interfere with the transmission of that essential electrical signal. The several medications Josh was allegedly given could add up, without debate, to significant compromise of that electrical transmission with the predictable result of death. Yet these medications were not found in his blood upon post mortem examination.

This, I believe, was a very clever ruse; a diversion to blame his death on medications, not on what I believe occurred: my son was smothered to death before Morley et al could finalize the planned harvest of his organs. Their plan was aborted only because a whistle blower at the hospital called the police, as mentioned before, and begged for their intervention.

Josh had a perfect nose, yet it was broken and punched in as evidenced in his autopsy pictures. I believe this is evidence that Josh was smothered to death. More information pointing to murder is overwhelming and is summarized in Chapter 18, The Killing.

Stealing From the Dead: Hiding From the Living

It is a fact that Bumrungrad and the Thai Police retained and secreted my son's body tissue: his blood.

Though I demanded that this blood be turned over to me, the hospital refused, as did the police. If one wants certifiable evidence of stealing Josh's body parts, look no further than their conversion of his blood.

A reasonable person would have to ask why. What was so bloody important about his blood? Though Bumrungrad made mumbled promises to turn over the blood, they never did. Josh was clean and sober when he entered Bumrungrad and wanted to stay that way. Hence, both Josh and I instructed Bumrungrad, in every way possible, to avoid addictive medication.

Bumrungrad deliberately ignored my and my son's entreaties and administered vast amounts of medications that reactivated Josh's addiction and also placed him firmly under the control of Bumrungrad and its chief evil-doer, Dr. Peter Morley.

Morley is known to have "managed" Josh's case, though he was an administrator, not a practicing clinician at Bumrungrad. Dr. Sukkitti, Morley's fall guy, admitted to Morley's complete supervision of everything concerning Josh.

The Associated Press: More Shame

While the AP had no difficulty issuing the above party-line piece on the Medical Tourism/outsourcing scene, they had a big problem in telling Josh's story.

The AARP and any responsible source would have had to investigate and read what I willingly published: Josh had a previous problem with drugs. He was violently allergic to opiates of any kind.

He should not have been given any drugs by a hospital morally and ethically duty bound to heal, not harm. Instead, Bumrungrad, immediately upon admission re-induced Josh's disease and also added a potent psycho-active cocktail to boot. There is no doubt in my mind, whatsoever, that this was deliberate.

Instead of news sources placing in context the "drug addiction" mantra, they deliberately justified their own sinister and underhanded agenda by suggesting that Josh was responsible for his own death and that someone with a problem had a life not worth living, or saving.

Sometime in 2006 after the www.bumrungraddeath.com website was live, a bright intern reporter from the AP called and asked for an interview. He said he had been blown away by what he read on my website and wanted to know more.

I met with the AP's prize-winning prodigy reporter and spent over two days going over, in meticulous detail, the story as I then understood it. The reporter produced a series of four pieces on Medical Tourism. One dealt exclusively with Josh. The series was never published.

First, the journalist told me that the AP editors needed the pieces to be shortened. We live in a sound-bite world and they wanted sound bites. The reporter obliged but still nada. Repeated stalls intervened; the author became frustrated, finished his internship and disappeared into the ether.

I contacted the AP's Chief Editor, Scott Gillespie, and asked why these seminal pieces had not made their international and national news feeds. The editor acknowledged that the subject was indeed important but he could not comment on why the AP decided to spike the story. The self-effacing Bumrungrad version (multiple feeds from the AP) has since issued but Josh's story was never told.

I participated in a 20-minute interview segment on XM Satellite Radio that was broadcast internationally. Also, I was filmed for a segment on European Public Television, but nothing in the mainstream media in the United States.

Where the U.S. media appear to have an insatiable appetite for one side of the story, they have shown consistent disinterest in exposing the dark side, the underbelly where sad truths reside, hidden from public view.

Stepping Forward

I have been contacted by many patients and families injured at overseas hospitals, particularly Bumrungrad. These are the stories of real people that never surfaces in the media.

Though I posted many similar instances on our website, www.bumrungraddeath.com, media members visiting our site have apparently focused on one thing: finding a rationale in which Josh was not worthy of living—that he deserved to die.

Interestingly, few American patients or families have wanted to be identified. Foreigners have no problem is calling a spade a spade:

09 March 2007:

A comment from a former Bumrungrad patient from Germany:

A few years back my husband and I visited Bumrungrad. My husband suffered from joint pain in both thumbs while my problem was an excruciating hip problem. I could hardly lift my left leg more than 5 cms.

My husband was offered to have his thumb joints fused. The doctor was not able or not willing to discuss the limitation afterwards.

I was told only hip replacement would solve my problem, not even physiotherapy would give me relief.

We returned to Germany to get a 2nd opinion. A German hand surgeon was outraged at the idea to fuse the thumb joints. This operation is no longer done. Apparently, there had been gatherings of hand surgeons prior to our visit. At this gathering the latest surgery possibilities were discussed.

I had physiotherapy in Germany and still have my original hip. The problem wasn't the hip at the time but a lower back problem. Despite the fact that we worked in Cambodia at the time, we never ever returned to Bumrungrad. We did have the impression that doctors would sell you whatever you were prepared to accept whether it was appropriate or not.

Americans Remain Silent

One need only do some simple web searches to see how extensively Medical Tourism has been lauded by the American media. The Los Angeles Times, in its Sunday issue of July 30, 2006, reports about the wonderment of vast cost savings.

In this article, Daniel Yi reports the efforts of Arnold Milstein, a consulting ambassador-at-large selling and rationalizing foreign care for high-paying corporate clients. Arnold Milstein was even singing the praises of medical outsourcing to the Congress where he lobbied about the miraculous phenomenon of medical outsourcing.

The only opposing voice at the Congressional testimony in 2008 provided by the American Society of Plastic Surgeons, who were obviously unhappy about having their livelihood stolen by cheaper options overseas.

Once it becomes clear that international pricing may benchmark costs for care in the United States reimbursement levels for doctors and patients will plummet to new lows and will be on par with fees and costs charged in Cambodia, et al. More specifically, insurers are anticipated to say: "Well, if we can get it done in Thailand for X, then we will only pay X for the same thing in New York or Chicago or Peoria."

The Associated Press, in one article, briefly reports another side to the Medical Tourism discussion: "This is not the solution," said California Hospital Association spokeswoman Jan Emerson. "In fact, this could make problems worse."

"Hospitals must deal with rising costs just like other parts of the health care system", she said," and California hospitals lost $6.65 billion in 2008 caring for the uninsured. Exporting the best-paying patients, she said, "Will only add to the woes of the entire healthcare system."

Not to worry. Milstein, in this same report, says, "The perception will change gradually, as more patients go through the experience." He can wait. Milstein and Mercer are raking in big bucks while the pressure builds and the big boys get ready to play hardball—with your life.

Some admit that American health care is good but inaccessible. What they fail to say is that the access is controlled by the money men. The less access, the more money falls into the money men's eager hands.

Lulled Into Illusion

Examining the media as it relates to healthcare would take volumes. Canadian Marshall McLuhan, scholar and author, devoted his life to understanding the impact of the media on the social mind and the social "unconscious," as the great Carl Jung had envisioned.

McLuhan discussed the effect that the media have, regardless of content, on the sensorium, the array of ways information invades the essence of our being.

Like being carried away, psychologically and psycho-physically, the constant repetition of the media, playing the same theme time and again, will ultimately lull vast populations into believing and becoming comfortable with any idea, however Draconian or absurd.

George Orwell conjured up terrible pictures of a Big Brother, controlling everything. For me, in my youth, his book was terrifying. At that time, 1984 seemed a long way off. I comforted myself then that I would not have to worry about such things. Besides, the illusions of youth are sweet and the sting of the real world had not yet set in.

Now, 1984 seems like ancient history. George was actually off his game a bit. Things did not happen quite as he had envisioned. They have become manifest at even more stupefying and horrific levels than the pictures Orwell painted in his seminal work.

We are the living witnesses to this societal tragedy, a tragedy with its roots in the near complete subjugation of free speech and the destruction of the First Article of the Constitution of the United States: the right to speak one's mind openly and freely.

With the corporate mutiny carried out in nearly every nook and cranny of the United States, the exchange of free ideas is in great peril.

The shocking similarity of reportage on Medical Tourism (or Medical Outsourcing) has stunned me. But it has also awakened me to the reality that this subject, obviously of tremendous personal importance, is but one of thousands in which the *politico corporativos* have taken what they believe is their permanent place at the head of the societal table.

As McLuhan put it, advertorials wash through our brains, selling consistent messages that tell us all will be well if we just believe. What I have not been able to believe is that Josh's story appears to be the only one that has gained any traction or attention in the United States and elsewhere in the world.

Reporters seeking to legitimize Josh's story have asked me, "Where are the other people who have been damaged? We need more examples of who died! Who else was maimed? Show us these and then maybe our interest will be piqued again."

Ebola Zaire in New York?

One case of Ebola Zaire in New York City, just one case, would throw the entire world into a panic.

Since when does the number of fatalities become the gate to reporting on whether we are sitting on the brink of an enormous new social trend: offshore medical care as a mainstay of healthcare in the United States?

Smooth Operators

At the beginning of 2008, I received a series of telephone calls from a man in San Francisco, the scion of a wealthy family in the Bay Area.

His mother had been admitted to Bumrungrad for cosmetic surgery that included a tummy tuck, liposuction and breast enhancement. After day one of her marathon surgery, she was back in the OR the next morning for her face lift (despite having done poorly with the trauma of day one's procedures), the final scheduled procedure for her body makeover.

Shortly into the second day of operations, the woman from San Francisco suffered a stroke on the operating table and, as her frantic son explained, was in a coma in the intensive care unit at Bumrungrad. He said his father had accompanied his mother for the procedures—procedures that would have been forbidden in responsible facilities anywhere in the world, given her medical condition. Clearly, any surgery on day two was absolutely contra indicated.

Not for Bumrungrad, however. Not only did they take a sick woman who was at terrible risk of death from surgery of any kind, they scheduled her for back-to-back major surgeries.

As it happened, I was on my way to Bangkok and made myself available to meet with the father and to see what I could do to move his wife out of Bumrungrad, as was the son's wish.

He told me that he had read Josh's website, that he would do anything to help me and that, together, we would fix "these bastards" for their malicious practices. When I reached Bangkok, the scion's dad did not return my calls. He had sunk into a deep clinical depression, blaming himself for having allowed his wife to talk him into this completely irresponsible and inappropriate sojourn into hell.

I traded calls with the son in San Francisco. He told me that the entire family was pressuring him to back off, to keep this ongoing tragedy out of the press and the public eye. He told me that he was upset about the pressure placed on him—pressure to be silent.

Finally, the son and I had a conversation in which he told me not to make any further efforts to contact his dad or to help his mom in any way. His father was deeply depressed, his mother was in intensive care and the family did not want anyone to know.

I discovered, through my inside contacts at Bumrungrad, that his mother died the following morning. She never regained consciousness.

This was not the only such story I've heard from those who contacted me. I cite it, though, because it is sadly representative. For reasons that are, at least, difficult to explain, people experience great shame and blame themselves for being duped into things commonplace at a joint like Bumrungrad but unimaginable in the Western World of medicine.

The kind of silence and shelter from the light sought by this family is exactly what places like Bumrungrad count on. Few, if any, will step forward and become confrontational, even when they are people of huge means. As long as this kind of avoidance of confrontation continues, places like Bumrungrad will be veiled from the public light, the only light that can force them into some semblance of humanity.

When Joshua was killed, I had no hesitation in shining a bright light on everything I could find. This is what Josh would have wanted. When I first sensed what they had done and finally confirmed their evil, I was and remain fortified by a sense of justice. I am sounding an alarm so that others will not be suckered by the media and by the marketing machine, which does not care for any human life.

I subscribe to the theory that conspiracies can involve implicit, de facto participation in which like-minded forces align without deliberation to commit terrible crimes. I also believe that there are explicit conspiracies in which participants conjoin with knowledge and intent to do wrong. I would say that the implicit participation of the media has resulted in conspiracies to persuade an anxious public into believing something that is fundamentally wrong.

Whether implicit or explicit, the result is the same: manipulation of minds and distortion of facts for the benefit of "the masters" who have no regard for who lives or dies.

Medical Tourism is Here to Stay

I do not believe that Medical Tourism will disappear, even if millions read this book.

However, I believe that Medical Tourism should be strictly regulated by international agreements.

Without broad protections and regulations, people will be led unknowingly and without safeguards to death's door.

Without enforcing high professional standards and potent financial sanctions, the fifteen minutes of Medical Tourism fame might well turn into a full-length feature for generations. This portends disaster.

Fifteen ~ The Killing

On this Father's Day of 2009, I now write a gift for my son. He gave me so much in his short life. Josh's sense of humor was razor edge and, like his old man's, zany!

I often recount the jokes and stories we shared, the ones that he asked me to repeat, over and again, his favorites—just so he could guffaw until his sides split with laughter.

His desire to make others laugh was, I hope, a genetic predisposition I passed to his smiling soul.

His absence remains profound: the torrents of tears; the pain that remains terrible. It weakens me.

Knowing what I have discovered does not make his loss any easier.

Knowing who killed Josh, knowing the details of how his life was taken, has not protected me from pain.

None of this has been easy for me. Writing this chapter, in particular, has required me to muster courage and strength I did not know I possessed.

The Stars Align

The constellation of information concerning Josh's murder aligned to clearly show the brazen way Josh's life had been snatched.

After being buffeted by the Thai Police, glad-handed by the United States Government, lied to by Interpol, ignored by the Thai Military Commander and Chief, shuffled aside by the Thai Commandant of Police and treated gratuitously by numerous beat and duty officers, I was set to consider anything!

Feedback from www.bumrungraddeath.com started to flood in. After a year if days and nights considering fighting fire with fire, I decided to try the pen.

My son's killers are today walking free, along with their numerous accomplices who covered up the crime, obstructed justice and distorted the truth.

Approached by Assassins

Professional assassins, a fixture in Thai society, contacted me upon learning of Josh's murder; they said that they were "Josh's friends." They wanted justice done in his name. They wanted money. Murder Inc.

I was given the tempting opportunity to push dial M. After agonizing reflection, I decided that truth would serve up living punishment, which is worse than death.

I decided to stop Bumrungrad and their cohorts from carrying out their vicious mission. I would throw a wrench into the workings of corrupt big-business interests whose trade is to prey on the flesh of the unsuspecting.

As I have said before, the murder of Joshua was carried out by trigger men and women-the doctors and administrators at Bumrungrad International Hospital. They were hired, after a fashion, by a highly corrupted cadre of criminals who pose as health insurance providers, hospital owners and, indirectly, the United States Government.

Their un-indicted co-conspirators are the governments around the world who have neither the skill nor will to regulate medical care. Additionally, though fully aware of the vicious trade in human organs, the United Nations and the major governments around the world have, by their silence, condoned a practice which is rapidly growing out of control.

My tactic, up to the publication of this book, has been to carpet bomb the world with information: information I pray will open doors and save lives.

The perpetrators of the destruction of quality care and patient safety shamelessly are hiding—in Washington D.C.'s office buildings, in the HQs of the insurance cartel, in the executive offices of Bumrungrad, in the lawyers' lair, in clandestine operating rooms, among the turbid doctors and nurses who have sold their souls, in pharmaceutical companies or pathetic travel agencies. Like vultures, they circle until dinner is served!

Hence, I do not believe for a second that Josh's murder is an isolated event.   A careful reading of the world's press and academic journals makes this abundantly clear. Further, I have received hundreds of reports about deaths and injuries at Bumrungrad.

The Details

In reflection, this book is about two murders: Josh's murder and the murder of truth at its most basic, life-and-death level—your life, my life, and the lives of countless millions.

In trying to interweave the complex story of the assassination of my son, I have also endeavored to reveal facts that illuminate corruption and deception intended to trick and fool the world's public into believing that the Medical Tourism pill is really good medicine.

I feel the public needs to know what is possible. There is nothing romantic about being killed in a "luxury hospital" in exotic downtown Bangkok or Bangalore. Nothing.

Lumpini and The King of Siam

The police station opposite Lumpini Park in Bangkok is featureless and unexceptional. Unlike the grand palaces of Thailand's upper echelons of power, this is a workplace with diverse precincts that include embassies, hotels, luxury department stores, bars, whorehouses and corporate headquarters. I can never forget Lumpini.

I have spent days at Lumpini, meeting with police officials from beat cops to commanders, from detectives to spies sent to befriend me.

Despite eighteen governmental coups in seventy-five years, one thing can be counted on—Thailand has the best law enforcement money can buy.

If you happen to find yourself at Bumrungrad recuperating from surgery and you hear gunfire on the street below, don't worry, it'll pass.

With luck, the airport won't be blockaded as you attempt to flee to safety.

Bumrungrad might even send you to their center in Dubai for a little R&R.

Yes, Bumrungrad owns, operates who contracts with over 70 hospitals throughout the world. The United Arab Emirates is one of their favored spots.

Long Live The King

One thing is sacrosanct in Thailand's recent history: King Rama IX.

The King of Thailand: King Bhumibol Adulyadej (Rama IX), born in Cambridge, Massachusetts.

For the Thais, the King is God on Earth. Even joking about the monarchy with its extensive royal enclaves of descendants can land anyone in a rat-infested jail forever, perhaps even worse. No questions asked.

The King of Thailand, the oldest living monarch in the oldest monarchy in the world, is often depicted in full-dress military uniform. Born in Cambridge, Massachusetts and educated in Switzerland, the King has maintained undisputed power. Interestingly, Thailand—in Thai, 'Free Land'—is anything but free. Though advertised as a Buddhist nation, it is anything but.

Instead of compassion, as espoused by the historical Enlightened One, Buddha Shakyamuni (c. 563 BCE to 483 BCE), King Rama IX has stood well out of sight, while allowing nearly twenty governments to come and go under his reign and operate with impunity. They might think of this as royal privilege; I think of it as royal narcissism.

Military and police power is an inherent foundation of Thai life. So is the absolute rule of Thailand's powerful titans of industry. These titans of industry have come to exert a clenched-fist authority over Thailand. They are the same group of people I ultimately found to be at the end of the food chain—the controllers and corporate faces of Bumrungrad.

The King appears to adore and defer to them.

Press Release Details of Murder Charges

I issued two press releases after hours of testimony given at Lumpini police station. Lawyers and translators were there to field the continuous, often ridiculous, requirements of the police. These press releases are a continuing part of my campaign to keep the hundreds of thousands who have read about Josh informed. These releases can be viewed on www.bumrungraddeath.com. They are important documents and will help to dimensionalize the reader's understanding.

The first officer in charge of Josh's case was completely against having me file murder charges against Bumrungrad. He flatly refused to accept any documentation or testimony on the subject of murder. He was only interested in the doctors whom I alleged to have been involved, not the executives of Bumrungrad.

The "blame-it-on-the-doctors" game is played out in the United States daily. Doctors and nurses are expendable and the powers that be are happy to serve them up as a sacrifice.

Most doctors in the United States are covered by heavy malpractice insurance policies sold by the same insurance company's patient healthcare coverage. Executives, hospitals and insurance companies are almost never held liable, for anything. Even if they are, armies of retained lawyers are prepared to drive anyone into poverty if they dare engage in litigation. The willingness of the Thai establishment to sacrifice its own doctors was, therefore, interesting and significant to me.

Subsequent to my protests about being muzzled by the "cop du jour," he was transferred to the hinterlands. It was hard for me to understand why an ordinary cop would want to squelch my charges of wrongdoing. As my education increased, it is now completely understandable: he was bought, I was sold.

I include these press releases as part of my running narrative to help dimensionalize the important details of what was happening with my critical intersections with the Thai authorities.

The March 2007 press release follows:

Father of Joshua Files Murder Charges, 19.March.2007

Last June, 2006, the father of the deceased was stopped by the Thai police from issuing a full statement which excluded what James Goldberg, believes and is informed actually happened to his son Joshua.

On Feb 26th, Mr. Goldberg was allowed to present full evidence and to file a full complaint with the Thai Police in Bangkok of 1st, 2nd and 3rd degree murder charges against Bumrungrad Hospital and various individuals. Other aspects of the complaint include Thai versions of obstruction of justice, document falsification, evidence tampering, cover up etc.

Named for first degree murder by Mr. Goldberg who is informed and believes that Dr. Peter Morley, Chief of International Medicine at Bumrungrad and the attending physician at the time of Joshua's death, Dr. Sukkitti Panpunnung are guilty of the pre-meditated murder of Joshua Nathaniel Goldberg which is believed to have happened around 9.00 PM on the evening of 23 Feb 2006, Bangkok time.

Mr. Goldberg is working with the American Embassy, the Thai Police and other official agencies of the Thai government to see that those who murdered his son are brought to justice.

Obstruction of justice and other charges have been brought against Mr. Mack Banner and Mr. Curtis Schroeder who Mr. Goldberg is informed and believes were involved in evidence tampering and cover up.

Over one year has passed since the death of Joshua Goldberg at Bumrungrad Hospital. The police became involved when a whistle blower at the hospital called the police to urge their intervention in what the caller described as a strange and nasty situation. Since that time, the Thai police conducted their own autopsy and are continuing investigations.

It is essential for readers to understand that this involves allot more than malpractice . . . and it is also vital that readers understand that any attempt to collect information from Bumrungrad or the US based company, The Joint Commission, which Accredited Bumrungrad, have refused, as evidenced the correspondence including in this site to respond to questions put by the family in ANY way whatsoever.

Mr. Goldberg, said in New York, that he will not rest until his son's killers are brought to justice.

The stink I made about "cop du jour" number one who prevented me from submitting murder charges resulted in a change of the guard. Regardless of the change of the officer in charge, he was still very much on guard.

The proximate press release was issued subsequent to my naming the murderers, in charges filed at Lumpini police station over one year after Josh was killed.

To my knowledge, none of the doctors or nurses involved in Josh's treatment were interrogated. Their testimonies would have been invaluable, in that several of those present were listed on the hospital records as having been in attendance at Josh's Code 3, a procedure we now know never took place.

Despite my pleas to seize the EKG, purportedly used during the purported Code 3 procedure, the police never set foot in

Bumrungrad. That machine, said to have had Josh's last breaths recorded, contained a hard drive which, if examined, would have offered conclusive evidence that his death at 6:35 AM on the morning of February 24, 2009, Bangkok time, was a complete fiction.

Medical Tourism: All That Glitters is Not Gold

Another important press release follows. In this public release I confirm a reward of $2 million dollars for information leading to the arrest of the suspects I named to the Thai Police and the U.S. Government in my official report. Neither the Police nor the U.S. Government had been helpful or were seeking to prosecute. Consequently, I attempted to flush out people who would speak, motivated by compensation.

Father of 23 year old who died at Bumrungrad Hospital, Bangkok, Thailand, files murder charges against hospital administrators and doctors.

Roslyn Heights, NY -- (SBWIRE) -- 03/28/2007 -- Self proclaimed "leader" of the medical Tourism or outsourced healthcare industry, Bumrungrad Hospital of Bangkok, Thailand, has had murder and other charges filed against it by the father of Joshua Goldberg who died at the hospital on 23 Feb 2006 for what Mr. Goldberg's forensic experts and Mr. Goldberg is informed and believes to be pre-meditated murder. "The evidence is overwhelming as evidenced by the hospital records, the post mortem analysis and the deep investigations we have conducted". Mr. Goldberg has not yet publicly disclosed his views as to motive but intends to do so after the police investigation has been finalized.

The complaint of murder was added on 27 Feb 2007 at Lumpini Police Station in Bangkok by Mr. Goldberg, father of the deceased. Previously, Mr. Goldberg had made malpractice, document falsification charges relating to his son's death at Bumrungrad last June but was not permitted to complete the complaint by those then in control of the Police in Bangkok.

Mr. Goldberg, whose website, http://www.bumrungraddeath.com, provides an in-depth and transparent analysis of the causes of his son's death. This website was established in May of 2006 and has had well over 250,000 visits from the world over.

Previously Mr. Goldberg had offered a $2 million dollar reward for information leading to the death of his son.

Settlement talks with Bumrungrad have produced no result except complete silence from Bumrungrad, at one time, owned in large part by Tenet Hospital, a US corporation that is the second biggest hospital owner in the United States. Additionally, Mr. Goldberg sought help and explanation from the Joint Commission, which Accredited Bumrungrad, but was also met with complete silence.

"The press has largely had favorable comments to make about the growing phenomena of medical Tourism or outsourcing, but little opposing thought has worked its way into the press", said Mr. Goldberg, in New York on 27 March 2007.

"The fact is," explained Goldberg, "that the US healthcare system has been the victim of corporate greed and outright theft over a period of years since Medicare was enacted . . . according to World Health Organization's survey of 2002, the US ranked 39th in the world in healthcare quality but spent more than 3 times more, per capita, than any other country on earth!"

"Additionally, Accreditation, granted by the Joint Commission of Oakbrook, Illinois has issued over 40,000 Accreditations nationally and now has begun to do so internationally... without sanction by the US Government to do so... over all the Accreditations granted by the Joint Commission, only 1/10 of 1% have ever been revoked... thus making Accreditation something for sale ... and not, as Congress, intended, to be enforced."

Goldberg named Dr. Peter Morley, the Hospital's International Administrator and Dr. Sukkitti Panpannung for first degree murder charges and at least 11 other individuals, including Mack Banner and Curtis Schroeder, both senior executives of Bumrungrad, for cover up, evidence tampering, document falsification, obstruction of justice, etc. ....all are employees and executives at Bumrungrad International Hospital.

Upon reaching the milestone of finally leveling murder charges, I thought there might be a chance for justice. I was wrong.

After a three-day testimonial affair at Lumpini in which tens of thousands of dollars were spent on translations, legal fees, voluminous copies of legal records, color copies of post-mortem photographs, CD file record copies etc., my final signature was affixed to the last page of a 50-page statement to the police.

The supervising officer promised me that they would get on the case. They told me that if I returned in thirty days they would be ready to proceed with finalizing formal charges—thirty days, that is, if the Thai Medical Council, though not required by law to do so, would opine favorably on the merits of the case.

To this day, the Thai Medical Council has remained silent. Why should they speak? They are in the back pocket of Bumrungrad, Sophanpanich and the Bangkok special interests, interests especially concerned that Josh Goldberg and his annoying father disappear for good.

This is the hook. The police appear willing but erect a fictitious roadblock—the Thai Medical Counsel, a government agency supported primarily by "contributions" from places such as Bumrungrad.

The Thai Medical Council are said to never act. They are paid handsomely to do nothing.

Chulalanghorn Pathology

Subsequent to Dr. Vertkin's face-to-face meeting with Dr. Kornkiet, the Thai police pathologist who performed the post mortem on Joshua, the unconditional agreement that he had reached with my forensic specialist began to waver.

We suspect that Dr. Kornkiet was told to soften his conclusions, thus opening the door to contrary arguments that would shift culpability away from the hospital.

When I discovered this, Dr. Vertkin contacted Dr. Kornkiet by email and fax to re-establish and revisit the issues on which they had reached collegial agreement.

The report and correspondence between the Thai pathologist and my forensic expert has already been captured in previous chapters. It memorializes the stance which, in the face of hard evidence, could not be medically avoided, no matter how great the business and financial pressures on Kornkiet. The death of Joshua Nathaniel Goldberg did not happen as reported and the facts were deliberately distorted and covered up.

No one has disputed any of Dr. Vertkin's assertions. In the record, the transcript of the meeting was sent to Bangkok, Police Pathology, for comments and modifications by Dr. Kornkiet and his associates. There were no disagreements with the forensic findings of either Dr. Cohen or Dr. Vertkin.

Dr. Vertkin received a note from Dr. Kornkiet and the entire police pathology center, approximately ten days after the above report was forwarded to Thailand for comment, stating that he had nothing to add.

They were in complete agreement with her conclusions.

Bumrungrad refused to comment or share their supposed internal "audit" of my son's case. One can only speculate whether such an audit took place, or, if it did, how it could be objective since it was conducted by the very people involved in the crime.

The Thai Medical Council remained silent despite the medical affirmations shared by both their colleagues and our specialists.

Talk: I'll Give You Two Million Dollars!

I posted two rewards for information leading to the conviction of the accused. The first reward was for one million dollars, the second for two million dollars.

Though my website traffic dramatically increased with the publication of these releases, not one person stepped forward.

In Thailand, a million dollars for a nurse or a doctor is a fortune, enough to ensure that two or three generations would not have to worry about money.

This is not to suggest that one or two million in the U.S. would be insignificant. However, this is money that an average hardworking Thai would have to think long and hard about turning away. They all did.

The fear of retribution in Siam is so entrenched and profound that even the temptation of a treasure chest delivered to the front door could not remove the dread that if someone talked, he or she and their family would be hunted down like wild pigs and slaughtered for betraying the big boys in the big buildings.

Blowing the Whistle

Surely, since Josh's story was by then well known in Thailand and especially in Thai medical circles, it is easy to imagine that a nurse, an orderly or a doctor must have been tempted.

We do know from the police that a person at Bumrungrad who wished to remain anonymous called the police begging them to come immediately to Bumrungrad to intervene in the foul play that was afoot.

The police responded, but by the time they arrived, Josh had been transported, fully clothed and without any sign at all of resuscitation, to Bumrungrad's morgue.

Not only did Bumrungrad tamper with the crime scene by removing the victim prior to examination by police, they were careless enough to deliver a fully clothed victim to their mortuary, supposedly minutes after they claimed to have revived him!

A Tale Told by Fools: Or Ghouls

This is the essence of the argument propounded by Bumrungrad concerning the death of Joshua. Without shame, I have created a parody of the actual events that Bumrungrad has used. My sarcasm is contrived. My disgust is not.

> We discovered Josh unresponsive at 6:00 AM;
> He was barely breathing;
> We immediately called in a Code Blue (Code 3) Procedure;
> The crash cart was rolled in within minutes;
> Before we could electrically jump-start his heart, we performed manual cardiac resuscitation;
> We immediately cut off Josh's clothes, inserted an IV and entubated to administer oxygen;
> We tried, desperately, for 30 minutes, to revive him, but he was pronounced dead at 6:35 AM;
> We discovered that someone called the police and so, to prepare our guest for his trip to the police pathology lab, we fully dressed him in his street clothes;
> So as not to be accused of being untidy, we removed all traces of our attempts to revive him, taking out the IV lines, withdrawing the breathing tubes and cosmetically covering over the electric-shock skin burns attendant to our several attempts to revive him;
> We healed all his internal wounds such as cracked ribs and bleeding airways caused by our interventions;
> Just to be sure, we even purged his body of the 20 drugs we had given up to the time of his death, leaving just a few to show that we were doing something; As to the multiple drugs he was administered during the Code 3, we washed those out of his system as well;
> We rushed his limp body down to our morgue just in time to meet the policemen and their doctors who had arrived to transport our dearly departed patient to the police morgue for autopsy;
> To be sure all would go well and that our patient would not have to wait the typical three days it takes to get to have an autopsy performed, we accompanied Josh to the police hospital and encouraged the police pathologist to perform his post mortem examination immediately upon arrival at the City morgue;
> We then stayed involved, to assure that the results of the post-mortem examination would meet or exceed our expectations; we certainly would not want to disappoint the young man's family;

- ➤ Back at the hospital, our "team" convened a meeting to discuss the terrible tragedy of a young man who died at our hospital/hotel, a few hours before he was to be discharged;
- ➤ During our post-game analysis, we discussed what we could have done better; Dr. Morley, in charge of this case, said that next time we should have made sure that the victim's stomach had been pumped in case someone might discover that the time of his death was two hours after his last supper (or 12 hours earlier); Dr. Morley explained how people could get the wrong idea and that inquiring minds might discover that we had lied—about everything;
- ➤ After the meeting, our whole Code 3 team and all of Josh's doctors left the room, turned out the lights and went about their rounds, hoping against any odds that inquiring minds would never inquire.

They Were Wrong

My imagined account is only a diversion, to distract attention from what I know is a far more heinous reality: Joshua N. Goldberg was put to death by Dr. Peter Morley and Dr. Sukkitti Panpunnung. They suffocated their unconscious patient upon learning that their plan—to extract his organs—had been foiled.

Their attempts to distract from the truth were flawed by hubris, and ignorance:

- ➤ An internal autopsy had been ordered two days before Josh died;
- ➤ His Code 3 medications had been called into the pharmacy two days before the alleged Code 3;
- ➤ No Death Certificate or Cause of Death was ever entered into his hospital chart;
- ➤ No discharge or death summary was ever completed. This is standard procedure.

All these actions are standard procedure for any hospital, especially one supposedly staffed by Board Certified doctors and accredited by the Joint Commission.

Delusions of Psychotic Minds:
Arrogance or Unbridled Narcissism?

Whatever mindset explains the machinations of my son's killers; these are surely very sick and evil people.

In my considered opinion, the insanity of providing bogus EKG strips to give life to their Code 3 caper was an act of madness of which only a true psychopath would be capable.

Death Threats: I Must Have Done Something Right!

I have received numerous death threats and was told by the United States Embassy during my last visit to Thailand in Spring 2008 to leave the Capitol. They could not, and would not, be responsible for my safety.

Despite having asked for assistance from the United States Embassy on several occasions, to supply bodyguards, my government flatly refused. Despite death threats, the U.S. Embassy officials in Bangkok stated that it is not the responsibility of the United States of America to protect its citizens while abroad. As a consolation prize, they would gladly provide a list of local bodyguard agencies.

Shortly after European Public Television aired an interview with me filmed in Bangkok, I received several death threats and thinly-veiled offers of help from government officials and Thai journalists who offered me "safe passage" and "safe house" sanctuary until they could arrange to spirit me out of the country.

Does this sound like a thriller movie to you? It did to me as well, until a trusted confidant in Bangkok, an Aussie who had opened doors and befriended me despite risks to himself, told me that the word was out to shut my mouth. The Thai power brokers behind Bumrungrad wanted me silenced.

The threats still filter through. The police were totally disinterested. They told me that they had more important fish to fry. I'd like to know what kind of fish.

Gloating: The Police Take Fiendish Delight

I would be derelict in my reporting duties to skip over a jaw-dropping episode played out while I delivered my testimony at Lumpini.

After two days of recording my deposition, the subject of the fictive nature of Josh's Code 3 finally had reached the head of the inquisitional queue.

This awful subject is important since there is hard physical evidence that Bumrungrad lied, completely, about all the circumstances surrounding Josh's death, including their self-proclaimed valiant attempts to save his life.

As Dr. Anna Vertkin, the forensic specialist, discovered in her careful examination of the autopsy photographs, and after having flown to Bangkok to meet with Dr. Kornkiet, the pathologist who examined Josh's body, it was clear, and Kornkiet agreed, that there were no indications, whatsoever, of any resuscitation.

The macabre photographs taken by the Thai pathologist were indispensable to the record.

Copies of these ghastly photographs had been made and entered into evidence by me. As I slid the photos, one after the other, over the soiled Formica table in the Lumpini Police Station, the investigating officer, hunkered down behind his computer screen, held them up for his comrades to see. They snickered and commented jokingly in Thai.

When Dr. Vertkin and I arrived in Bangkok to meet with chief pathologist, Dr. Kornkiet of Chulalanghorn University, where police autopsies are performed, I was alerted to the alarming nature of the photographs taken during my son's post-mortem examination.

Dr. Vertkin urged me against reviewing the photographs. But I knew that as upsetting as this would be I had to know firsthand exactly what was being discussed.

The horrific reality, I reasoned, would help me to find the horrific truth. I was right. I was also wrong: The price I have paid in recurrent nightmares, burned into my unconscious, is beyond measure.

To make sure that Bumrungrad, the Joint Commission and all their other gang members could not dispute the palpable reality of this critical evidence, the photos are posted with a **WARNING** on my website, www.bumrungraddeath.com. It's not that I want you to see what they did to my boy. It's that I want you to see what they didn't do.

Appealing To a Higher Power

Ultimately frustrated by the Thai Police and abandoned by the United States Embassy (who, by their own reckoning, had had enough of Josh and me), I prevailed, in a last ditch effort, on the Embassy to carry a letter to the Commander of the Royal Thai Police.

Thailand has a population of sixty two million—ten million reside in Bangkok alone. Bangkok has one of the largest per-capita police force ratios in the world. I had prayed for some cooperation from "on high." My prayers were once again not answered.

The letter below did evoke a response from the Royal Thai Police. They brought in the Thai division of Interpol. I was temporarily gleeful.

But the young Interpol detective, despite initial gusto and promises that an indictment would be handed down at the beginning of 2008, quickly backed down and was removed from the case.

He had received instructions from other, unknown powers to back off. Obviously, higher powers had received orders from even higher powers to forget it.

I secretly recorded the interview with Interpol and captured the bluster of the young Interpol Officer and his colleagues. A digital recorder, hung around my neck and secreted under my shirt, recorded it all.

The next day I would face again the excruciating 24-hour flight back to the United States. A swim in a beautiful garden pool at the Nai Lert Park Hotel seemed appropriate.

I entertained hopeful thoughts while floating effortlessly in the hotel's gorgeous pool. When I returned to my room to shower, the digital recorder that had captured the precious promises by Interpol was gone.

I had been warned that this hotel was used for clandestine meetings and was also an ideal location for all manner of operatives to spy on people. I didn't think, until then, that I had entered the ranks of persons worthy enough to be spied upon. It seems as if I had touched on stuff too hot to handle. The Embassy told me to get out of Dodge: I did.

Luckily, I dumped the digital voice files to my computer immediately upon returning from the Interpol interview. My laptop was locked in the hotel safe. I still have the Interpol interview on record.

The following letter to the Commander of the Royal Thai police is inserted below. Like most all communications to anyone involved in the crime or the investigation, no response was received. This correspondence is included in my narrative since it captures a comprehensive summary of the events up to July 2007 and makes an official request of the highest Thai authority to become involved in adjudicating my son's murder.

To: The Commander and Secretary General
of The Royal Thai Police
From: James Goldberg 2 July 2007
Special Investigation into the Death of Joshua N. Goldberg
at Bumrungrad Hospital, 23 Feb 2006

Dear General and Commander,

My son, Joshua N. Goldberg, died at Bumrungrad Hospital on 23 Feb 2006.

I filed a complaint in June 2006 with the Lumpini Police accusing approximately 10 individuals of various forms of criminal wrong doing leading to the death of my son. The investigating officer, at that time, refused to allow me to complete my complaint, which at that time, was to accuse at least 2 more individuals of pre-meditated murder in the first degree. These individuals are Dr. Peter K. Morley and Dr. Sukitti both of whom are on the staff of Bumrungrad Hospital.

The officer in charge also refused to allow me to make charges for obstruction of justice, evidence falsification and tampering and accessory to various forms of manslaughter and murder in the first degree, as it is so called in the United States.

In March 2007, I returned to Lumpini to complete my complaint against Dr. Morley and Dr. Sukitti and to add additional charges for cover up, falsification of documents, obstruction of justice against Mr. Mack Banner and Mr. Curtis Schroeder, both American citizens. The investigating officer was newly assigned as the former officer had been transferred to another facility. I believe his name is Lt. Col. Sumart.

I have additionally instructed my lawyers who are empowered to act for me, the firm of Herbert Smith, to also name this week the Board of Directors of Bumrungrad Hospital whose Chairman is Khun Chai Sophonpanich for their role in covering up the circumstances of my son's death. I have communicated directly with Mr. Sophonpanich in his capacity as Chairman of

Bumrungrad's Board and as a majority stock holder in Bumrungrad.

Additionally, an American organization which accredits hospitals, called the Joint Commission, is, I believe, in possession of critical information which they have failed to release to me. The Police should issue a warrant for this information.

One of the alleged assailants, Dr. Peter K. Morley, head of Bumrungrad's International medical business, was, I am informed, convicted in Thailand about 7 years ago for practicing medicine without a license and sentenced with a fine and suspended sentence.

I have presented a wealth of evidence in addition to the medical opinions of two world famous forensic doctors, both from America, who I retained to engage in a detailed analysis of exactly what happened to my son. These documents are on file, translated into Thai, with Lumpini.

Two of the world's leading forensic specialists were retained by me to perform a detailed analysis of the case and have come to a common conclusion that my son's death was at least the result of gross negligence, dereliction of duty and deliberate infliction of actions which contributed to my son's death.

Dr. Morley, I believe, has a criminal record, in Australia, but the Australian Federal Police will not release this information to me but will to Lumpini who has failed, despite my insistence, to request it.

In March 2007, I specifically told the investigating officer that more than ONE year had passed since my son's murder and that virtually nothing had been done. He promised me, at that time, that the investigation would be given high priority and that when I returned to Bangkok, from the US, in approximately 1 month, that further interrogations and collection of evidence would be accomplished.

The Vice Counsel of the US Embassy, Mr. Ted Coley, had arranged for me to meet with the Lumpini police on the afternoon of 8 May 2007. I waited for approximately 2 hours and was eventually told that the officer would not be available to meet me. No apologies or explanations were given: this is after one year of attempts to bring justice to for my son.

Following this, I re-contacted the US Embassy and asked for their help in rescheduling the meeting. This was set for Thursday, 11 May 2007. This time, the investigating officer did see me and my attorney from the law firm of HerbertSmith Ltd which has world wide offices including here in Bangkok.

During that interview with the investigating officer, I was told the following:

1. Pending a report from the Thai Medical Counsel, Lumpini would not proceed with its investigation. This report was requested in writing from the Medical Counsel by Lumpini 3 times in writing and numerous times by telephone. The original request was made nearly 10 MONTHS earlier.

2. Despite having given very specific evidence to Lumpini they have failed to seek warrants, interrogate suspects, seize computer records, conduct any on site visits at Bumrungrad nor have they taken any action whatsoever.

3. Records requested from Bumrungrad pursuant to the investigation were produced and are virtually insignificant and many, based on my first examination of them, are falsified.

4. I produced well over 150 pages of information plus forensic reports, yet Bumrungrad produced less than 20 pages of information. It is my understanding that Bumrungrad took months to produce even these scant few documents.

5. Apparently, Lumpini has given my evidence to the Thai Medical Counsel, who, as I understand, has rarely if ever contradicted or taken action against any doctor.

6. Lumpini claims that they will not investigate my son's murder further until the Medical Counsel renders their opinion, based on evidence which I have presented and WITHOUT the benefit of any serious investigation on the part of Lumpini.

7. I believe, this is an unacceptable and improper procedure for ANY police force to not take a case where solid and professionally evaluated evidence has been presented which demonstrates probable cause.

As the aggrieved father of my only son, I cannot and will not allow this to continue.

The excuse that nothing could be pursued in terms of further police investigation without the "opinion" of the Medical Counsel is absurd as there are many other charges which I have made that have nothing to do with the practice of medicine and are, therefore, not appropriate for the Medical Counsel's advice.

Despite having police forensic specialists to interpret the medical aspects of my son's murder required Lumpini has failed to take advantage of any other resources in the Thai government to get the bottom of this case.

This is a truly serious situation. I have withheld further action pending a true police investigation; but this has not *happened.*

The consequences of pressing criminal charges in the US and other places where Bumrungrad does business will bring shame on Bumrungrad, and, unfortunately, on the whole of Thailand.

The economic and social consequences which Thailand will suffer as a result of what surfaces from the investigation of Bumrungrad will wash over onto all of Thailand and its attempt to become a major and serious force in the world of medical outsourcing and medical Tourism.

I have tried to avoid such a confrontation and exposure of Bumrungrad's egregious practices in the interest of maintaining good relations between our two countries. The exposure of Bumrungrad's misdeeds (which are NOT limited to my son's case) will have a negative effect over ALL of Thailand's medical Tourism/medical outsourcing business as well impact airlines, hotels, restaurants and tourist dollars in general. My son is buried in Thailand, as a Monk, and I must return there for the rest of my life to visit his shrine.

I ask that there be direct intervention and supervision of this investigation by your office or your delegated representatives. I ask that you consider this case as symbolic of whether the rule of law can be depended upon by the increasing number of people who are seeking or who are sent to Thailand for medical treatment. I ask that warrants be issued to seize the computers of Bumrungrad Hospital and the medical equipment alleged to have been used in what I strongly believe is a falsified scam deliberately staged by Bumrungrad to disguise the true cause of my son's death.

I ask that Dr. Peter K. Morley be interrogated and that I have the opportunity to be present for this questioning. I ask that the Thai police request that the Australian Embassy revoke the passport of Dr. Peter K. Morley as I consider him to be flight risk. I recommend that Dr. Morley be held without bail until his role in this murder is thoroughly clarified. I have also asked that numerous other individuals be interrogated; their stories will simply NOT match-I am absolutely convinced.

I believe that the second person most importantly involved in this crime(s), Dr. Sukkitti of Bumrungrad Hospital be thoroughly interrogated and detained until his role can be thoroughly clarified. I believe Dr. Sukkitti will, for fear of his life, tell the entire story and reveal what all of the forensic evidence collected in this case clearly suggests terrible wrongdoing leading to the death of my only son who had gone to Thailand to be ordained as a Buddhist Monk.

Bumrungrad's CEO, Mr. Mack Banner, informed me during a surprise visit I made to the hospital last Friday, that Bumrungrad had conducted its own internal and confidential investigation, yet when I was asked to see the results, Mr. Banner refused.

Additionally, when I went to talk to Dr. Sukkitti, Dr. Morley appeared within 5 minutes with guards who restrained and physically beat me while Dr. Morley ran away & down the hallway to avoid having to answer any questions which I posed to him.

For this disgusting display of brutality, I ask that Dr. Morley be further charged for ordering the physical abuse of an American citizen and that he be held liable for battery and assault. I reported this incident to the American Embassy and quickly departed Bangkok for fear of my life.

I have returned to the United States for a brief period of time to attend to some important business, but am prepared to return to Thailand on short notice to participate in what I hope will be a true investigation by the police.

I believe that this case is far above the ability of Lumpini to handle and that an alternate authority be sought, perhaps by transferring the case to the DSI, who I believe, based on my limited knowledge of your laws, is best suited to handle a case which is complex and which does have the financial and moral fate of Thailand at stake. Therefore, this case is appropriate for the DSI, however, if you have other suggestions, I would welcome them.

I have been in close contact with the US Senate and Congress about this case and I have met with and have the blessings of the US Ambassador to Thailand, Mr. Ralph Boyce. Mr. Bartlett, the Consul General of the US Embassy has been informed of this matter and has been gracious in jumping over standard protocol to place this communication directly in your hands.

I stand ready to inform any and all individuals regarding the details of the case. I have already had my forensic medical specialist meet with Dr. Kornkiet, of the Police Hospital, to make certain that both physicians were in complete agreement about the state of my son's body when as yet unnamed informant called the police to alert them that something was very wrong. Absent of that, the record shows, Bumrungrad, against the law, was intending to autopsy my son, undoubtedly with a self effacing result and to finish burying the reasons behind the death of my son.

I have been told that you are a man of ethics and honor. I respectfully place myself in your hands and ask that you communicate your intentions in this matter directly to me through Mr. William M. Bartlett, Consul General for the US Embassy in Bangkok.

Respectfully and with Sincere Pleas for Your Assistance,

James Goldberg

The significance of having been continually repulsed by the police cannot be underestimated.

The Thai police are the handmaidens of the power elite.

The fact that cop after cop, Commander after Commander and General after General did everything in their power to make me go away is significant. I'm just a piss ant father who would not stand to have their "Boys from Brazil" strangle the life out of his son. Obviously they read the tea leaves and saw that big time trouble was brewing.

Crying the Blues?

Things are not broken for the American Medical Money Machine. Business has never been better.

What they have done and are doing, helped by the kinds of ex-Arthur Andersen accountants (several now running the operations of UnitedHealthcare AKA AARP) who brought you ENRON and the contrived California Energy Crisis, imperiling millions of people, is to hedge their bets and forage into new opportunities for grand larceny. The architects of United Healthcare in recent years are Andersen alumni.

The creators of Medical Tourism are now positioned to continue unabated, anywhere in this wide world. They have been working on this expansion for years.

Recall that Tenet invested in Bumrungrad in the early nineties. Other companies have also been laying the groundwork for at least the past two decades.

The American Medical Money Machine is not alone in their pursuit to dominate medical care internationally. British BUPA, a poor cousin of United, is working hand in glove with United to extend their network of care globally. The main difference is that BUPA, the British private health insurer, grosses about $10 billion in annual revenues versus the nearly $80 billion reported by United.

No other country comes close to The American Medical Money Machine in their offensive push to exert lock-tight control over the world's medical markets.

In my opinion, the American insurance cartel makes the Mafia, at its height, look like kindergarteners napping on mats. They are the modern mob, but this time they have gone well beyond having a plant or two in government: a judge here, a cop there, a DA anywhere, a handy politician everywhere.

This time, they own the U.S. government.

Recent articles about the ownership of Senators and Congressmen in the healthcare industry reach an astounded public daily (2009). These same people who are elected to regulate and set policy are setting policies for their own gain.

The Circle is Unbroken

The management and Board of Directors of Bumrungrad did what any upstanding and responsible management in a questionably ethical corporation would do: they covered their tracks and denied everything.

But what of those people who accredited the Bumrungrad operation, the Joint Commission back in Oak Brook, Illinois?

Maureen Potter, ousted Director of the Joint Commission International, accidentally reported to me many other complaints and Sentinel events at Bumrungrad. She told me that six people died for unexplained reasons at Bumrungrad the year prior to Josh's murder.

During one of my visits to Bangkok, a gentlemen from the Midwest who had traveled to Bumrungrad for a hip replacement, was found dead on the roof of Bumrungrad! This incident was not reported in any newspaper or television station in Thailand-English or Thai.

Maureen was subsequently thrown out of her position. She had apparently let too much slip.

Harold Bressler, the Joint Commission Corporate Counsel was officially instructed to stonewall me. In short, everyone at the Joint Commission was told to batten down the hatches and shut their Midwestern traps or they, too, would meet the fate of ousted Nurse Potter.

My two telephone conversations with Bressler were more like monologues: I did the talking and he answered with balderdash or silence.

The immensity of the malfeasance surrounding Josh's death was now in sharp relief and granular in detail.

I remained confounded by the question: Why would the Joint Commission risk it all to aide Bumrungrad in covering up killing Josh?

His was but one case; but this one case had gotten out of control and had surfaced to worldwide visibility. This was not good for the fundamental agenda of the Joint Commission, abroad and at home.

I had entered into the fray thinking that the Joint Commission carried with it enormous power: the power of the purse. Without the flow of money enabled by their accreditation, Bumrungrad would be on its ass.

The American Medical Money Machine Equation:
$=Accreditation

I approached the Joint Commission thinking that I would have a muscular ally. Instead of exerting their fiduciary powers in the interests of justice and fairness, they viciously turned on me to defend and cover for their accredited pals half-a-world away. It is astounding that they mobilized their awesome powers to shut down one person.

I realized what they knew all along—the little known, secretive and covert Joint Commission, was an indispensable constant to The American Medical Money Machine equation: $=accreditation.

In other words, the Joint Commission adds the illusion of legitimacy to a foul business. The government has given the Joint Commission control over the stop cock.

They can turn it on or off at will.

From 1965, when they were first empowered by Congress, the JC they have let the money hose flow unfettered in the U.S.

They are now casting the aura of legitimacy over places like Bumrungrad with only one aim in mind: keep the liquid gold flowing without interruption, in Chicago or Jakarta, Boston or Brazil.

Their hidden agenda and mission is to protect and shelter the astronomical financial interests of the members of their tribe.

They have done so in the U.S. since Medicare was enacted in 1965; they are now fully entrenched in providing the same cover for U.S.-dominated healthcare interests globally.

They are good friends to have.

All of the members in their club know about—and gladly pay for—what is most certainly the most sophisticated protection racket of all time.

The discovery of the sacred and pivotal role filled by the Joint Commission is the terrible point where the whole tragedy of Josh's murder came full circle.

The Joint Commission, to be sure, obstructed justice, covered up crucial evidence and became a party to a terrible crime. I discovered that this is their business.

This is what they are paid to do by the American Medical Money Machine, the very people who represent the tyranny to which a whole country has fallen victim. This little known organization wields nuclear power.

When this blatantly hit me, it was as if someone had planted a pitchfork in my skull. I walked around for days in a daze. No thoughtful person, however insensitive, can avoid the becoming nauseated by learning of this terrible and hidden power.

I Can't Believe This!

I set out to see if anyone else had connected the appalling dots, chards of information, I had unearthed. What I found were scattered pieces, suggestions and theories.

What I did not find was the story I tell here: that things haven't been so bad at home for the bad boys that they've never made more money and stand to gain dramatically more while an entire society cowers in the corner wondering what the politico corporativos are going to do to them next.

As of 1 October 2009, the Congress of the United States appears poised to go along with the program of big business. By denying the creation of a government administered healthcare program, they are effectively giving the criminal insurance cartel trillions more to steal. Not one word about oversight has been in any of the Congressional debates.

Carry Me in On My Shield

I hasten to point out that the consequence of this vast financial chicanery is not abstract in any way. It means the loss of life. It means the mistreatment of illnesses, the avoidance of responsibility for quality care and patient safety. These may appear to be financial crimes on the surface, but they go far beyond financial rip off and fraud. The actions of the insurance cartel, the hospital owners, the HMO's often result in death and suffering. Connect the dots!

If this happened to me, what will happen to you?

In my opinion and based on copious research my son was killed with premeditation by people who dress like bankers.

I have spent untold energy in bringing my son's killers to justice. I trust that this exposé or personal memoir on which I have labored for over three years will be an essential change agent in holding the healthcare industry cult of demons accountable for snuffing my son's precious life.

I foresee and aspire that this work will help to cast new light on the insidious plot to kill my son and with even greater importance, to explain how the killers in the club are actually murdering the interests of the public, making fodder out of healthcare and a joke out of safety.

My academic and professional training in philosophy, technology and business have provided me with appropriate tools to engage in pitched battle with the forces I am examining.

I have spent much of my career advising enormous corporations on technical and business strategies to achieve dominance in their chosen fields.

Much of my work, ironically, has been in healthcare technology. I am no stranger to the halls of multibillion-dollar medical device and pharmaceutical companies who strive to achieve dominance in their respective markets.

I had not, however, engaged in working with insurance interests or hospital corporations. My work focused on the technical side of innovation.

I have put my son, his life and his death in a spotlight for the entire world to see. I've exposed his memory to those who have maligned him and attacked me.

Placing him on worldwide display is not an easy thing to reconcile; I still struggle with having done so.

One of the overriding reasons I have exposed both my son and myself to the slings and arrows of this outrageous fortune is so that those of you contemplating stepping into this mess will think long and hard about following through. I do so to fore warn those who are foolish enough to treat in the world of medical outsourcing.

For those committed to overseas procedures, in treatment or in transit, it is not too late to free yourself.

In the back section of this work I have provided some important guidelines which will protect you.

It is vital to see past the Pepsodent smiles to the snarls and sneers behind them.

Getting the Point

The micro examinations into Josh's death, I pray, will enlighten and increase understanding of what happened to Josh and may well happen to you.

Before stepping back to examine the macro picture of Murder Inc., I want you to know a bit more about the human life that was snuffed at Bumrungrad and covered up by countless layers of authorities, agencies and companies.

Sixteen ~ World Access: Medical Assistance

Joshua had a health insurance policy with Blue Cross of California. Blue Cross, as with most other with most other U.S. health insurance providers, contracts with World Access to administer benefits on its behalf for its policyholders who receive medical care abroad. They are called third-party administrators. In the world of insurance, they are often called "specialty insurance providers."

Here is how World Access describes the Medical Assistance aspect of its business in the "About Us" section on their website (www.mondialusa.com):

Medical Assistance

Mondial Assistance Group's Medical Assistance network is by far the largest of its kind in the world. International and local network teams share responsibility for controlling the quality of the services provided. They apply strict selection and performance criteria in evaluating service provider support. The Medical Network is capable of handling any type of medical situation from the most simple to the most complex.

Thailand is among the world's most popular tourist destinations. If you have customers traveling to Thailand or a neighboring country, then there will be times when illness or accidents necessitate Medical Assistance. Mondial Assistance Thailand can quickly mobilize Medical teams when the need arises. We can arrange Medical escorts on scheduled flights, or deploy private aircraft in more serious cases. Once hospitalized, we provide Medical Supervision to liaise with the treating Doctor in order to keep you and the patient's family and friends well-informed.

Mondial Assistance Group's Medical Assistance network is by far the largest of its kind in the world. International and local network teams share responsibility for controlling the quality of the services provided. They apply strict selection and performance criteria in evaluating service provider support. The Medical Network is capable of handling any type of medical situation from the most simple to the most complex.

Thailand is among the world's most popular tourist destinations. If you have customers traveling to Thailand or a neighboring country, then there will be times when illness or accidents necessitate Medical Assistance. Mondial Assistance Thailand can quickly mobilize Medical teams when the need arises. We can arrange Medical escorts on scheduled flights, or deploy private aircraft in more serious cases. Once hospitalized, we provide Medical Supervision to liaise with the treating Doctor in order to keep you and the patient's family and friends well-informed.

Created in 2000, Mondial Assistance Group is the result of the successful integration of Swiss-based Elvira Travel Insurance and France's SACNAS-Mondial Assistance, two companies with 75 years of cumulative expertise in travel insurance and service solutions. In 2000 and 2001, the Mondial Assistance Group acquired World Access (USA), World care (Australia) and AutoAssist (Thailand). Mondial Assistance became the Group's Global Brand in 2006, paralleling the worldwide launch of a new logo, representative of its people-focused business and new common values. Today the Group's global corporate brand is supported by a portfolio of specialty product brands. The Group is equally owned by AGF and RAS, both members of the ALLIANZ group.

Major Milestones

Note that World Access (now Mondial) is a wholly-owned

subsidiary of the world's largest insurance company, Allianz. Other businesses of Mondial include Travel Insurance, Ticket Insurance, Medical Insurance for Travelers, specialized Concierge services, and so on.

Josh's primary provider, Blue Cross, transferred its responsibilities for patient management to what was, in 2006, World Access. Note the promise made on the World Access website on coordination and information exchange with a patient's family and physician attendant to foreign medical care and hospitalization:

"Once hospitalized, we provide Medical Supervision to liaise with the treating Doctor in order to keep you and the patient's family and friends well-informed."

Though Josh's hospital chart contained my contact information and that of his doctor in the United States, no communication was received from World Access. Considering the contents of the transcript below, the communication should have been abundant.

Only when I demanded the hospital administration records that I assumed were kept by Blue Cross did I learn that World Access was in fact the responsible party.

The administrator's role is, or should be, to represent the interests of the insurance company—Blue Cross in this instance—and the patient's. World Access admits the importance of family involvement and the necessity for coordination with a given patient's regular physician. Had that been done, had World Access or Blue Cross contacted Josh's doctor or me, he would most likely still be alive! Judging from both the World Access and my numerous telephone conversations with Josh, the administrator never contacted him either.

The issue of Bumrungrad's culpability in this is clear: the very JCI standards with which they are bound to comply—as a function of their accreditation—were entirely disregarded. The only communication I received from Bumrungrad during the entire episode was to announce my son's death. Yet the Joint Commission International standards spell out clearly that hospitals are obliged to openly and honestly communicate with family members; that family and the patient's regular physician are key elements in successfully treating a patient abroad. Not surprisingly, from what I have recounted in this book, Bumrungrad did not comply.

When I confronted the Joint Commission about Bumrungrad's flagrant failure to comply with the Commissions "standards," they pointed out the fundamental fraud in the whole accreditation process: compliance with their standards was voluntary. The Commission accrediting institutions abroad does so without any intention of enforcing their set standards. Further, the Commission seems to be unconcerned that their standards are not followed.

The first thing that all the foreign hospitals accredited by the Joint Commission say about themselves is: WE ARE ACCREDITED BY THE STANDARD BEARER OF THE UNITED STATES FOR ACCREDITATION OF HEALTHCARE FACILITIES.

This is a fraud, plain and simple, foisted on the public. This leads one to believe that accreditation has meaning and substance when it is only PR and Marketing hype.

This manipulation of truth has spawned a profitable business for the Joint Commission and Bumrungrad. This brazen, unfettered and callous deception makes a mockery of all individuals considering care abroad.

This applies to Bumrungrad. It also applies to over two hundred hospitals in other countries to whom the Joint Commission sold their Gold Seal.

Joint Commission International (JCI) Accreditation.

Organization Accredited by
Joint Commission International

If a hospital is serious about quality and safety, it seeks independent confirmation.

First Asian hospital to get international Accreditation:

Bumrungrad was the first Asian hospital Accredited by the Joint Commission International (JCI), the international arm of the organization that reviews and accredits American hospitals.

Their checklist includes over 350 standards, for everything from surgical hygiene and anesthesia procedures to the systems in place to credential medical staff and nurses. JCI sends a team to re-review hospitals at 3-year intervals. Bumrungrad was first accredited in 2002, re-Accredited in 2005 and 2008.

I fault the United States Department of Health and Human Services for not bringing sanctions against this organization when matters like this deception are brought to their attention. They are required to do so by law but have consistently ignored their fiduciary duty and public trust by not policing the Joint Commission. This is an outrage.

I am particularly sensitive to this kind of fraud. Without knowing what the Joint Commission seal of approval meant, I assumed that Bumrungrad was a good place, the kind of place to which I could entrust the care of my son.

I sent Joshua to Bumrungrad because I fell into their trap. I was frantic to get him treated when he first complained of his sore ankle. I bought the PR, the Gold Seal. It was the biggest mistake of my life. I hope it will not be yours.

An administrator's responsibility should be a kind of in loco parentis. But examining the transcript of the entire administration of my son's care at Bumrungrad is shocking:

- ➤ The number of disconnections and dropped calls;
- ➤ The unavailability of doctors or officials at Bumrungrad;
- ➤ The broken promises to call back;
- ➤ The language problems;
- ➤ The delay and outright refusal to supply records
- ➤ The lack of a definitive diagnosis after ten days of hospital care;
- ➤ The promise to send reports post mortem-reports that were never received;
- ➤ The lack of action by World Access and Blue Cross to inform Josh's doctor and family;
- ➤ The complete lack of alarm, response or action to the news given to World Access, in item 37, that the "above named passed away."

Contrary to their website gloss, the pictures of the Bumrungrad "medical hotel," I have described what goes on behind their closed doors.

A transcript of text between World Access and Bumrungrad reveals what you may expect. Examine this document carefully. It speaks volumes.

Particular attention is called to item #37.

Pertinent Notes from Issue 346127 Joshua Goldberg

Note #	Summary	Detail	Date Time Added
1	EMAILED INTAKE FROM HOSP	Requesting GCL--no medical info, no DOB. Only Dx and tmo name	02/13/2006 12:36PM
2	REQUESTED BENEFITS VIA EMAIL	Hardeep and Doug	02/13/2006 12:36PM
3	MEDICAL REPORT RECEIVED	faxed to RN for review	02/13/2006 4:27PM
4	BENEFITS OBTAINED	relayed by Hardeep Chase Precert is not required	02/13/2006 4:27PM
5	GC NOTE	RN RECOMMENDS GC FOR INPT HOSP ON FEB 12,2006-PENDING VC/TC SCRN	02/13/2006 11:22PM
6	*****GCL FAXED TO HOSP**** 1 DAY 2/12/2006--2/13/2006	/	02/14/2006 1:20PM
7	ADDL MEDICAL INFO RECEIVED--	faxed to RN for review	02/14/2006 6:50PM
8	med report reviwed	mri results from 2/13-spine-mild narrowing of 14-5 w/ disc bulging causing lt lat resess and mild l5 transveres root abutting no indication on report what tx plan is-need more information	02/15/2006 12:28AM
9	WAC--Hosp	Transferred multiple times...spoke to Dr. Sira's office but no one is too certain of when he can be reached. Advised will c/b later	02/15/2006 10:42PM
10	AC------->Hosp	Interpreter # 4417 (Sam / Thai) assisted TMO office ph# in Interested Parties actually goes to hosp switchboard Attempted to transf to RN station for TMO Line died---recording that call cannot be completed ~~~~~~~~ Attempted again a bit later, This time no Thai interpreter available Staff answering did not speak English	02/16/2006 1:11AM
12	AC----->Billing	Trying Ms KITIYAWADEE for assistance (She¿s off today) Reach colleague Mr Pondej instead Advs¿d we need treatment plan	02/16/2006 1:26AM

		We have not recived the additional notes that it says were sent to us- could someone please look into this-the only med reports we have received have dx and mri result and labs-and is from 2/13-we need tx plan-if you have this additional med info pleas fax if not let us know and we will contact hosp thankyou	
		Susan Combe RN/Case Manager World Access Medical Department Phone: Tollfree: 1-800-720-8909 　　　　　Collect: (519) 742-1902 Fax.　　(519) 742-2256 Email: WAMD@worldaccess.com (Legal Disclosure)	
14	EMAILED HOSP TO REQUEST	an update--asked for most recent medical report so that extention can be sent	02/17/2006 2:17PM
15	MEDICAL REPORT RECEIVED	appears to be a little written info and more lab values -faxed to RN for review	02/17/2006 3:49PM
16	GC NOTE	RN RECOMMENDS GC FOR INPT HOSP FROM 2/12-2/13-PENDING VC/TC SCRN	02/18/2006 12:53PM
20	WAMD to TMO office	0200 called to office, doctor not there , transfered 3 times, eventually transferred to the nursing station where pt is . Advised that pt is still admitted, doctor is busy with pt , they advised us to call back later. Thanked . Michelle RN	02/20/2006 2:14AM
21	MEDICAL REPORT RECEIVED	dated 2/16/2006--faxed to RN	02/20/2006 12:16PM
22	1345 Received faxed medical report	pt admitted for sever back pain and many episodes of weakness and numbness to the lt foot EMG- lt paroximal sciatic neuropathy MRI of Lumbar spine- unremarkable Currently client has severe pain requiring analgesia Dexamethasone 4 mg iv given client to be hospitalized another 7 days Fax dated 2/16	02/20/2006 1:50PM

23	...need to determine what to client is receiving	Kate 10 days is an extended period of time for medical information received	02/20/2006 1:54PM
26	WAC--Dr. Sita	Kate pt has been transferred to the care of Dr. Sikitti Called office and able to speak to him Pt remains admitted for pain control—he requires morphine q4h to control pain, not responding well to treatment EMG, EEG, MRI all negative--difficult to account for level of pain he has CPK rising to over 3000 at present will try to have him d/c in the next few days	02/21/2006 2:51AM
27	GC note	DK to go 2/13-2/24 pending vol5c	02/21/2006 2:51AM
28	New TMO	Dr. Sikitti Panpunnung	02/21/2006 2:52AM
29	Med Director Dr Peter Morley---->WASC	Req GCL ext---wants to know progress AC reviewed issue Advs's some delay as RN hed to reach TMO, TMO changed etc He confirmed current TMO Dr Sita as listed in Note below Advs'd we will attempt to fax GCL ext this shift or next If AC unable to do on Overnight will email Day Assistance Colleague Jason transf to AC	02/21/2006 3:23AM
30	Ms Kidcawadee----->WASC	She is also req GCL ext Advs'd hed just spoken with Dr Peter Morley Advs'd Overnight or Day shift could now fax as RN had ok'd Thanked	02/21/2006 3:29AM
31	***GCL FAXED***Feb 12 - Feb 24 / 2006	12 Days Fax Successful Hard copy to Scanning for Imaging Copy saved to H Drive : Shared Folder as well	02/21/2006 4:09AM
32	Ms Kidawaddee ->WASC	Wants to know when faxed GCL will arrive Advs'd just sent successfully 5 minutes ago	02/21/2006 4:12AM

	AC held while Ms Kiddy checked fax machine	
	She confirms GCL arrived – all pages	
	AC Advs'd if pt stays past Feb 24 RN will MC again	
	Advs'd GCL ext can be sent again after RN GC's	
	She understood	
	She can fax RN or email	
	Assistance updated med reports as well	
	Thanked	
	Original Message-----	
	From: Catherine Ibarra	
	Sent: Tuesday, February 21, 2006 4:21 AM	
	To: Assistance Group; Overnight Assistance; Kim Boynton; Marla Moreira	
	Cc: Assistance Overnight Group; John Tabb, Steven Armstrong	
	Subject: 345127/ J Goldberg / THAILAND / GCL EXT FAXED	
	Good Day to all,	
Emailed Assistance	The Hospital Director Dr. Peter Morley and Ms. Kiddawadee have phoned several times tonight. Since our good RN¿s have now GC¿d –the GCL ext has been faxed (successfully) per their request	02/21/2006 4:18AM
	Hard copy has been sent to Scanning for Imaging.	
	A copy has been saved to H Drive / Shared Folder as well.	
	The Hospital has confirmed receipt of the GCL to Feb 24.	
	Please see Notes 29 ¿ 32 for details.	
	Thank you,	
	Catherine Ibarra	
	Assistance Overnight	

33

#			
36	1525 WASC AC->WAU. asked about HNPP-is this diagnosis or treatment Adv'd this	is a disorder Copied and pasted info from Internet. Need to know what treatment pt needs. AC will follow-up	02/23/2006 4:28PM
		Original Message----	
		From: TPPS [mailto:lppa@bumrungrad.com]	
		Sent: Thursday, February 23, 2006 10:53 PM	
		To: Kim Boynton	
		Subject: RE: 346127 Goldberg,Joshua HN 101319727	
		Importance: High	
		Hi Kim	
37	EMAIL FROM HOSP-PATIENT DIED ON 2/24	Greeting from Bangkok. HNPP is a special laboratory test for level of palsy, we would be informed that the above name was passed away this morning (Feb 24, 2006). Thank you very much for your always kind assistance. As for last medical report we will send to you via fax. Have a nice day. Kind regards, Kitty	02/24/2006 5:53PM
38	GC NOTE	RN recommends coverage patient's hospitalization up until pt expired on 2/24 subject to VC and TC of policy. RB RN	02/24/2006 7:30PM
40	Mr. James Goldberg ----> WASC	Patient's father called to request copies of medrex and case notes, as he is investigating son's death at hospital. AC relayed that she will need to get permission for this. Mr relayed cell #516-319-1767 and home address for sending copies: 118 Village Road, Roslyn Heights, NY 11577 Both thanked	07/21/2006 1:10AM

AC asked if permissable to send case notes, etc. to Mr. Goldberg. Susan Yates responded that she would like to speak with him to clarify reasons why. AC sent email with cell phone number and brief explanation of earlier phone conversation.

Hello Susan,

AC spoke with Susan Yates

This is the case we briefly discussed last night. This young man had a previous drug problem and went to Bumrungrad Hospital for an illness / though the diagnosis is not really clear. In short, he died at the hospital 2 weeks later, and his father has examined medical and autopsy reports with experts who say he had various contraindicated medications in his system when he died. His father, Mr. Jim Goldberg, feels the hospital has not been forthcoming with him, and the FBI, US Embassy and Thai police are currently investigating the situation.

07/21/2006
1:14AM

Mr. Goldberg would appreciate copies of the Case Notes and any medical reports received by WASC. He asked me to relay to you that he will happily sign a release of liability for World Access, and that he is very grateful for the management of the case performed by WASC.

He stated that he is available at any time to take your call, but would prefer a call before 11am or so. (He is located in New York.) His cell phone number is 1-516-319-17■.

41

Stakeholders

Many stakeholders live on the continuum of medical Tourism/ outsourcing. The role of the third-party administrator, like World Access, is not common knowledge. Yet the vital role it plays on the ground, supposedly to protect your life or that of your loved one, is undeniable.

Big money is changing hands here. World Access, AKA Mondial, should earn their keep or reap what they sew.

Would you call this negligence? I do.

Seventeen ~ Organ Trafficking

If not all this were enough, a new thread was woven into our terrible tapestry and must necessarily be described.

Sometime in late 2006, I received an anonymous email. The writer suggested that if we were looking for a motive for murder, we would do well to investigate whether Josh had been "sacrificed" for his organs.

I had been struggling with motive. Aside from a purely psychotic or vengeful act, I could not understand the motivation behind this suspected crime. Why would Bumrungrad go to such extremes in fabricating hospital charts, arranging for a Code 3 resuscitation two days before Josh actually died and arranging for an autopsy well before my son's actual death? What would justify the extent to which they went?

Why was my son dead?

Had Josh seen something in the hospital that Bumrungrad would do "anything" to conceal?

I may never know. Josh's room had three beds. The patient in the next bed had complained that Josh was snoring on the night of his death. We tried to contact this patient but his name was expunged from the record and Bumrungrad refused to give access to him. A private investigator I hired located the patient's home, but the young man had been recently murdered and no suspects had been identified. Coincidence?

Was Josh killed because of his last name, an act of anti-Semitism? Bumrungrad's operations are intimately bound with the U.A.E., Dubai, Qatar and other Middle Eastern and Southeast Asian countries, some of which are known to be anti-Semitic.

Had he, of his own free will, found a drug and ingested it?

From the beginning, Morley suggested that Josh had obtained "lollypops" or Thai 'street speed' and that this drug had caused his death.

No such drug or any of its chemical derivatives were found in post- mortem examination. Additionally, Josh was said to be so highly medicated with opiates given by the hospital that an amphetamine would have served to revive and not kill him. Finally, Josh detested any medications that stimulated the body and mind. He would have never ingested anything of the kind.

Had the pharmacy made a terrible mistake by mixing known contra-indicated medications? Why were there no doctor "overrides" when the Bumrungrad electronic pharmacy system was supposed to have published them? (Standard procedure)

Certainly. I learned that there were no doctor override orders in his hospital chart. I also learned, from an employee of Bumrungrad's software subsidiary that the pharmacy system was not even operating at the time of Josh's death. Bumrungrad represented that it was operative. The pharmacy department disclaims any knowledge of mixing contra-indicated medications.

Why was an order for an autopsy found in the hospital records that were dated two days before he died?

I believe because Josh's death/killing was pre-meditated. The degree to which Josh's hospital records had been falsified or forged make it abundantly clear that Josh's death was not a matter of malpractice or medical mistake.

Why had Code 3 medications been ordered two days before Josh allegedly died?

Why had the hospital asked the insurance coordinator, World Access, to extend his stay for another ten days on the night before his demise?

Bumrungrad provided no viable reasons. To the contrary, they have ardently resisted ANY attempt to unearth the facts.

Why were the nurses' rounds for 10:00 PM and 12:00 AM not recorded in his hospital chart?

Josh was already dead by the 10:00 PM rounds. This was the first and only time in his 11-day stay at Bumrungrad where the 10:00 PM and 12:00 AM were skipped.

Why did the hospital records reveal a consultation with the hospital pathologist (the doctor who performs autopsies) two days before Josh died?

Arrogance, and a belief that no one would read them as carefully as our forensics people, lay at the root of the hospital's criminal negligence. They didn't know with whom they were dealing. The medical investigation completed by Dr. Vertkin more than confirms this.

Those reportedly present during the Code 3 at 6:00 AM simply did not add up.

The autopsy evidence clearly reveals that Code 3 never took place. The records had been entirely fabricated and names of attendees were inserted by Dr. Morley, I presume, of people loyal to him or whom he could trust. I contend that none of the people listed were even in the hospital at the time of Josh's demise.

There were far too many inconsistencies and contradictions in Bumrungrad's records. One by one, I went through all the possibilities and scientifically eliminated all the probable causes under consideration. All the questions I had were put under a high-powered microscope were rationalized and/or answered.

When the completely unexpected suggestion came to look into Organ Trafficking as a motive, I was dumbfounded. The theory brought together and explained a number of discordant facts, yet there was no way that we could access carefully hidden inside information.

Beaten by Bumrungrad Thugs

During my last visit to Bangkok in mid-2008, when I entered the hospital to get answers from Morley and Sukkitti, the two I felt were directly responsible for Josh's death; I was physically beaten and removed from the property.

I did not hit back. They bruised my ribs, gave me a black eye and smashed my camera. They threw me into the street in the midst of heavy traffic and speeding cars.

Since organ trafficking was introduced as a possible motive for murdering Josh, I began an extensive search for academic or other studies that detailed organ trafficking. This effort resulted in unexpected fruit: organ trafficking is big business and is very much alive and well in South East Asia.

This update was posted on www.bumrungraddeath.com:

Thai Doctors Kill Patients & Harvest Organs, 12.July.2007

I am informed and believed that Bumrungrad is involved in these kinds of activities. I provided Mr. Mack Banner, the VP of Operations for Bumrungrad to confirm or deny that Bumrungrad was involved in these kinds of activities. As with all other matters, Bumrungrad feels, I believe, that they are simply ABOVE the law . . . and remained silent.

It may well be that Bumrungrad is ABOVE the law . . . since, in Thailand, the law is largely for sale to the highest bidder . . . .and big money does buy big silence. No wonder that the new Prime Minister has called for massive police reform. Some recent articles are provided in the News and Update section which illustrate the recent police reformation.

Upon close examination of all the forensic evidence concerning the death of my son, I now feel that I have identified the most likely motive . . . that Josh was killed to harvest his organs. Were it not for a whistle blower at Bumrungrad who called the police, I believe this would have happened.

The Joint Commission, in May of 2006 informed me, by accident, that at least 6 other Sentinel incidents were reported by Bumrungrad in the year immediately before Josh's death. A Sentinel incident is an unexplained death.

When pressed, both Bumrungrad and the Joint Commission

*would not reveal ANY information about these 6 other deaths . . .
.probably Americans.*

*In addition, while my Forensic specialist and I were in Bangkok to
meet with the police coroner, an American was found dead on the
roof of the hospital. He had gone to Thailand; we told by the US
Embassy and died on the roof. The hospital is reported to have
said that the many lost his mind . . . . more likely he was heavily
drugged . . . .and wanted out. But Bumrungrad does not let go of
the possibility of making money that easily.*

*By every hospital standard known, roofs of hospitals are always
locked . . . .since, desperate patients would seek an end to their
suffering if given the opportunity. Yet, on one amazingly hot
Bangkok afternoon, this man found his way onto the roof . . . .and
was found dead. What did he see? Why was he there? He had
come for a hip replacement . . . but instead, was found dead on the
roof of a 15 story building in blazing heat. Why? No answers to
these questions were forthcoming from Bumrungrad and from the
Joint Commission . . . .and the police investigation . . . as far as I
am aware, has gone no where? Why?*

Medical Tourism . . . My Foot!

Should anyone doubt that the speculation concerning organ
trafficking is a figment of the author's imagination, this article in
the Thai Press reveals that where there is smoke there is fire.
This article was published in the Bangkok Post in late 2007.

*Thai doctors charged with deliberately declaring brain death to
get organs.*

*Three doctors and an administrator from a Thailand hospital
have been charged with conspiracy to commit murder following
accusations that they deliberately declared 2 patients brain-dead
and falsified documents of other patients to make it easier to use
their organs for transplantation.*

*The charges, which carry the death penalty, resulted from a police
inquiry showing that the team had not followed correct
procedures when declaring organ donors brain-dead. The
investigation found that from 1996 to 1997, about 100 illegal
kidney and liver transplants were performed at the*

Vachiraprakarn Hospital in Samut Prakan. Donor's relatives allegedly received $525-2625 per organ in kickbacks from the hospital.
The inquiry was launched in February after Thailand's Medical Council accused the hospital of illegally trading in human organs.

The Council found 9 cases where people who were not relatives of the organ donors had allegedly signed transplant consent forms.

In 29 other cases, the Council learned that organs were allegedly removed by doctors without the consent of the donors' relatives. The Council revoked the license of one surgeon and suspended the licenses of another surgeon and a neurologist.

The case has highlighted the fact that Thailand has no effective laws controlling the trade in human organs.

A key element in discerning the truth is to put as much light as possible on the people who have been involved. If they open up, great. If they do not, we can take comfort in knowing that they obviously have something to hide.

This is the text of a press release I released from New York in June 2007:

Motive for Murder: Harvesting of Human Organs

New York, New York, 25 June 2007

"After extensive research and continued silence by Bumrungrad Hospital, Goldberg is informed and believes that Bumrungrad Hospital should be investigated for engaging in harvesting organs for transplant from victims who are plunged into chemical comas."

These additional charges were filed with the Bangkok Police under the same case # as previously filed: (Criminal Complaint number is 1484/2549).

"Though given the opportunity to respond, Mr. Mack Banner, CEO of Bumrungrad, has refused to respond to the following email letter from Mr. Goldberg: This was sent on 22 June 2007", stated Mr. Goldberg.

I have informed the International Police as well as the Thai police and the American Embassy that you conducted, as you indicated, an independent investigation of my son's death. I know that this report was never turned over to the police nor was the entire hospital chart ever produced.

Of course, I have full possession of the entire chart . . . .which seems to have disappeared from your computer system; lest I am sure you would have produced it for the police instead of the insipid 10 or 12 pages; many falsified. The actual chart is over 200 pages!

Are you now willing to admit that your hospital engaged in the business of harvesting of human organs for profit?"

Yours Truly,
James Goldberg

The Pent-Up Need for Replacement Parts

In the United States alone approximately 60,000 patients are on the waiting list to receive a donor heart each year. Only 2,000 heart transplants are conducted in the United States yearly since the donors are scarce and the organ must be transplanted within four hours of harvesting.

After four hours, as anyone knows who has studied this subject extensively, the chances for survival go way down. Longer time periods for transplantation apply to kidneys and livers but speed of transplantation from harvest to transplant is critical to survival rates.

A similar number of patients are on the "waiting list" in the EU as the scarcity of organs there is also substantial.

Hence, 58,000 people with end-stage heart disease in the U.S. and a similar number in the EU will die each year for want of an appropriate or available organ.

In the demand for human organs, properly matching donor and recipient are critical components of the equation. The current marketplace does not support the market need against the available supply. Enter organ brokers, the latest movement in organized crime.

This is big business, and where a need exists someone will figure out how to fill it.

A brief examination of discussion groups, blogs and the like, reveals a wealth of public information about the horrendous and bloody crimes are happening in South East Asia: fodder for organ brokers. This is taken from the recent United Nations proceedings near Washington, D.C.:

2009 Johns Hopkins Model United Nations
At Conference XII

March 5-8, 2009 ● *Baltimore, Maryland.*

Another sticky issue is the non-consensual aspect of organ trading. With-out question, there is money to be found in organ trading, and money often causes people to act unethically. Because those involved in the trade (like the donors) desperately in need of money; many will stop at nothing to receive organs for trade. In numerous countries, including Thailand and India, murders and subsequent organ harvesting have made the news lately, making the existence of these illegal markets, which are subject to no regulation, downright dangerous to the public.

They are mainly sold to Thailand . . . . (The Epoch Times, March 17, 2006)

This is Astounding!

STATEMENT OF HARRY WU-A Famed Chinese Dissident and Journalist (Excerpts)
Re: Sujiatun Issue
Harry Wu
JUNE 8, 2006

In March 2006, the members of Falun Gong planned an investigation of the "death camp" at Sujiatun in northeast China, where they claimed the Chinese government was secretly imprisoning Falun Gong practitioners and harvesting their organs while still alive for profit. However, this "Sujiatun Auschwitz" allegation was based on nothing more than the testimony of three "witnesses".

Three-quarters of the 6,000 arrested Falun Gong practitioners have died, having their hearts, kidneys, retinas, and skins harvested and their bodies disposed of . . . Since 2001, the concentration camp has secretly detained thousands of Falun Gong practitioners. The hospital removed their kidneys, livers, and corneas.

After the organ removal, the emptied corpses were sold as models to the "Biological Plastic and Chemistry Factories" that sprung like mushrooms because of the sufficient supply of dead bodies and others were disposed of right on the spots. Investigations show that the organs were taking from the arrested Falun Gong practitioners alive.

Due to the exceptional brutality, many participating medical staffs suffered from serious psychological problems and there have been reports that some medical workers committed suicide because of the mental pressure . . .

The organs from the Falun Gong practitioners have become the main supply of China's underground organ trade. (The Epoch Times, March 17, 2006).

Question: Where are these organs usually sold? Do the higher authorities in the government know about this?

Answer: They are mainly sold to Thailand, but I believe they are also sold to other regions of the world. (The Epoch Times, March 17, 2006)

I have worked as journalist in China for some time now, and have been exposing the situation of Falun Gong. Most of the people know that there is a Masanjia Labor Camp in Shenyang City, Liaoning Province, that there is a Dabei Second Prison near the Masanjia Labor Camp, and that there is a brainwashing center located in the Huanggu District Police Department. You may not know that there is another facility especially used to torture Falun Dafa practitioners in the Sujiatun District. Up until now, nobody has dared to do an interview to report this place.

Most prisons and labor camps have detainees going in and out, and eventually information will be brought out. But this Sujiatun Concentration Camp has not had anyone come out yet; therefore, the people outside find it very difficult to know what is happening inside.

During my other interviews in Shenyang, I learned that there are very few Falun Dafa practitioners still detained in the Masanjia Labor Camp or in Dabei Prison, because they have been sent to this concentration camp in Sujiatun. (The Epoch Talk about mind blowing and uninformed, Forbes, one of the Forbes Richest Americans, pines for a new day when the dream of capitalism can fulfill all needs—on the open market. Times, March 9, 2006)

Back at the Ranch: The Big Sell

Media mogul Steve Forbes reveals his views and attitude towards transplants abroad.

In his August 13, 2007 article, **Open-Heart Surgery—90% Off,** Steve Forbes writes:

About 7,000 Americans die each year because they are unable to get lifesaving organ transplants, primarily kidneys. (Author's Note: it's more like 100,000.)

Back in 1984 Congress passed the National Organ Transplant Act. It outlawed the commercial trade of organs and set up the monopolistic United Network for Organ Transplantation.

A patient who can find a willing—and fit—donor among family or friends can get a transplant immediately. Those who cannot are left to fend for themselves. The hunt for foreign organs is now big business in the U.S.

Not surprisingly a growing number of sick Americans are

desperately trying to make their own arrangements for organ transplants overseas, particularly in China, Pakistan, India and the Philippines (Author's note: Let's not forget Thailand)

FORBES and other publications have written stories about the often murky world of brokers who arrange surgeries in foreign hospitals, which is very different from those involved in medical Tourism.

The academic literature is replete with references to organ trafficking in South East Asia and other parts of the world. The literature on this subject is extensive. Therefore, I have extracted certain relevant slices to illustrate that human organs are big business.

Though I have no direct, verifiable information that Bumrungrad is involved in such activities, I thought our readers might be interested in what is going on behind the scenes in the countries where Medical Tourism is flourishing.

These anecdotes represent the kinds of revelations uncovered in the academic journals. I do not intend, here, to be encyclopedic in this examination of organ trafficking. That would take volumes.

What's important here is the trend towards selling human organs whatever their source. People who believe they are going to get an organ that will provide them new life should consider:

- The high infection rate in foreign surgeries;
- The medical health of the "donated" organ;
- The skill and experience of the surgeon;
- The likelihood that the surgeon is a financial partner in the process of acquiring the organ;

Rejection or other post-operative problems might occur after the recipient has returned home that other surgeons and doctors will, for reasons of liability, refuse to treat.

My research revealed that India continues to be a primary site for a lively domestic and international trade in kidneys purchased from living donors.

In South Africa, the radical reorganization of public medicine under the new democracy and the channeling of state funds toward primary care have shifted dialysis and transplant surgery into the private sector, with predictable negative consequences in terms of social equity.

Meanwhile, allegations of gross medical abuses, especially the illegal harvesting of organs at police morgues during and following the apartheid years, have come to the attention of South Africa's official Truth and Reconciliation Commission.

Residents of the Gulf States travel to India and Eastern Europe to obtain kidneys made scarce locally by fundamentalist Islamic teachings that will in some areas allow organ transplantation (to save a life) but draw the line at organ donation.

Japanese patients travel to North America for transplant surgery with organs retrieved from brain-dead donors, a definition of death only recently and very reluctantly accepted in Japan.

To this day, heart transplantation is rarely performed in Japan and most kidney transplants rely on living, related donors (see Lock 1996, 1997, n.d.; Ohnuki-Tierney 1994).

For many years, Japanese nationals have resorted to various intermediaries, sometimes with criminal connections, to locate donor hearts in other countries, including China (Tsuyoshi Awaya, testimony before the International Relations Committee, U.S. House of Representatives, June 4, 1998) and the United States.

Until the practice was condemned by the World Medical Association in 1994, patients from several Asian countries traveled to Taiwan to purchase organs harvested from executed prisoners.

The ban on using organs from executed prisoners in capitalist Taiwan merely opened up a similar practice in socialist China. The demand of governments for hard currency has no fixed ideological or political boundaries.

Patients from Israel, which has its own well-developed but underused transplantation centers (see Fishman 1998, Kalifon 1995), travel elsewhere to Eastern Europe, where living kidney donors can be found, and to South Africa, where the amenities in private transplantation clinics can resemble those of four-star hotels.

Turkey is emerging as a new and active site of illegal traffic in transplant organs, with both living donors and recipients arriving from other countries for operations. In all these transactions, organs brokers are the essential actors.

Because of these unsavory events, the sociologist-ethnographers Renée Fox and Judith Swazey (1992) have abandoned the field of organ transplantation after roughly forty years, expressing their dismay at the "profanation" of organ transplantation over the past decade and pointing to the "excessive ardor" to prolong life indefinitely and the move toward financial incentives and purchased organs.

A decade ago, when townspeople first heard through newspaper reports of kidney sales occurring in the cities of Bombay and Madras, they responded with understandable alarm. The same people now speak matter-of-factly about when it might be necessary to sell a "spare" organ.

In India, wealthy people have shown willingness to travel great distances to secure transplants through legal or illegal channels, though survival rates are low.

Between 1983 and 1988, 131 patients from three renal units in the United Arab Emirates and Oman traveled to India to purchase, through local brokers, kidneys from living donors despite reports of poor medical outcomes with kidneys purchased from individuals infected with hepatitis and HIV.

(See Saalahudeen et al. 1990). (Most Arabs now travel to Thailand for Medical "Tourism.")

Laws in India prohibiting organ traffic have produced an even larger domestic black market in kidneys, controlled by organized crime expanding from the heroin trade (in some cases with the backing of local political leaders).

In India, the kidney business is controlled by the owners of for-profit hospitals. They cater to foreign and domestic patients who can pay to occupy luxuriously equipped medical suites while awaiting the appearance of a living donor.

I believe this is part of Bumrungrad's modus operendi.

Using organs from executed prisoners is fairly widespread in Asia.

Awaya (1994) goes even farther, referring to transplant surgery as a form of "neo-cannibalism." "We are now eyeing each other's bodies greedily," he says, "as a source of detachable spare parts with which to extend our lives."

Brokers in Southern California promise clients delivery of "fresh organs" anywhere in the world within 30 days of placing an electronic mail order.

The headline message from all of this is: despite assurances by the likes of super capitalist Steve Forbes that one should take comfort in knowing:

> ➢ that foreign Medical Tourism meccas are accredited;
> ➢ have Board Certified doctors;
> ➢ are willing to deliver great medicine in style;
> ➢ are filling the needs of an important market.

Well, Steve Forbes, remember: fools rush in where wise men fear to tread! These accolades are deceptive and misleading.

Accreditation means nothing, even if by a U.S. based company. Hospitals and doctors lie about their U.S. or European Certifications.

The come-on of luxury accommodations is absurd. Most

genuine doctors are wary of glitz. They want money focused on the delivery of great medicine, not great hotel accommodations. As to filling a market need, Medical Tourism/ transplantation fills a need, but how well and at what cost?

Testing, Testing: For What?

Bumrungrad performed numerous tests on Josh during his eleven days at Bumrungrad. Forensic analysis of the kinds of tests that were performed is highly instructive.

The following tests were unnecessary, given my son's symptoms. These tests were primarily focused on infections and organ functions.

According to my forensic expert, Dr. Anna Vertkin, M.D., these tests appear to be aimed at qualifying Josh's organs for transplant and not related to any symptoms Josh presented:

➤ Lumbar puncture—there were no CNS symptoms and a CT Scan with unremarkable results; since Josh had no fever, no elevated white count, no confusion, no headache, etc, this dangerous and painful test was only done to determine if there is an occult infection transmittable to others. (i.e. organ integrity).

- ➤ Rickettsia and Tick Typhus—no symptoms presented justified these tests, concern of transmittable diseases;
- ➤ Hepatitis B and C—nothing to justify these tests except searching for transmittable diseases;
- ➤ Various blood cultures—nothing present suggested an infection—this would only be interesting vs. transplant integrity;
- ➤ Lyme Disease antibodies—again nothing presented by Josh justified these tests; they were searching for transmittable disease;
- ➤ Urine for protein electrophoresis—nothing presented suggested this, a test to determine kidney function and integrity;
- ➤ Requests for gnathostomiasis antibodies—searching for transmittable disease by organs, not relating to his illness.

In addition, Josh was scheduled to have been discharged on February 23 or 24, 2006 but was not, for reasons never explained.

It should be said that after ten days in the hospital, Bumrungrad had not diagnosed what was wrong with Joshua. We only discovered, post mortem, that there were two bite/fang-like marks on his left ankle. We believe that Josh had been bitten by a snake, a krait, a viper local to Chang Mai, or a cobra. All these deliver a neurotoxin and a hemotoxin—which explains the symptoms my son presented.

Because the toxins quickly disappear one cannot test accurately for them but must diagnose on the resulting symptoms—loss of feeling and paralysis in the left leg. Bumrungrad says that it has experience with tropical medicine and with snakebites yet they never once mention this as a possibility.

From the hospital records and the discussion the doctors and accountants at Bumrungrad had with the third-party administrator, World Access, the hospital had apparently begged World Access for more time to treat Josh and had asked for Josh's hospital stay to be extended.

The morning after having made this request, Bumrungrad emailed back saying, "We would be informed that the above name was passed away this morning, 24 Feb 2006. Thank you very much for your always kind assistance. As for the last medical report we will send to you via fax."

It is important to note that World Access, under contract with Josh's insurance company, Blue Cross of California, failed to inquire into the reasons and causes of the death. Also, Bumrungrad never provided the last medical report as promised; World Access never demanded that this be provided.
This mutual cooperation between the administrator of benefits for Josh, World Access and Bumrungrad, is very troubling. Instead of being attentive and applying their supposedly superior knowledge, the insurance companies appear pre-disposed to simply look the other way.

Hospitals Are a Great Place to Qualify Donors!

Hospitals are a terrific place for secret organ harvest. Why: Bumrungrad delayed the release of my son once, on 20 Feb 2006, for unknown reasons. He was again scheduled for discharge on February 24 but was said to have died that morning.

> The patient is totally under control;
> Patient tissue type and organ integrity can be determined;
> Very little time lapse from harvest to transplant: a key to successful organ transplanting;
> Recipient match to donor easy to determine;
> Recipient ready while donor is harvested;
> Outside services are not required;
> Both donor and recipient are charged—no middle man;
> Cooperation of all staff within the confines of the hospital can be bought;
> Harvest to order: the hospital has a handle on its most suitable inventory and can match waiting recipients with donors.

I had encouraged the police to search admission and procedure schedules for transplants since I feel strongly that they had scheduled to harvest Josh—probably multiple organs—and transplant to matched recipients.

A day before he died, his care was transferred from his attending doctor to Dr. Peter Morley, Chief Administrator of the hospital, a cardiologist and Nephrologist (heart and kidney specialist). Josh was an ideal candidate for harvest: great health, alive, no relatives or friends in attendance.

We do know that on the night/morning of 23/24 Feb 2006, a whistle- blower called the police to intervene over something mysterious going on at Bumrungrad. His body appears to have been rushed to the Bumrungrad morgue, fully dressed and without any signs of resuscitation when the police pathologist arrived.

Photographs in evidence attest to this but the police were unwilling to do anything.

I have given Bumrungrad ample time to respond to these charges. They have not. I have informed the Joint Commission of this and they too responded with . . . nothing. The police did not intervene to question the people most likely involved and the Thai Medical Council did nothing whatsoever. Their endorsement of probable cause is mandatory for the police to take action and file formal State charges.

Blocked, Blocked, Blocked. It happened to me; it will happen to you.

The United States of America: Human Rights?

I have attempted to illustrate what is afoot in China, Thailand and throughout South East Asia with regard to organ trafficking. In favor of concentrating on economic issues, the United States appears to have taken its focus off human rights issues. Organ-trafficking crimes are and may continue to be overlooked.

Consequently, the medical tourist is and will continue to be a stranger in a strange land, without portfolio and alone. Don't expect any help from home.

Effectively, this is equivalent to the FDA stopping inspections of food suppliers. Left to their own devices, history tells us, the industry will self-police with disastrous consequences. Temptation for short cuts is too compelling to ignore; the bottom line will rule. This is the world the U.S. and other leading Western powers have chosen to ignore.

We believe that the same model of logic can be applied to the organ-trafficking trade. Without regulation, the players will do as they wish.

The media are more than willing to fill up airtime with accolades about places like Bumrungrad. The literal explosion of information and media attention around the subject has been without precedent. People like good news, an answer to what ails.

In their rush to sell you the Brooklyn Bridge, these "talking heads" do real damage to the public. They are irresponsible for not looking deeply into the dark side of what's truly happening in the world of Medical Tourism.

This is a murky, onerous and difficult subject about which it is difficult to get hard data. However, comparing multiple points of information, one may see that serious crimes are being committed.

I may never be able to prove that my son was killed for his organs, though all the signs point to it. Whether Josh was murdered with this intention in mind is, in a real way, not the point. The point is that a reasonable and informed person should consider that Medical Tourism is like an un-licensed rogue? elephant: unfettered, rampaging uncontrolled.

No matter what the appearance of propriety may be, the reality is that places like Bumrungrad can do anything as long as it makes money.

The subject of organ transplantation and the black market is only one issue in the overall context of Medical Tourism. But because of its heinous nature and dark doings, it is an important bellwether to examine. If the "industry" with self-proclaimed leaders like Thailand's Bumrungrad operate in what must be construed as highly suspicious ways, what does this say about their integrity in all the other areas in which they are involved?

The stink, in my view, permeates everything they touch. Bumrungrad and all the other Medical Tourism destinations that do business in unregulated, uncontrolled countries without policing are free to take the path of least resistance, and they do.

Germany, France, Switzerland, The U.K., Australia, Canada etc. are countries, like the U.S., where there is at least a semblance of oversight. In the shady world of foreign medicine, the government is strictly hands off, especially when the leaders of the government and private powerful interests are one and the same.

Organizations like Bumrungrad thrive on being beyond the reach of control. They can live and thrive because of it. No matter how good the deal, one should never lose sight of their defining reality.

I admit that the information presented here, as it relates to Josh's death, is circumstantial. What is not circumstantial, however, is a discussion I had with a person who Dr. Peter Morley knew back in Australia. It seems as if Morley, Dr. Morley, had a long-standing interest and fascination with organ trafficking as a means to a large end.

Removing the Stone of Folly by Hieronymus Bosch.

Eighteen ~ Medical Tourism, Your 15 Minutes of Fame Is Over

Steve Forbes: Media Mogul, Former Presidential Candidate

"Medical Tourism is an exciting glimpse at the huge savings, productivity gains and medical advances that could be had if we got genuine consumer-controlled healthcare here—as well as overseas."

Medical Tourism is a response. Medical Tourism is a marketing concept. Medical Tourism is a proposed alternative to healthcare at home.

This phenomenon, born from the minds of marketing people in Thailand, has spawned a patchwork quilt of big and small players looking to jump on a new and potentially profitable bandwagon.

Take a moment to search the Internet for Medical Tourism. As of summer 2009, a Google search of "Medical Tourism" cited 1,770,000 references. There are thousands of big and small players trying to sell you health care. Check out Google Images, you'll find 336,000 images devoted to Medical Tourism alone.

Medical Tourism is being marketed aggressively. Bumrungrad is seen to be at the epicenter. The hospital has entered into alliances with travel agencies the world over.

Travel agencies have fallen on hard times due to global recession (2008-2009), Internet offerings, and commission cut backs from airlines, hotels, and cruise operators. Once part of a robust industry, travel agents are eager to jump on what could be a new lease on life.

The idea of taking advice from a travel-agent-cum-medical-concierge is shocking. Untrained, unregulated and avaricious, these brokers are anxious to sell you anything you will buy.

Imagine getting advice from Mom and Pop Travel Agent, Main Street U.S.A. "Hello, I'm interested in a gall-bladder procedure. Have you any recommendations? Any discount or promotional deals available?"

Emerging countries seeking to bolster their local economies regard Medical Tourism as a boon. In addition to having more people fly in for a round of golf, they can now look forward to having people drop in for a bypass on their way to the beach.

In countries with marginal infrastructure to regulate most industries, medical operators such as Bumrungrad can carry on their business as they see fit, and with impunity. The interests of industry and government are so closely aligned as to be indistinguishable.

So rapidly has this concept caught fire, the "industry" has given rise to an international association and annual meetings. The 2009 conclave was in Singapore in June. Here's what the Medical Tourism Association said about their 2009 conclave in Singapore:

Interest in Healthcare Travel has been rising, not only among individual customers but also among insurance companies and businesses. Medical Tourism is entering a new phase, one in which individual patients will not be the only consumers of medical Tourism. Their employers, insurance companies and governments are also part of the equation.

Healthcare Travel Exhibition & Congress 2009 represents the splicing of two of the world's largest industries: Health and Travel and Tourism. It is bound to have a huge effect and attract wide participation.

There are about 6 million tourists from a worldwide 600 million tourists with special needs. The Healthcare Travel industry is growing at 15 to 20 per cent annually and it's estimated that total gross medical Tourism revenues will rise from $56 billion today to $100 billion by 2012.

The speakers list is headed by movie star dashing, Ruben Toral, former director of marketing for-Bumrungrad. Now on his own, with likely assistance from Bumrungrad, Reuben is leading the worldwide charge (pun; intended).

Ruben Toral, President, International Medical Travel Association Ruben Toral, CEO of Mednet Asia Ltd., is a recognized leader in medical Tourism and healthcare globalization.

With over 15 years experience in healthcare marketing, Ruben has built companies, brands, physician networks and has distinguished himself as a thought leader in the area of healthcare globalization. He is the Conference Chair for The Healthcare Globalization Summit, external advisor the Joint Commission International Task Force on Globalization and board member to the International Medical Travel Association.

Ruben is an accomplished speaker and writer on the topics medical Tourism, healthcare globalization and lifestyle medicine. His insights appear in business, travel and trade publications like Fast Company, Medical Travel Today, Business Week and Spa Asia.

Ruben Toral, Mr. Medical Tourism.

Soft Spot?

Ruben Toral does not occupy a special place in my heart. He was the henchman tasked by Bumrungrad to slander and malign Joshua. It is a textbook move to make the victim wrong, diverting blame onto others. He divulged the private files of my son to AARP who then proceeded to libel Josh by inferring that he was a drug addict who took his own life.

What prospective patients for the Medical Tourist machine need to realize is that they are being enlisted into a very deliberate effort to get your business. The "industry" has big money behind it. Their interests are tied to the very people from whom patients are trying to escape: medical care at home.

Hossana: Gimme That Old Time Religion

The people who are trying daily to sell you on Medical Tourism are interested in self-aggrandizement and self-enrichment. Toral was a Bumrungrad flunky who earned his wings and is now a "recognized leader in Medical Tourism and health care globalization."

Apparently, in his spare time, Mr. Toral is also an expert in Asian Spa facilities.

In a few short years, Mr. Toral has, with Bumrungrad's backing, emerged as the bandleader for international Medical Tourism.

Since Bumrungrad's interests extend way beyond Thailand, through Asia and into the Middle East, they benefit by the elevation of the whole industry, not just Thailand.

Toral is their torchbearer. But he receives his marching orders from Schroeder and Banner back at Bumrungrad (Bumers).

Medical Tourism literature has little or no mention concerning patient safety. This is not surprising. It's the last thing on their minds. The advice of many marketing gurus is: Sell Sizzle—Not Substance! The Medical Tourism cartel has apparently taken this to heart.

The way in which Medical Tourism is being pushed is reminiscent of the early days of Oral Roberts, one of the first television Evangelists in the United States (1957). As a boy, I would sit before the black-and-white TV in awe and true wonderment as one crippled person after another was healed on the stage, given new life and the lord.

In 1977, Roberts claimed to have had a vision from a 900-foot-tall Jesus who told him to build City of Faith Medical and Research Center and the hospital would be a success.

In searching for a proper analogy for Medical Tourism, no

comparison comes as close, for us, as Pentecostal Evangelism. The opportunity to make money by pushing religion and salvation over radio and television was too tempting for early hucksters to ignore. In its infancy, unregulated television had no problem in having throngs of lepers, cripples, bedridden and the cancer stricken find instant salvation, right in front of the awestruck viewer's eyes.

Medical Tourism: Too Good to be True

Medical Tourism makes similar claims to Old Time Religion: a panacea without side effects.

Visions of luxurious, clear, modern, well-equipped hospitals filled to the brim with the best Board Certified doctors practicing in prestigiously accredited facilities, at a fraction of the price and with care to rival the best in the world.

Breaking a 2,500-Year-Old Code of Honor

Instead of the sacred relationship envisioned by Hippocrates, which binds a patient and a doctor together in a sacred trust—the patient literally putting his or her life in the care of the physician—we have now the invocation of a compelling selling proposition.

Patient care, envisioned by the ancient Greeks, focused on the prognosis and care of the patient—what is going to happen to that patient. The diagnosis was only the beginning.

As medicine becomes dominated by corporate needs, ancient wisdom has gone by the wayside. The need for a thoughtful process that considers individual sensitivities has given way to a hard sell for a soft proposition.

We forget the wisdom and experience of those who have gone before us. Aphorisms 1.1 captures the delicate considerations attendant to the care and well-being of a patient:

Life is short, art long, opportunity fleeting, experiment treacherous, judgment difficult.

Come, Join Us!

There is a cult-like quality to the phenomenon of Medical Tourism. The language around the concept has been manufactured. The true nature of the proposition is cleverly disguised.

Had I not had close experience with the likes of Toral, the AARP, the Executives at Bumrungrad, the officials at the Joint Commission and the experience of my son's death at their unclean hands, I might well be in the same boat as those who look at the Medical Tourist proposition from a distance.

Fate did not deal me the cards of an uninvolved bystander. I have seen the under belly of this creature. I have smelled its breath.

I can understand and empathize with those standing at the sidelines thinking that outsourced care is a real solution.

When our backs are up against the wall and we are pressed to make a choice, we decipher the information available, mix it with our intuition and decide.

We hope that these pages are assisting in revealing information not previously known. I hope that with this revelation of the true character and nature of the brokers of this economic oppression, better and informed decisions can now be made. Before there was an excuse; now, there is not.

The Driving Forces: Why Alternatives Have Been Sought

The Western world, which gave rise to Medical Tourism, can be characterized by:

- Excessive expense of healthcare; up to 90 percent higher than foreign care
- Difficult access to healthcare providers
- 45 million in the U.S. without health insurance
- Astronomical cost of prescription medication
- In British Commonwealth countries, very long waiting times
- Promise of quality care

- Procedures and medications available and not yet approved in the U.S.
- Difficult or nonexistent follow-up care when patient returns home
- Problematic assessment/care resulting from varying languages
- Recourse for malpractice or problems; virtually non-existent
- Slated to become big business; according to McKinse, $2 billion gross by 2012
- Regarded by U.S. industry as alternative to domestic care; largely as a money saving measure
- Covered by insurance if facilities participate in insurance plan and are Accredited (read: Joint Commission for U.S. participants)
- Some insurance companies such as World Access and British BUPA are accrediting hospitals on their own accord; United Health appears to be laying similar plans
- Doctors drained away to higher paying positions in medical tourist hospitals, leaving depleted quality of care for nationals
- Unions regard this as a threat to their members
- U.S. doctors see this as a drain away from resources at home
- Insurance companies see this as another windfall opportunity to increase profit margins. Corporations see this as a way of escaping the vice grip of their health benefit obligations.
- U.S.-based companies are active participants and owners in the foreign matrix of medical tourist care facilities.

In all cases, credibility for foreign institutions is contingent on accreditation by the Joint Commission International. Without their accreditation patients would not come nor would insurance pay!

The concept works largely on blind faith.

While it is true that big changes in the U.S. are afoot as this book is being penned, the underlying forces and problems are likely to

---

Economic Based Health

The head of *Forbes* magazine in this excerpt looks at health care as if he were shopping for a used car.

Open-Heart Surgery--90% off
Steve Forbes 08.13.07, 12:00 AM ET

A fast-growing phenomenon—"Medical Tourism," which will be a $40 billion industry by 2010—is showing how we can "solve" the healthcare financing crisis.

The hospitals and physicians are <u>usually first-rate</u> and, amazingly, can provide operations at 10% to 30% of the cost in the U.S.

They are certified by Joint <u>Commission International,</u> a not-for-profit subsidiary of the Joint Commission, which accredits U.S. hospitals. The international Accreditation process is as rigorous as it is in the U.S.—but without the unnecessary bureaucratic paperwork.

Take No Comfort

No informed person should take ANY comfort in Accreditation by the Joint Commission. With due respect to Mr. Forbes, the international process is nowhere near as rigorous as it is in the United States. Mr. Forbes comments are dangerous and misleading.

Mr. Forbes opines that the doctors are "first rate" but fails to say how he knows. Again, based on my research, this is dangerously misleading hype. In fact, the skills and experience of the doctors at these facilities ARE a MAJOR issue given that they practice medicine in largely unregulated environments.

Say whatever they may say about themselves; until this new industry is regulated and are able to meet the acid test of truth, one should look with great suspicion on doctors who take kick backs for prescriptions and receive personal payments for unnecessary procedures, tests and medications.

If this sounds like what occurs in the United States, it is. The difference is that abroad the profit margins are higher; the hospitals and doctors are unregulated.

Package deals abound for procedures; one from column A, two diagnostic tests from column B, one surgery from column C.

The twist on the package deals, negotiated by insurance companies is what additional services can be sold which jack up their total take.

Not unlike cruise ships who sell cabins inexpensively, the surcharges for use of the spa, wine at dinner, crew tips, side trips at port, transfer services, a gift or two at one of the arcade shops, a little gambling; before you know it, you've doubled or tripled the cost.

Are You Guilt Tripping Me?

Guilt trips are a specialty at Bumrungrad. I had a hard time imaginng this until I heard it for myself while waiting to confront one of my son's killers, Dr. Sukkitti.

A couple in the cardiology waiting room at Bumrungrad was asked by the "sales" nurse what kind of scan the patient would like. An X Ray was included in her "package" but the doctor thought that a CT Scan or an MRI might be better; the surcharge for the CT was x and the MRI, y.

Understandably and predictably, the patient didn't know the difference and asked the nurse which one she would recommend. Well, said the nurse, if you want to be absolutely sure, the MRI would give the doctor the best picture—and, if you really want the best of the best, we just got a new motion picture MRI that would allow the heart to be filmed AS IT BEATS—this, for y plus dollars.

The patient conferred with her husband for about twenty

seconds and signed up for the video MRI.

The same tactic is used with medications, alternative diagnostics additional procedures etc. What begins as a great deal transforms into a significantly higher price than originally cited? In the United States, this is called bait and switch.

Tools of the Trade

The abundant services becoming available around Medical Tourism remind one of Frommer's Guides to Europe on $25 dollars a day.

Book authors/publishers such as Patients Beyond Borders and its partner Medeguide, offer new online services which connect patients to doctors online; the precursor to foreign medical treatment.

Ruben Toral's company also represents and advises United Healthcare. What goes around comes around. We see this phenomenon repeating time and again; it is no accident.

Toral comments, "Through this partnership, Medeguide now offers visitors a one-stop source of information that enables them to easily search and find the right destination, doctor, and treatment."

Josef Woodman, author of Patient's without Borders and Mr. Toral's partner, says he is going to be a speaker in an important, upcoming

AARP Event:
(As of 6/ 10/ 2009 Woodman is not listed as a participant)
AARP Presents Vegas@50+

The 2009 National Event & Expo, scheduled from October 22–24, will be at the Sands Expo and Convention Center, Las Vegas, Nevada, where the party never stops. You won't want to miss these three days and nights of concerts, celebrity speakers, engaging educational forums, hundreds of interactive exhibitors, giveaways, and much, much more. Meet up with old friends, bring the family, and make new friends. We'll show you a good time!

Wait a minute, AARP is controlled by UnitedHealthcare; remember Dr. McGuire and his historic resignation and $ billion door prize?

Dwell on this for a moment. AARP, a 40-million-member organization, is a front for UnitedHealthcare, the nation's largest health insurance provider. United is also an organization that has been fined billions for Medicare fraud and numerous SEC infractions.

UnitedHealthcare's largest shareholder is a founder of the largest chain of pawnshops and check cashing operations in the United Sates David Burke.

Burke is also in the business of making quick, high interest loans. Some call this loan sharking.

Without casting aspersions on Mr. Burke, former Chairman of UnitedHealthcare, the FBI and the DEA believe that the U.S. pawnshop industry has direct ties to the South and Central American drug cartel and that the Pawn industry is suspected of money laundering and gun running in cahoots with the drug cartel down south.

Forty million members of AARP don't have the slightest idea about any of this. I think they should.

Machiavelli Move Over

I don't fault Toral and Woodman for trying to do business. What I fault them for is their covert agendas.

The corporate company they keep and represent intends to dominate and control of a vast portion of domestic and international healthcare dollars. They pay only lip service to patient safety and quality care.

Since health care represents one-fifth of the U.S. gross domestic product, because United is the largest health insurance company and because AARP represents about one-sixth of the American population of 300 million, the numbers involved are extraordinary.

In 2008 UnitedHealthcare grossed $70 billion in revenues.

AARP is a brilliant, self-financing arm of United. The company's approximate annual budget of $1 billion is paid for by nearly $700 million in United commissions. The rest comes, happily for them, from member dues and the smorgasbord of other services and goodies AARP offers. This is brilliant marketing; it is also brilliant mind control.

AARP: Star-studded Cast

Among the illustrious cadre of speakers in the queue for AARP in Vegas, note the two highly visible journalists set to espouse their views [from AARP's 2009 Convention Invitation/Rooster of Speakers] to include but not limited to:

John Hockenberry is an American journalist. He has won four Emmy awards and three Peabody Awards. Hockenberry accepted a position in early 2007 as a Distinguished Fellow at the Massachusetts Institute of Technology's Media Lab. He is the co-host of the daily, new morning drive news program, The Takeaway with John Hockenberry and Adaora Udoji, co-created by Public Radio International and WNYC and editorial partners, the BBC World Service, The New York Times and WGBH Radio Boston.

Soledad O'Brien is an anchor and correspondent for "CNN: Special Investigations Unit." She also covers political news and reports for special programs, such as CNN's in-depth look at African Americans 40 years after the assassination of Dr. Martin Luther King, Jr. She joined CNN in July 2003 as co-anchor of "American Morning." She was part of the CNN team that won a Peabody Award for coverage of Hurricane Katrina. Previously, she had been a weekend anchor and correspondent for NBC, covering the Space Shuttle Columbia disaster and Pope John Paul II's historic visit to Cuba. O'Brien is a graduate of Harvard University with a degree in English and American literature.

How motivated would either one of these journalists be to use their bully pulpit to dig into UnitedHealthcare or its ties to AARP? Big money buys big cooperation.

Either Mr. Hockenberry or Ms. O'Brien are unaware of the polluted waters in which they are swimming (which I hope is the case) or, worse, they are aware and don't care!

This is the kind of power behind Medical Tourism and the AARP cum UnitedHealthcare Group. The very places we turn to for some ray of truth are found beholding to "The Man."

It seems likely that corporations like AARP need not deliberately control information distributed to the masses. A simple invitation to speak and a handsome honorarium is all that is needed to buy silence.

This represents the subtle lay of the American landscape. This is the interwoven fabric of corporate control draped over free speech. This is the infrastructure who is trying to sell you Medical Tourism.

These excerpts are representative of hundreds I have received and reviewed. No case, however, has surfaced to the level of my son. Josh has become the benchmark for wrongdoing in the Medical Tourist boom. He will not soon be forgotten.

Things They Don't Want You to Know

The Sun-Herald
August 27, 2006
Bumrungrad Breast Infection, 26.August.2006

HELEN (not her real name) had breast surgery at Thailand's

Bumrungrad International. The hospital room was as luxurious as promised, but her post-operative care left her in a potentially life-threatening situation.

"When I was discharged I began getting dreadful pain in my left breast," she said. "They put me on antibiotics but then the stitches began to come apart and it began to weep."

After 21 days in Bangkok, Helen, 57, flew back to Sydney, where a plastic surgeon diagnosed an infection and performed further surgery . . . . Helen was left with terrible scarring that she is hoping to reduce with more surgery.
No comment was available from Bumrungrad hospital.

Bumrungrad Horror Story from Cambodia, October 3, 2006
As a resident of Cambodia . . . we've found Bumrungrad's care to be "spotty," and the hospital, overall, to have become very profit-oriented.

.My newborn son was separated from his mother for 3-days while in an intensive care incubator, without her once being offered to visit her child.

Only when we became aggressive about "What's going on? Why can't we see our child?" The so-called "intensive care" was actually not very intensive, probably unnecessary, though expensive, and it appeared that food was being withheld from the infant during the whole process.

We won't be going back to Bumrungrad.

Keep up the good work!

======

New South Wales Feels Impact of Medical Tourism
26 August 2006
Risky scalpel tours cut into taxpayers' pockets

Louise Hall and Connie Levett

August 27, 2006
Luxury room, deadly bugs

AUSTRALIANS suffering from botched cosmetic surgery overseas are costing taxpayers thousands of dollars when they undergo remedial and reconstructive surgery in NSW public Hospitals.

Plastic surgeons are reporting dozens of cases of complications including infections, hair loss, "hideous" scarring, paralysis and failed implants from cut-price "scalpel Tourism" packages. "Over there, you are a tourist and you are on your own and there is no backup if something goes wrong, whereas in Australia if something goes wrong, we have the Medicare system," he said.

"It is not easy to salvage these cases, [so] is it really fair for Australian taxpayers to foot the bill when something goes wrong overseas?"

The Federal Government is so concerned about the risk of complications from discount or uncertified medical establishments that it has a special travel advisory warning for "medical Tourism" in Thailand.

Parliamentary Secretary to the Minister for Foreign Affairs, Teresa Gambaro, said there had been an increasing burden on embassy staff helping Australians suffering complications, primarily in Bangkok but also in the Philippines, Indonesia, Argentina, Iran and Ukraine.

"It is an increasing cost to the health system... in Asia there are only a few really good surgeons," she said.

She said her clients were girls in their early 20s wanting low-cost breast augmentation and liposuction and women over 35 wanting multiple surgeries.

Chairman of NSW Health's surgical services taskforce, Dr Patrick Cregan, said people opting for cheap overseas surgery risked having unqualified surgeons.

Eye-to-Eye with the Devil

By the time my investigation started to concentrate on Medical Tourism, I realized that I faced enormous forces.

St. Wolfgang and the Devil.

Shining bright lights on the multifarious interests that had combined to strip America of its formerly viable healthcare system is a long and tough process.

I take comfort in knowing that history is full of examples where great changes were enabled by lone rangers. I continue to brace against the wind, realizing that individuals can be powerful agents for social change.

I made a promise to my son never to stop digging up the truth, no matter what the risk.

Coming Full Circle

Is it any wonder that alternatives to American health care problems are being created and marketed? Look at what the powers that be have left in their wake.

The irony: the same sources seeking to outsource you caused the problems, which led to the need for outsourcing. They operate on the other side of the world and are waiting with open arms to receive you again.

The trend towards Medical Tourism will further degrade American medicine. It will also negatively impact the countries to which foreigners are being sent, since the attention of their medical programs will turn toward the profits that foreigners bring to their shores at the expense of the care of their own peoples.

Backstage: Behind the Fall

The same interests that created the problem have now created their own "solution:" Medical Outsourcing/Tourism. Whatever the noise, we must listen to the music. The music being played is the same, on either side of the ocean.

The devastation of American health care did not happen in a void. In 1965, when Medicare was enacted, this country was unquestionably #1 in the world in medical excellence.

Since 1965, and the passage of Medicare, the United States has fallen to below 40th in quality rankings, according to a 2002 World Health Organization (WHO) survey. (The World Health Organization has been infiltrated and associated with the Joint Commission! Imagine, a Commission which has overseen.)

Corruption without Borders

The corruption of the healthcare industry is vast, beyond comprehension. Billions have been collected by Federal and State governments for Medicare and Medicaid fraud from insurance companies and Hospital corporations. This is non trivial.

In summer 2006, for example, Tenet Corporation, AKA National Medical Enterprises, was fined $900 million by the Federal government for Medicare fraud. Tenet, one of the most egregious offenders in the secret world of healthcare criminality, was given four years to repay. The case was settled on the Court House steps. No one went to jail.

Tenet had three hospitals damaged in Katrina's rampage through New Orleans. Tenet took close to $400 million from their property-insurance coverage, closed the hospitals and voila, they were more than half way into paying the Federal Government with four more years, at about $125 million a year, to finish this latest round of fines.

For Tenet, this is doughnut money. For New Orleans, it is yet another disaster, being deprived of an adequate healthcare system. Ethics has never been the concern of Tenet.

Tenet has been investing in foreign facilities for years. Whether Tenet has indeed parked its Bumrungrad interest in proxy is not the issue. Vital here is that major American health care corporations have been quietly laying the foundation for the next wave of patient care: exportation. Bumrungrad has labeled this Medical Tourism. Don't be fooled, it is patient exportation enabled by financial incentives that appear to, but do not, solve the American dilemma.

A Parting Shot

This, from the August 17, 2009 issue of the venerable publication Global Travel News, should remind you that the Medical Machine is alive and well.

International Hospital Accreditation Skyrockets 1,000%
By eTN Staff Writer | Aug 17, 2009

In the last five years, the number of JCI (Joint Commission International) accredited public and private hospitals around the world have increased by nearly 1,000 percent. Up from a mere 27 hospitals and healthcare organizations with that accreditation in 2004, currently over 250 such entities in 36 countries have now been accredited by the JCI. This extremely high standard of "American accreditation" now instills a new level of confidence in US citizens seeking affordable healthcare alternatives abroad. With the US Congress currently locked in a fierce battle over how to solve the national healthcare crisis, Josef Woodman, author of Patients Beyond Borders, joins Sandy Dhuyvetter on TravelTalkRADIO to discuss this extraordinarily relevant trend.

Nineteen ~ Reflections and Projections

Historical Perspectives: A Look Back and a Review

During summer 2009, an extraordinary ground swell of explosive public outpouring, some of it violent, has erupted in town-hall meetings and on the streets. The subject of healthcare is an intensely personal experience for 300 million people in the United States.

Not since the riots of Newark and Los Angeles, the protests at the Democratic Convention of 1968 and the marches on Washington against the war in Vietnam, or the Million Man March, have the American people become as vocal and animated.

They are angry, very angry. Yet they don't know where their frustrations should be directed. In short, the world has been seeing free-floating rage against the government of the United States.

Healthcare goes to the fundamental underpinnings of society. Healthcare issues carry an importance for people similar to national security. In concept, the people have transferred authority to the government to provide certain safeguards and functions. Originally, these functions were limited but have expanded wildly over time.

For many, healthcare is seen an entitlement. Indeed, Medicare's power resides in the Senate Finance Committee, which oversees entitlements, of which federally-funded healthcare is perhaps the largest program.

Medicare and Medicaid were originally envisioned as support for the underprivileged. That has changed over time to the point where people of all economic strata have sought to take part in government-funded Medicare and, on the State-support level,

Medicaid. The economic and logistical strains placed on the system have swollen to the point of bursting.

Private insurance, except for the very wealthy, comprising a small percent of the populace, is not available for people over 65. Instead, supplemental insurance to fill in gaps in Medicare are sold by most medical-insurance operators.

Setting aside the question of why Medicare came to include those who could afford to pay their own way, the United States, as of 2009, has close to 50,000,000 people without any form of medical insurance.

The healthcare-reform movement of 2009 seeks to include those 50,000,000. The consequences are staggering but necessary.

As it is, clear class and geographic distinctions exist concerning the quality and accessibility of care. But as the Baby Boomers swell into the ranks of the retired, the stresses on the healthcare system are being distorted to the breaking point.

As Medicare has sought to contain the downward spiral into oblivion, the government and the insurance cartel have sought to cut costs.

Benefits have become marginalized and reimbursement levels for healthcare professionals have been steadily declining. The ever-decreasing level of payment to doctors has forced many to flee from medicine. They simply cannot afford to practice healthcare.

Patient visits with their doctors, when they can find one, are under four minutes. Doctors must crank that many patients through their office to just stay financially even. Clearly, the quality of care suffers under such pressures. Yet the liability for performance remains high.

Hospitals, seeking to manage their profits, cut doctors and nurses from their payrolls whenever possible. This places excessive burdens for those on duty. Burdened with too many patients and too little time for individual patient care, mistakes are made. Doctors and nurses are regularly blamed while hospitals and administrators are rarely subjected to litigation.

Fraud by hospitals is rampant, as is fraud by the healthcare-insurance cartel that contrives every means possible for not paying on either government funded or private care.

Now comes the prospect of 50,000,000 more patients seeking those same, dwindling resources. This is the eye of the perfect storm. Complete breakdown and chaos is not only likely, it is certain.

Fraud in healthcare admitted by the Department of Justice is estimated to exceed the yearly budget for the Pentagon: over $600 billion! Laws are on the books to regulate this kind of malfeasance and in some cases, outright criminality. They are rarely enforced.

The healthcare-insurance cartel pays big bucks to make sure these laws are not applied to them. Now, on the eve of healthcare "reform" in 2009, the very robbers who have had their way for decades are not going away. Instead, they will be given even more money to "manage."

The insurance cartel has covered and hedged its bets. Win or lose, they will win.

They are masterminds at creating distractions and diversions that defocus public attention from their graft and vicious attack on individual patients and "non complaint" doctors.

They want the public distracted and uninformed or, worse, misinformed. They have the geese that lay the golden eggs and they are not about to let them fly the coop.

As if the unbridled thievery in the U.S. were not enough, the insurance cartel has been creating a new "alternative" for disgruntled U.S. patients: Medical Outsourcing AKA Medical Tourism.

I have discussed the consequences that this movement holds for the U.S. as well as for countries that are literally jumping with joy at the prospect of enriching their own coffers through the prospective economic miracle of Medical Tourism. It's a hideous trap.

What Does All This Mean?

I have no doubt that for many, reading this book has been an unexpected journey and, I hope, a profound one.

I never anticipated the events that led me to write this book and to become an ardent activist. The distant call I received from Dr. Morley in the middle of the night marked the start of discoveries I had never imagined and could never otherwise have known.

Writing this recantation of my experiences has caused me to relive, in magnificent, granular and excruciating relief, every detail. This has been a horrible blessing but a necessary one.

In continuing and deepening my investigations, I have had many opportunities to reconfirm and solidify my understanding and conviction.

The current brouhaha in Washington D.C. over healthcare is churning the public mind and the entrenched interests to realign and strengthen their respective positions: the public to regain their lives and the entrenched interests to make sure that nothing changes. Nothing.

As a student of words, I cannot help but be struck by the use of the word 'reform,' as in Healthcare Reform. Reform means to reshape something that exists.

We know that what exists is fundamentally, totally broken. Why have the powers that be not used the world "replace?"

Replace means to put something new in the place of something already there, like replacing a President, buying a new system to perform work, or firing a bad employee and replacing them with a new one.

Yet nowhere in the healthcare debate raging in the summer of 2009 is there talk of replacement, only reform. This is a profound revelation of the unconscious state of mind. I regard this as a manifestation of the continued insinuation of the interests of the cartel and their cohorts to not only maintain but actually to extend their reach into the lives of the citizenry. They do so in concert with the government of the United States who, as we have seen, supplies the economic fuel to power the giant private engines of the cartel.

This is a tragedy but unfortunately true. The illustrations of the politico medico industrial complex are too abundant to deny. Only the kinds of mindless and ignorant people who can deny the Holocaust could deny the blatant march on the rights of Americans and by extension, the citizens of the world, now being waged over healthcare reform.

I have discussed my belief that conspiracies can be either implicit or explicit. I do not subscribe to a conspiracy where all the parties in collusion meet secretly to plot their tactics. What I believe, however, is that the opportunity for stealing the spoils of war or business of any kind is so tempting, so obvious to those trained in larcenous thinking, that insects and rodents from different nests in different places all know that food has been left out overnight and that it is time to raid the kitchen.

The food of which I speak is being served buffet style. This is the kind of conspiracy that explains the cartel. With the amount of additional money to be injected into the system, we sit at the beginning of an orgy fit for the Kings of the cartel. You and I, our children and our children's children will be picking up the tab while the vultures continue to pick through every last piece of meat.

Graphic talk, but not out of place. We are talking trillions of dollars.

I cannot predict what will come from the efforts afoot in Washington. I suspect it will not be good. Since I don't feel comfortable in opining about will happen, I will withhold my views that I will share after the fact.

What I do feel comfortable in discussing are the necessary elements which, if absent in the reformation of healthcare, will spell certain doom.

As to the issues of Medical Tourism, I will stand with the proposal I sent to the United States Senate, attention Senators Grassley and Bacus, Co-Chairs of the Senate Finance Subcommittee on Healthcare. I am reproducing the proposal here for your reference.

Clearly, despite my protests, the dialectic of exporting patients for cheaper care to Third World countries will not stop. But it must be controlled and patients protected far more than current law or contractual agreements provide.

I hope that by instituting the kinds of mechanisms I have suggested to Congress, the cartel in the U.S. and its foreign buddies will no longer be in a position where they are free from responsibility. If you have further suggestions as to similar or other mechanisms, please let me know by contact at info@theamericanmedicalmoneymachine.com

The difficulty writing this manuscript in deciding what to leave in and what to remove has been extreme. Culling through the thousands of data points and realizations that I have uncovered has made prioritizing arduous yet critical. Other books will come as the story unfolds.

The K.I.S.S. Principle (Keep it Simple Stupid)

Moses and the tablet, before he broke them in two.

Though Moses descended with 613 Commandments, only ten are generally still recognized. Keeping 613 or even 127 concepts at top of mind means pruning, necessary in going intelligently forward.

As Lincoln wisely suggested: "I'm sorry I wrote such a long letter. I didn't have the time to write a short one." Heeding Lincoln's entreaties for brevity, I have tried to extract the most important takeaways from my confrontation with destiny.

This concerns me. I want what I have learned STICK permanently in my readers' minds. This is stuff too important for any of us to forget.

The Joshua Doctrine

In memoriam, I have dubbed these suggestions, questions and prognostications The Joshua Doctrine:

(1) Anything that interferes with the sacred relationship between a doctor and his patient will doom everything else.

(2) As long as the cartel maintains control, money will be stolen and the entire system will suffer.

(3) Without bringing the robber barons to justice for sins they have already committed, the cartel and its cohorts will continue to plunder unimpeded; not until an example is set will there be any fear of reprisal.

(4) As long as evidence-based medicine is used to rule the practice of medicine, patients will suffer and good doctors will flee practice.

(5) Unless insurance companies are stopped from practicing medicine without a license, the relationship and trust between doctor and patient will be impossible.

(6) Sentinel Events need to be reported and shared publicly, as a matter of law.

(7) Hospital statistics need to be open to inspection by all; doctors should provide references so that patients can check with others as to the quality of care they should expect to receive.

(8) The Joint Commission must be abandoned and a new and objective form of accreditation and regulation introduced that is not subject to bribery and corruption.

(9) The Joint Commission must be held responsible for its part in the destruction of American healthcare, its executives tried for treason and fraud, its tax exempt status revoked retroactively and its past tax heavens revoked and repaid to the public in compliance with laws incorporated in the Social Security Act Amendments of 1965.

(10) Past HHS Secretaries, including Donna Shalala, should be investigated for breaking the laws incorporated in the Social Security Act Amendments of 1965.

(11) Every lobbying firm in Washington should be shut down; as long as permanent campaigns are funded by interests seeking to buy influence, we are dead ducks; lobbying must become an artifact of the past; only publicly-financed campaigns can restore a real democracy' s democracy of which we have been robbed.

(12) No elected official can maintain any interest in any organization over which they have authority; if this means paying Congressmen and Senators more, fine; but they simply cannot be on the take when they have sworn to give to their constituents' good and thoughtful statutes, not the best laws money can buy.

(13) Without these replacements in basic policy, we will be rearranging deck chairs on the Titanic; this will only prolong the agony, but the ship will go down as sure as the sun will come up.

(14) Is It too late?—the directional significance of offshore care;

(15) No wonder that alternatives to American Healthcare are being created and marketed; look at what the powers that be have left in their wake.

(16) The irony is that the same sources seeking to outsource are the ones who caused the problems that have led to the outsourcing; they are also the ones, on the other side of the world, who are waiting with open arms to receive you again, but now they can operate with full impunity and patients will have no recourse.

(17) This trend will further degrade American medicine and will negatively impact the countries to which foreigners are being sent, since the attention of their medical programs will now be turned towards the profits that foreigners bring to their shores.

(18) The move to Medical Tourism or outsourcing is, in itself, troubling; it is even more significant, however, for what it portends for American healthcare; as of now, Medical Tourism is a blip on the screen, though Bumrungrad claims, at times, 400,000 patients a year and at other times 50,000; the sources standing to benefit from the medical 'stay-cation' business will proffer higher numbers, never lower; there are no straight answers as to how big this phenomenon is, but this is beside the point: that domestic and foreign interests want you to travel for treatment; where the absolute numbers of dollars they make will be lower, in concept, the profit margins will be higher and the opportunity for unregulated skimming enormous.

(19) The key points to the Medical Tourism program are: the cartel and foreign operators are prepared to wait till Medical Tourism takes hold; whatever way the public may be sold, none of the facts or figures are reliable; organizations like Bumrungrad are free to sell you the fountain of youth—and they do—without fear of reprisals from false advertising or fraud; Bumrungrad and the other members of the Medical Tourism establishment are outside the jurisdiction of U.S. and International Law (note: Thailand does not participate in any treaty that would hold it accountable for its actions regarding medical Tourism. This is true for most of the other major markets who are hawking their medical wares).

(20) Perhaps the more significant reason, I speculate, that Medical Tourism bodes poorly for healthcare systems in the U.S. is that the pricing structures from abroad will most likely be used by the cartel to set pricing standards at home.

(21) This means that reimbursement levels will be adjusted downward from current levels and benchmarked against pricing abroad; I have already discussed how doctors are hurt by ever-declining payment schedules and how patients suffer terribly in having to participate in higher premiums for declining services; the introduction of the foreign-pricing model will make this mess even worse.

(22) They will argue, I surmise, that a patient can get the same treatment abroad-equivalent in every way to the U.S. so why should the insurance company or employer pay more when the same thing is available for less, even if it is an ocean and a continent away?

The Producers

A relevant sidebar might interest you: when I interviewed a former CBS Television Producer who was part of the now famous 60 Minutes episode that provided pseudo legitimacy for Bumrungrad, I asked him what was the basis—the key point that 60 Minutes wished to make? His answer: care at Bumrungrad was equivalent to care at home. Full stop.

People die at hospitals in Chicago and at Bumrungrad. Hospitals in L.A. have Board Certified doctors, so does Bumrungrad; hospitals in New York are accredited by the same agency as Bumrungrad; these points of comparability were cited by the former 60 Minute producer.

I pointed out that his logic was flawed. Though marred, legal recourse exists for mistakes at home, none abroad. I reminded him of Schroeder's Marching Mantra: **"If there's a mistake, we fix it; but the idea of suing for multimillions of dollars for damages is not going to be something you can do outside the U.S."** He had no response.

I reminded him of the dubious ownership status of Bumrungrad vis-à-vis Tenet Healthcare. He replied that if he was a patient in for a bypass, why would hospital ownership concern him?

Taken aback, I responded that if I were to go under the knife at the shop of known criminals with a historical record of heinous acts resulting in many deaths, I would want to know. What reasonable person wouldn't?

Would you check into a hotel known to be infested with rodents carrying the plague?

The retired producer said that they did not have time in an 11-minute segment to show all sides of the question. They knew of previous deaths at Bumrungrad but this was not considered significant. 60 Minutes had 11 minutes to present the good, but not the bad or the ugly.

How convenient and tragic, especially considering that the CBS endorsement became the de facto imprimatur of approval of Bumrungrad and, in a broader sense, medical outsourcing. You can't unring that bell! I wish I could.

Patients: Last to Be Considered

As long as the patient/doctor relationship is degraded, whatever solution may ensue will most assuredly fail.

Things to Come and Cautionary Notes

Overcrowded emergency rooms now serve as primary-care resources for a vast percentage of the population. This is likely to continue and worsen.

It is increasingly harder to get a timely doctor's appointment whether you have insurance or not, whether you are "connected" or not.

Patients will be even more surprised to be denied claims by insurers (entities that in actuality practice medicine without license), who will be overriding doctor's recommendations.

To justify these claims denials, statistical recipe models will be used. Get used to being a statistic and to having your treatment plan painted by numbers.

Soaring deductibles and co-pays place heavier burdens on individuals. This is taking place while healthcare plans, hospital chains and insurers become more profitable than ever. This will continue with impunity. The big insurance players' hold over governmental behavior will not loosen. The government will reign supreme. Shut up and take a number.

People of moderate, low or fixed income must often choose between food and medications and often do not fill or refill prescriptions because of the costs, particularly the elderly. This will become worse. Insurance coverage will be forced on people and premiums will be collected by the IRS. Healthcare plans foisted on the public by the government will benefit the cartel and will underpay and shortchange the patient, again.

The Joint Commission has violated the law since 1965. They have been aided and abetted by the HEW and now the HHS. Their deeming authority should be withdrawn by the United States Government based on fraud, dereliction of duty and for their participation in cover-up crimes, aiding and abetting, racketeering and other crimes of deceit.

The JC claims to be not-for-profit but it goes beyond any charter that describes the nature of these types of organizations. The JC is a for-profit organization in business to make money. They write in their literature about profits and the bottom line.

This is hardly the talk of a charitable or scientific/educational organization. Their tax-exempt status is wholly misplaced. It should be revoked and they should be held accountable for and taxed retroactively to 1965, when they were first chartered by the United States Congress.

The Joint Commission International (JCI) should be sued by the Justice Department for committing fraud by illegally employing the implicit authority of the U.S. Government in drawing business to those entities that pay the JCI and the Joint Commission for its services.

They have also violated truth-in-advertising laws and should be held accountable in both the U.S. and World Courts for perpetrating a fraud on the American and international public by illegally using the implied authority of the United States Government for their own interests.

If the Joint Commission or any other agency with similar ethics and lack of social conscience is permitted to operate, the cartel and medical money interests will eat the medical system alive.

The HHS should be sued for its failure to set fees and to oversee the Joint Commission. Please note that the American Nursing Association, during the summer of 2006, sued HHS for its failure to oversee the Joint Commission in assuring that proper staff/patient ratios be maintained.

Individuals found to have participated in accrediting hospitals and secreting information that could have saved the lives of others, had they followed their charter of publicly sharing Sentinel Events, should be criminally prosecuted to the full extent of the law. This also goes for HHS officials involved in looking the other way. They are co-conspirators in these vast rackets.

Any company found to have participated in any of the crimes committed by HHS and the Joint Commission should be fined and held criminally responsible for their actions. Specific individuals involved, based on whatever statute of limitations applies, should be prosecuted by the Justice Department to the full extent of the law.

A new oversight body should be established to oversee and implement the mission originally designated for the JC in 1965. This new body should be free of industry connections and should maintain a completely non-partisan position. The composition and function of this body should learn from the terrible mistakes and financial destruction of the American Health Care system under the watch of the Joint Commission. This body should report to a public board and be accountable for its actions.

The recent association between the Joint Commission and the World Health Organization should be declared illegal. The Joint Commission collaborated with the WHO to establish international safety standards.

When considering how dangerous and infected U.S. healthcare institutions have become on the Joint Commission's watch, it is ludicrous that the WHO would team with the overseer to permit the destruction of the once proud and superb U.S. healthcare establishment.

The implied use of the name of the United States Government is being compromised by the activities of the Joint Commission and will continue to diminish the integrity of the United States around the world. This must be brought to an immediate halt by the United States Government.

I propose The United States Special Patient Protection Act, to require the Joint Commission to disgorge all information, since its formation, in its possession regarding their operations, findings, Sentinel Events, financial dealings etc.

Further, this Bill will propose that a Patient Safety Treaty be established in which participating countries offering Medical Tourism, providers and insurers are held responsible by the U.S. Federal Government for malpractice, patient injury and/or death of U.S. citizens who receive medical treatment outside the United States and its territories.

Mandatory insurance and a special world court must be established to hear litigation brought by harmed parties. Insurance companies, anywhere in the world, must be forbidden, by law, to participate with or compensate any healthcare facility that does not participate in this treaty.

Evidence-based medicine is another way of saying treatment by statistical analysis and formula. Though evidence-based medicine is a tool that should help individual physicians make diagnostic and therapeutic decisions on how best to treat patients, those who support evidence-based medicine most vocally are interested in cost, not quality.

Treatment of patients is complex. More variables are at play than can be accounted for in any database. The individual judgment and intuition of physicians adds a level of sophistication that even the most advanced medical informatics cannot synthesize or predict.

Corporate nursing staffs are in the business of containing costs and are often compensated with incentives for denying treatment rather than acting in the patient's best interest. The door closes to that patient who knows far more than someone sitting on a telephone half a world away.

Evidence-based medicine is a valuable directional tool. I do not doubt or disagree with that. I have personally been involved in licensing medical informatics and understand, in detail, where it is useful and where it is not. These systems will never replace an experienced physician. They will assist in decision-making but will not replace it.

Insurance companies want to use evidence-based medicine to justify the denial of care, using seemingly scientific and objective resources to validate their position. But these systems are not comprehensive and should never replace the human mind, whose computational and multi- dimensional powers are not even close to replication by any computer system.

By pointing to evidence-based medicine as "the" standard, insurers are looking to save money by justifying decisions for patient treatment, not for patient well-being. It's as simple as that.

The movement is growing in the U.S., backed by the need for big business to find a means of justifying denial of care. The bottom lines of the insurance companies reflect how well this is working and will continue to work.

If this trend continues towards evidence-based medicine, which I contend no one in Washington truly understands, we are toast! Evidence-based treatment and reimbursement must be made illegal, not the standard of care being proffered by the cartel.

Insurance companies have large nursing staffs, overseen by a rubber-stamp doctor who does not evaluate individual cases but is there to serve a legal requirement. The criterion: that a doctor is approving medical decisions made by these corporations.

These activities must be immediately stopped and made illegal, with criminal penalties imposed on all levels of offenders from the CEO to the "Customer Care" Call Center Staff. Only then will the wanton abuses currently being inflicted on the public be stopped.

Recent changes in Medicare provide that it will not pay for treating hospital-acquired infections. If a patient gets sick while in the hospital, the capped amount that the hospital will be paid will not cover the costs of treating the patient who acquired the infection after admission.

The stated intention of this policy is to encourage hospitals to "clean up their acts." The reality: patients will likely be discharged sooner than wise treatment standards dictate, so that the hospital is not stuck with the bill for treating hospital-acquired infections.

Capped payments have already motivated hospitals to discharge patients as soon as possible. I predict that early discharge will become even more exaggerated, so that hospitals avoid the risk of acquiring infections on "their dime."

In patient safety, the U.S. ranks around #37 by a 2000 World Health Organization survey, making a Hospital stay a serious and dangerous proposition.

While hospital corporations seek to sweeten their bottom lines, hospital-acquired infections are soaring.

Reduced budgets for janitorial services and high patient turnover are certainly to blame. Surface contact with bacteria and airborne organisms is a major concern. The world is seeing new and rapidly evolving, antibiotic-resistant bugs that mutate, while feasting on patients whose immune systems have been compromised due to HIV or therapeutic regimens for cancer.

These cases often involve drugs or other therapies that severely suppress the patients' immune systems, making them prey for the bacterial- and viral-infested environments in which they live.

Hospital visitors and workers who leave after their shifts carry new diseases that defeat various known antibiotics.

Existing antibiotics are overwhelmed by the rapidity with which these infections spread, through the innate intelligence of mutating organisms. The problem is of enormous proportions and is becoming even more daunting.

Hospitals must be forced to segregate immune-compromised patients, such as those receiving chemotherapy or radiation, or who have diseases that attack the immune system, such as HIV. MRSA—methicillin-resistant staphylococcus aureas—is a worldwide problem.

I am not being discriminatory—far from it. I have had many friends and acquaintances, bisexual and gay, who have died from HIV-AIDS. They, like any patients, deserve great patient care but simply cannot be mixed with the general hospital population. It has proven to be a recipe for disaster. I contend that the MRSA epidemic—it is an epidemic—can be traced to the commingling high-risk patients with the general population.

Unless such patients are isolated in special sections of the hospital, with dedicated heating, ventilation and air-conditioning systems, no amount of cleanliness or care on the part of hospital workers will stop the deadly march of MRSA.

Unless such isolation is mandated by law, expect hospitals to remain perhaps the most dangerous places on earth.

The majority of hospitals in the United States are owned by enormously powerful chains whose identities can probably be counted on the fingers of two hands.

The same consolidation trend can be seen in the insurance

industry, where ownership has been reduced to a few groups who either compete or often cooperate, cross marketing their various products and services.

Their profitability is astounding while the price at the premium pump grows, becoming a daily and visible reality to every American.

These are trusts and they must be busted. Failure to do so will assure the financial slavery of the populace.

Formularies (medications an insurance company will pay for) often challenge doctors and patients by excluding certain drugs, even for which there are no generic equivalents.

Though some drug companies provide support programs, their impact is modest when considering the vast profits of the pharmaceutical industry.

The raging battle—that somehow these same medications can be purchased from other countries at a fraction of the cost—is fought by the lobbying interests in Washington. The lobbyists are on the doorstep of every Congressperson and Senator, daily, ensuring that their interests are protected. These same lobbyists often hire law firms to write the very legislation that they wish to see enacted.

Prices must be normalized worldwide and this must be mandated by law.

Only doctors and patients can choose medications. If this power is not given back to the patient/doctor relationship, patients will be under-treated and mistreated. Expensive medications will affordable only by the wealthy.

Those unable to pay will die and/or suffer—it's that simple
.
All Blue Cross and Blue Shield companies in the United States belong to a common association headquartered in Washington: The Blue Cross/Blue Shield Association.
This organization bonds the disparately owned and operated

Blues into a holistic entity that shares ideas, programs, procedures and information.

The information they share transcends any HIPPA privacy laws and exposes every patient to having his or her personal information shared with every insurance company and government agency.

The participating Blues keep and share their data across company lines and use such information as they see fit, with impunity. They also sell access to their database to any other insurance company or class of organizations exempted in the HIPPA legislation passed under President Clinton.

In other words, the HIPPA law does not apply equally to all persons in the United States. While one may call the hospital to inquire about the medical condition or status of an adult child and will be denied such information, absent consent from that family member, the insurance machine is sucking it into their databases and selling that same information about an individual to whomever qualifies for exemption.

Amazingly, HIPPA guards information about a given patient from one doctor to the next, absent specific permission by that patient to disclose it. Those confronting this brick wall will gain no comfort from knowing that exempted organizations can access such personal information for a fee or through participation in a subscription database. While the rest of the world kowtows to the gods of HIPPA, insurers, governments etc. merely need to "log on."

The databases that insurers sell also track doctors. Doctors who rebel at the autocratic machinations of the insurance companies that largely dictate care decisions to physicians can find themselves "blacklisted" for life.

Once ejected from an insurance plan, with or without cause or due process, a doctor will most likely never work again in his or her chosen profession.

These databases—the sale and distribution of any information other than completely sanitized data—must be stopped, with severe criminal and civil penalties for failure to comply.

Congress must also reverse the HIPPA immune protections, which the insurance cartel bought for itself when HIPPA law was written (by the cartel) and enacted. The HIPPA privacy laws are an insult to the public. The protections afforded the medical industry are a brazen example of the cartel doing its best to get away with murder.

If these databases are allowed to continue to infect our society, every person in the country risks being blackballed or—by denial of care and manipulation of the system—killed.

A new kind of Grand Jury System must be established and put in the hands of the citizenry. These community-based Grand Juries should determine the merits of cases that should go to through the legal process. Of course, appeal mechanisms need to be put in place.

If there is criminal intent along with civil culpability, cases should be referred to the local District Attorney or, where appropriate, the U.S. Attorney.

These law-enforcement officials should be required to evaluate the cases and will be required to publicly disclose the basis for NOT pursuing a referred case. Appeals mechanisms should also be available.

If a matter is Civil, a special court should be established by the States and a lawyer, paid by the community, assigned to represent those who cannot afford one. With due respect to Public Defenders, whom I greatly admire, I am talking about retaining law firms that have the same skills and experience the cartel's lawyers bring to the table.

Only after we have equal access to the law will we stand any chance of righting our sinking ship.

All caps on liabilities should be removed. They are

unconstitutional and deprive the population equal protection under law.

Instead of making wrongdoers more vulnerable for their errors—I am talking about the insurance cartel—the trend has been to protect them by imposing financial shields to deflect responsibility. This must be stopped.

A little-remembered concept in American jurisprudence should be dusted off and polished for daily use: Citizen's Arrest. I am talking about having every citizen realize that he or she is, in fact, a legal deputy.

Check your local rules. Use them! If you don't feel bold enough to go to your insurance company to arrest their president, call the D.A. and the local police and swear out a complaint!

Because the local police are likely more interested in parking-meter violations and DAs are notoriously lazy and often corrupt, set up a community website and post details of the crime and what happens to your case. Keep it in the public eye and the roaches will eventually, God willing, run for darkness.

Throttle Back Medical Outsourcing/Tourism

As for medical outsourcing, AKA Medical Tourism, my counsel to the Senate Sub Committee on Healthcare states what I believe needs to be done in the interests of worldwide patient safety and quality of care.

I concede that free-market conditions, while they continue to apply to healthcare, will continue to expand medical outsourcing. But certain restrictions and safety measures can and should be adopted.

If it were within my power, I would restrict private insurance companies from paying overseas facilities that do not participate in the treaties I described to the Senate Sub Committee. This applies, as well, to Medicare reimbursement payable to overseas facilities by the U.S. government.

(See Appendix #13 for Specific Details Regarding Regulation of Medical Outsourcing/Tourism)

Some Personal Projections about Public Policy

I have developed an intuition by plunging myself into the congressional medico-industrial complex. My sense of what will work tends towards simplification, not towards the mind-boggling complications being entertained on this eve of healthcare reformation, summer 2009.

The lawyers who have crafted new government and industry involvement have fabricated ruses. They only portend that the fat cats get fatter and the sick get sicker, and never the twain shall meet.

The astronomical monies being considered for spending by the administration, for whatever the new policies are supposed to provide, are a folly, a joke at public expense. These dollars will go not to patient care but to the care and feeding of the cartel.

Just as World War II would have ended rapidly had someone put a bullet in the brain of Uncle Adolph, the swamp we are slogging through would be cleared, overnight, if the bastards from the American Medical Money Machine were thrown out.

Considering that no one in the permanent campaign business appears willing to allow that, what happens if they fail and the cartel wins? Who will pay for their next campaign? Only by publicly financed campaigns can Washington and the States be rid of the scourge of special interests. The devastation of healthcare in the U.S. illustrates no better example.

This crap must stop. They want to make it a super-complex issue. It isn't.

One Executive Order and the bums are through. Executive Orders have toppled major corporations, taken ownership in auto companies, banks and insurance companies (sadly, not in health insurance).

President Obama, wake up and smell the coffee. The Players you are fixing to reward are guys and gals you should be putting out of business—and in jail.

The following ought to be seriously considered:

(1) Catastrophic coverage: mandatory; Please remember that having healthcare insurance is NOT equivalent to having medical care! Healthcare insurance is measured by the healthcare industry in "billing events", doctors and patients measure medical care in terms of positive and realistic outcomes. They are entirely different animals yet are nearly always confused as being the same. They are NOT.

(2) Federal programs for the under-privileged, not for those who can afford to pay.

(3) Strict criminal penalties for fraud.

(4) Public needs to rely on personal responsibility and more self- education; don't run to the doctor when you can treat yourself; loosen regulations on prescription drugs; medications like antibiotics should be made available without prescription.

(5) Stop "Wars on Drugs"—a stupid, gigantic waste of money; legalize drugs and finance medical reformation.

(6) Heroic care at the end of life must be eliminated; if a family feels so inclined, it's on them; we must back-off from the killing expenses incurred in the last few days of life; I am as sorry for me as I am for you, but no one gets out of here alive; when the ticket is ready to be punched, punch it and don't leave the living to die an unsustainable financial death; we are the only country in the world with the obsession to hold on at all costs.

(7) Medicine is a service to be accessed when needed; you only get fixed if you need to get fixed;

(8) Basic services are provided by the government, the rest of (the people pay for insurance or free market, but not a free market controlled by criminals posing as honest business people.

(9) The cost of private-sector insurance coverage will rise to offset inevitable losses in Federal programs; the cartel is simply not going to abandon its monstrous greed—it will suck up money wherever it can find it, and you and I will pay more for less.

(10) Class distinction will become more polarized and crystallized—the well-heeled will be, well, healed and the rest will not.

(11) Offshore care will become more enticing for the wealthy but not in Third World places like Thailand; Germany, Switzerland and France will cater to wealthy Americans; people who bother to check will come to the same conclusion about a glamorous dump like Bumrungrad: this stinks and if you die, tough.

(12) Post-foreign-care follow-up will become a major issue and problem; when things go wrong, as the Australians have discovered, a medically-outsourced patient will be left hanging out to dry.

(13) Employers will restructure work weeks to under 30 hours to avoid mandatory participation for full-time workers.

(14) Greater numbers of the underemployed or chronically unemployed will arise as employers find every way possible to evade Federally-imposed programs.

(15) Chaos and confusion will be abundant; trying to figure out these programs will cause massive congestion and frustration.

(16) As databases track everyone in every way, emergency rooms will be places where nurses and doctors will be encouraged by law- enforcement officials to call the cops

if they find an outstanding warrant, missed child-support payment, delinquent tax bill or any other traceable infringement.

(17) Enlarged police forces and prisoner-confinement facilities will be inevitable; with increased accuracy and holistic databases, the number of people falling into the legal and penal system will dramatically increase, placing a burden on them all.

(18) Employers will become unpaid, de facto government agencies.

(19) Increased identity theft; as a result, many people will not want to be identified, using chat-room aliases, sometimes registering for services under a dozen different names.

(20) Denial of claims, since insurance companies will have access to all data and will pick off the weakest and most vulnerable.

(21) Recourse for problems will involve maneuvering a messy maze; few will dare or be able to afford the time and expense;

(22) A new career classification will arise: armies of statisticians and actuaries.

(23) Society will suffer from increasing malaise that springs from the growing reality of helpless and frustration; all but the strong will be tortured by the systems contemplated; the life of one will become more valuable than another: this stuff foments revolution.

(24) Demoralizing an entire society—a successful person's life is more important and therefore receives better care—one person's life is more valuable than another.

(25) Higher morbidity and mortality rates will arise from statistically managed care.

I hope that community health-education programs will arise to help people help themselves. The tribe and the family will have a real opportunity to resurge. This is how it has been throughout history: a way that our stratified, specialized and fractionalized society has forgotten. I think it's time to remember the foundation embedded in our historical roots.

We are tribal creatures who for eons cared for their own.

The Internet provides a fantastic basis for information, treatment, triage and support. New businesses, I believe, will spring up where government efforts, dominated by cartel interests, will simply become so obnoxious and odious that people will seek higher ground.

Without replacing healthcare into the hands of doctors and patients, the U.S. healthcare system is doomed. Corporate and government-dictated medicine must be dissolved.

The doctor knows best.

Twenty ~ Eulogy

Josh at nine, dreaming of an acting career.
His great sense of humor came through as Grouch Marx.

Josh in 2005.

Josh in Ghana, West Africa.
He traveled independently,
volunteering at orphanages.
He had a particular tenderness
with young children.

This is the text of the Eulogy read at ceremonies held for Josh in New York and San Francisco.

People who had not yet heard of his passing asked me, "Where is Josh?" I respond:

> ➤ He is everywhere
> ➤ And anywhere
> ➤ He is wherever you think he is
> ➤ He is where you think he is not
> ➤ He is here all of the time
> ➤ He is here none of the time
> ➤ But he is and will always be here: In my heart of hearts.

Josh is laughing in his special abandoned way. Josh loved the absurd.

On February 23, 2006, in Bangkok, Thailand, Josh went to sleep in Bumrungrad Hospital. He was being treated for an infection and loss of feeling in his right leg. He had been in the hospital for about ten days and was shortly to be discharged for outpatient treatment.

For reasons completely unrelated to his leg, Josh was discovered by the nursing staff at about 6:00 AM of the morning of 24 February. His heart was in ventricular tachycardia, an uncontrolled arrhythmia. This is what the hospital officials reported.

The hospital, one of the most publicized in South East Asia and accredited by the same agency that certifies hospitals in this country, had made a series of terrible blunders, the last of which appears to have involved mixing multiple medications known never to be combined. This deadly cocktail stopped his heart at 6:00 AM.

When attempts failed to revive him, Josh passed on into the loving hands of the universe.

Josh is now continuing his journey into the Pure Land and into a happy rebirth. He was ordained as a Buddhist Priest/Monk at Thamkrabok Monastery in Central Thailand. His ordained name is Pra Tatsawuttoe, or Teacher.

Teacher! How did the monks come to name him teacher?

We are here to pay homage to Pra Tatsawuttoe, Joshua, a being who, in life and death, continues to touch the hearts of so many. His passing has set in motion a series of profound teachings.

I was there when he l flew out of his mother, the first to gaze on his face. I thought that this beginning and the life that followed, with its many twists and turns, was the life of someone I fully believed I knew and understood.

This was not a simple matter in Josh's case, because of his brilliance, his mercurial interests, his willfulness and his complexities.

What I have come to realize is that I had little idea who Josh, Pra Tatsawuttoe, was.

I came to realize that the all-powerful forces of karma relegated my participation in his life to a small walk-on role, with no more than a line or two to recite in the play of his life.

We think we know who someone else is. Do we?

While walking up 6th Ave in New York three years ago I heard a voice call out to me: "Jim!" I turned 360-degrees but could see no one I knew. Then a man appeared, dressed in a funky baseball cap and sweats. That man was Gen Togden, my Buddhist teacher and friend.

It was the first time I had ever seen him without his robes. Gen is a man with the smile of a pixie and the compassion of Buddha.

I considered Gen to be a Bodhisattva (a living enlightened being) exercising his profound compassion for all through his supernatural abilities to help others find themselves. I considered him then—and still do—a holy being. Now, here he was on the sidewalk wearing a baseball cap and running shoes.

At that moment, I was struck by the high likelihood that no one else on that teaming street knew that they were in the presence of such a highly evolved being. He looked just like any another guy walking down the street.

On that day, if my consciousness had been more highly evolved, I might have been able to recognize perhaps a dozen more Bodhisattvas on my way to the subway.

But who would they be? The man with one leg and a kitten with an outstretched arm and a cup, a well-dressed executive going about something important, the bus driver who nearly ran me over?

The Buddha taught to regard everyone as a Buddha in one state of realization or another; everyone is capable of being awakened. Gen Togden took Josh, during some very dark hours, under his wing, setting up a place for Pra Tatsawuttoe to live with him in New York in his personal quarters.

As I sat in the rear of the temple in Thailand in which one hundred Buddhist monks chanted for two nights just prior to Josh's cremation, I was struck with amazement.

What had the monks known about Josh that I did not?

His tragic passing, at an age where his potential in this lifetime will forever remain unknown, has turned out to be the deliverer of the most overwhelming and profound teaching I have ever received.

I miss him terribly for the insane shticks we shared.

Josh was amazingly sweet, like Tupelo Honey—sweetest of all honeys.

You only needed to have glimpsed him for a second, to see his profound sweetness particularly with children and animals. He was a special and delicate being.

Josh graduated from the famed New York Institute for Natural Cookery, a full-fledged Vegan chef. He worked in soup kitchens, feeding the hungry and needy, when he himself was broke, down and out.

He detested political liars and charlatans. He could not stay away from political protest like The New York Republican convention, which landed him in jail, along with 1,500 others including AP photographers and reporters. He spent twenty-four hours of his incarceration on the floor of a pier on the Hudson used for housing buses, sitting in gobs of grease, oil and diesel fuel without food, water or legal representation.

I begged him not to do it but my voice was just a whisper in the distance. Pra Tatsawuttoe listened only to the music he heard in rustlings of his universal wind.

Josh was phenomenally brilliant, able to read and comprehend books, photographically, at unimaginable speed.

His tastes in music ran from Gangster Rap to Mozart, from Jungle, Rave to Les Miserables, from Bob Marley to Chopin.

His dancing was organic and fluid. He loved to dance. His was a whirling Dervish!

This was not an ordinary being who passed through town. This was a teacher.

Pra Tatsawuttoe was teaching that grasping too tight is like trying to chase and capture your own shadow; that evil is wrong; that delusions need to be dispelled; that we have a choice between pure wisdom and indulgence in pure illusion.

He taught that suffering is all around and that we have a responsibility to do whatever we can to remove the pain of others.

He believed that greed and self-absorption or self-cherishing is the root of all of our human problems.

His lessons: do something important with your life; take away the suffering of those who suffer, absorb it into your being so that they might be free of anger and fear.

This is the legacy of my son, Pra Tatsawuttoe.

Pra Tatsawuttoe had, from an early age, difficulties with eye-hand coordination. This led Josh to be a loner at school, often sitting out ball games that required close eye-hand coordination. This was disturbing but there was nothing we could do about it. The taunts of his classmates were heartbreaking.

Little did we realize, then, that Josh would become an expert on skis.

A few weeks before his passing, not having skied for a while, he went down double diamond slopes covered with moguls as high as hills, laughing hysterically, skiing backwards and, in the same kind of flash in which he was born, Pra Tatsawuttoe disappeared down the mountain with the sound of his voice tapering into infinity.

This is how I will remember Pra Tatsawuttoe, my little Joshua, my son, my friend, my teacher. Please remember him in your own way, but remember him.

Upon entering the chilling morgue of Bangkok, I stooped down to whisper in his ear, the mantra of Avolokitishvara. This is the mantra of pure compassion. Om mane peme hom.

Of the songs we sing in this lifetime, some are happy, some are sad, some harmonic, some grating, some stay in our minds, the lyrics always remain clear but some muddy with time.

The sweetest song of my life is the song of the pure and simple love of a father for his son. Pra Tatsawuttoe, Joshua's song is one that I will sing forever.

Imagine Josh filling his dreams for peace.

Picture his wish for us all—to find our on ways to happiness.

Afterwards ~ Remembering History and Keeping Promises

We make war with seeming impunity. We have evolved into near-complete destruction of the separation of powers contemplated by the Founding Fathers. We have allowed an Imperial Presidency to evolve when, in fact, it was the very thing we had fought, as embodied in British Imperial domination and unfair taxation.

Those four million people, the first Americans who put their necks on the block, knew that if the Revolution did not succeed, the leaders of that audacious revolt would have been executed en masse. It did work, but in less than three hundred years, we appear to have become the very thing we sought to escape.

Now, the consequences of this transformation are being visited on each of us in very personal ways. The health of you, your family and friends are at stake.

It should never be forgotten: At one time or another, we are all patients.

Whether we are currently robust and healthy, or sick and in need, we will all eventually require the care of what was once the world's most vaunted and respected profession.

I am not bound by abstract forces to stand idly by and watch terrible crimes being visited by unbridled corporate interests on our society. Neither are you.

My efforts are dedicated to the memory of my son and for the compassion that I have for the people of this great land and the world. As a student, I learned about a great country with a remarkable governmental and societal system. The reality of what I have found since the mid-1960s has been horribly different from what I studied as a hopeful kid in school.

Thomas Paine, one of the most prolific visionaries of the American Revolution, said that democracy is an awesome responsibility in which the citizenry can never give up on its diligence, lest its partnership with those vested to represent the people would grow quickly out of balance and runaway into the kind of imperial mess in which we are now living.

Putting aside the issues of war and peace, our responsibilities to be world citizens and co-participants, rather than hegemonic dictators to a world who now largely reviles us, let us simply focus on what happens to a society that does not care for its sick.

Please join me in being another who Does Not Walk Away! We can rescue and arrest the rapid decline of health care in America.

To take meaningful and deliberate steps to improve our health care, we must understand that evil forces are at play and are especially concentrated in the United States of America. Understanding what is really happening is the first step in making informed decisions about what to do next.

It is a matter of life and death.

Supplement A ~ User's Guide to Medical Tourism

The following list has been on line at www.bumrungraddeath.com for nearly three years. It has been copied and used in numerous articles written by others around the world. I'm glad.

Though the wording is specific to Bumrungrad and Thailand, the reader can easily substitute the name of the hospital and the country being investigated.

The recommendations are, in a sense, tongue-in-cheek. Without the authority of the countries or their institutions, a patient is at the mercy of whatever they may wish to say. Forget the truth. Yet the exercise of asking these questions may help potential patients understand what they are up against.

Most likely, with some exceptions, the questioner will be stonewalled, lied to and provided with fluff instead of substance.

Perhaps, if enough people put these kinds of hardball questions to the foreign doctors and institutions, they will eventually come to their senses. We doubt it, however, and feel that mandatory insurance and international treaties are required to protect the safety of the patient.

The kind of response to these kinds of questions will clearly demonstrate whether the institution under consideration is dealing in good faith.

Should they balk or resist, run, don't walk, in the opposite direction.

What to Ask For

(1) Make sure that you are accompanied by a relative or friend for your entire stay; preferably, that friend should

have medical knowledge and should monitor every test and medication administered; if there is any doubt about anything, your primary-care physician or other medical advisor at home should be called immediately.

(2) Be aware that doctors in foreign hospitals often receive a twenty percent kickback on the price of all medications they prescribe; this, naturally, encourages them to over-prescribe, since they receive more money for doing so.

(3) Ask for the credentials of treating physicians and be sure that they are verified with your Embassy or another independent source.

(4) Make sure that your health care insurance contains a rider to cover injury or malpractice from treatment abroad; I am unaware of any such policy, but the insurance market might respond if public demands are made.

(5) Ask to see evidence of licenses of all personnel to be attending the patient, including personnel in pharmacies.

(6) Ask for full disclosure on how many procedures of various kinds have been performed at the institution in questions, particularly the procedure you intend to have performed, and the complication rate: how many have they done, at what average cost and what was the rate of complications, morbidity and mortality.

(7) Ask to see a history of hospital-acquired infections and the number of patients affected.

(8) Ask for a history of pharmacy errors resulting in complications, injury or death.

(9) Find out what deaths occurring in the five years prior to your visit were caused by undetermined reasons.

(10) Research deaths or injuries that resulted in police reports

and investigations—also ask for the outcomes for each case.

(11) Research the number of police investigations for mishaps at their facilities—ask for specifics.

(12) Ask about the percentage of foreign patients who have returned for second or third procedures.

(13) Get a list of all doctors who are U.S. Board Certified or Certified in other countries, along with the evidence of that certification.

(14) Demand disclosure of the details of the hospital insurance covering malpractice and negligence; ask for details of their policy, limits and requirements for adjudication.

(15) Ask for a list of laws regarding medical malpractice and negligence laws currently in force in the country where the patient is considering treatment.

(16) Ask to see the list of all disciplinary or corrective actions required your prospective hospital by the Joint Commission for Hospital Accreditation or local regulatory authorities within the last five years; request, also, the results and copies of the correspondence, which confirms that corrective measures were, in fact, completed.

Supplement B ~ Visiting Us Online

My small team launched Josh's site, www.bumrungraddeath.com in May 2006. Since then, we have worked diligently to provide the interested public with a near-complete record of all events and investigations regarding the death of my son. I felt that considering how much I was learning, transparency and easy access to all of the information was vital. I still feel that way now.

Visitors to Josh's site can read current news and updates about the case, all of Josh's forensic records, our correspondence with the Joint Commission and Bumrungrad Hospital and much more.

We have a site for the book:

www.theamericanmedicalmoneymachine.com. As word spreads, we hope that this site will become a popular forum and patient exchange for topics relating to Medical Tourism and healthcare. A supplemental site also should be consulted, www.bumrungraddeath.com

We encourage comments, shared thoughts and suggestions about what's happening with healthcare in the reader's neighborhood.

Supplement C ~ In Training

To prepare for the writing of this book I have:

- Read well over four hundred400 books;
- Received and absorbed thousands of daily news feeds;
- Read existing and proposed legislation;
- Visited and digested hundreds of websites;
- Spoken with Pulitzer prize-winning investigative journalists;
- Made at least ten trips to Thailand;
- Met with dozens of Thai and U.S. officials;
- Consulted with the U.S. Senate Finance Committee and Sub Committee on Healthcare;
- Contacted more than 75 of America's most renowned trial lawyers;
- Worked with my attorneys in Thailand;
- Discussed Josh's case with International Police (INTERPOL), the Australian Police, the Thai Police, the Federal Bureau of Investigation (FBI) and the Central Intelligence Agency (CIA);
- Conferred with the U.S. Ambassador to Thailand;
- Been interviewed by European Public Television for a documentary on Medical Tourism, which aired throughout Europe in the summer of 2008;
- Confronted the Joint Commission;
- Copiously researched everything even remotely relating to healthcare in the U.S. and elsewhere in the world;
- Been approached in Thailand by professional assassins proposing to "fix" my problem.

For more than three years, my life has been consumed with trying to make sense about what happened to Josh and to a world seemingly gone mad.

For at least a year after Josh died, I was filled with anger and profound sadness.

I saw Josh born; I closed the door on his funeral pyre.

At times the weight has been so heavy, the nights so long and littered with horrific dreams that it has been close to unendurable.

During the second and third years, my thinking and writing slowly began to crystallize. So many thoughts filled my waking and sleeping hours, a cacophony that sometimes threatened to overwhelm my senses. I was daunted as to how I could make sense of all of this.

How could I tell two stories at once without confusing the reader, and myself? Indeed, the book eventually embodied the story of Josh and the story of a society—a monumental challenge, to say the least.

I learned that writing such a work involves finding a voice. Finding this voice has been a difficult and lengthy process.

I also had to elevate my mind above my feelings, to get enough altitude above the excruciating and continual pain to be able to speak without crying. This has not been easy. If one person reads and understands what is contained in these pages, it will have been worth it.

I received many letters of support. I am grateful for all of them. They helped me to understand that there were others who were paying attention—in several cases, very careful attention.

The following letter, from a gentleman in the United Kingdom, is representative and perhaps the most salient, of all I received. This bolstered my spirits and motivation to attack this work with passion and, I trust, clarity of mind:

Dear Mr. Goldberg,

Sir, first and foremost may I convey my condolences to you and your family for the terrible loss you have experienced in Joshua's needless passing away in the hands of a hospital that is less than forthcoming with the facts let alone candid with the truth.

I know your pain well having recently lost my father in less than satisfactory circumstances in a hospital in the UK. Suffice to say, I truly admire the laudable efforts you are going to, your stoic perseverance and your dogged tenacity in ensuring justice is obtained in Joshua's name and in Joshua's memory.

You not only obtain some sort of justice for Joshua but your battle also strikes a blow for all those less able to fight the large corporate system that ensures "secretive hospital / insurance conglomerates" hide behind giant legal companies with huge war chests to defeat the average member of the public whose hearts are already broken and whose coffers won't run to the levels required to even bringing the smallest of claims.

You are doing Joshua proud in even attempting to take on the mite of the hospital with their clandestine modus-operandi and that in itself is enough in many respects. But the fact that you might also actually make the hospital change their modus-operandi, suspend or even dismiss the negligent medical offenders as well as compensate you in the name of Joshua is wonderful justice for the little guys of this world. You are the modern day David and I wish you every success in slaying Goliath.

Having read every document on your web site tonight, I am appalled at the hospital's stance on all matters therein. The rapid deterioration of Dr. Morley's communication upon realizing you were not going to be dissuaded from discovering the truth neither bamboozled by his empty, baseless technical poppycock is horrifying. It's a real eye-opener as to how quickly these grey men conveniently hide behind the vastness of their organization and quite literally ensure the paper trail or lack thereof smite the enquiring family members down at the first sign of difficulty or indifference.

The lack of compassion, decorum or any semblance of common decency let alone basic manners emanating from the Bumrungrad Hospital is shocking, indeed it beggars belief.

I take my hat off to you sir and if I were in a position to offer any services I would happily do so. My area of expertise is close protection security in hostile regions of the world. So not particularly useful to you in your present predicament. But if there is anything I can do to assist you and your efforts in more practical terms, on any level, please advise me accordingly and I will endeavor to help.

Yours in sympathy and admiration,
TR, Great Britain

I knew that I had to get to an understanding, a complete understanding, for my sake and sanity and in honor of my only son.

The website I posted with the help of a few kind souls only three months after Josh was killed has drawn millions of visitors from around the world. An outpouring of comments and compassion has been expressed from around the planet, along with terrible insults and harangues.

I have also been contacted by dozens of others who have been the victim of bad doings at Bumrungrad. Informants and spies have come forth, a literal gushing of expression of all sorts from everywhere imaginable.

In summer 2009, I went to search the Internet and discovered that Josh's story is well known throughout the world and especially in Thailand. His case has been cited in dozens of articles, blogs, discussion groups, books, newsletters and the like. Try a Google search to see the incredible number of writings and opinions relating to Josh that have spread to distant places.

This grassroots growth has been very instructive; I planted seeds about three years ago, not knowing what would grow. I had one primary purpose: to bring light on everything relating to Josh's death. What I found in my ensuing worldwide investigation was astonishing. I wanted total transparency; where I had faced blocks and darkness, I wanted a living record, illuminating everything.

I have been gratified to see my hopes spring into a groundswell covering the world. I am sure that Josh is smiling. I am smiling, too, through my tears.

Waiting a lifetime, for this moment.

BIBLIOGRAPHY

o   The Buying of Congress, Lewis, Charles, Avon Books (1998), ISBN 0-380-87596-3

o   A Wrongful Death, Bing, Leon, Villard (1997), ISBN 0-679-44841-1

o   Life Sciences and Health Changes, Raymond, Susan (Ed.), Academy of Sciences (1998), ISBN 1-57331-148-0

o   To Do No Harm, Marath, Julianne M. and Turnbull, Joanne E., Jossey-Bass (2005), ISBN 0-7879-6770-X

o   Measuring Public Safety, Newhouse, Robin and Poe, Stepahnie, Jones and Bartlett Publishers (2005), ISBN 0-7637-2441-1

o   Medical Errors and Medical Narcissism, Banja, John, James and Bartlett (2005), ISBN 0-7673-8361-7

o   Wall of silence, Gibson, Rosemary and Singh, Janardan Prasad, Lifeline Press (2003), ISBN 0-89526-112-X

o   America's Tunnel Vision, Watson, Michael Towns, Horatio Press (2006), ISBN 0-9776203-5-2

o   Champions of Health Care Quality, Brauer, Charles, Greenwich Pub. Group (2001), ISBN 0-944641-45-8

o   Protect Yourself in the Hospital, Sharon, Thomas A., R.N., McGraw-Hill (2003), ISBN 0-07-141784-2

o   The Giant White Lie, Bogdanich, Walt, Simon and Shuster (1991), ISBN 0-671-68452-3

o   How to Get Out of the Hospital Alive, Blau, Sheldon P., M.D. and Shimberg, Elaine Fantle, MacMillian (1998), ISBN 0-02-862363-o

o   Code Green, Weinberg, Dana Beth, Cornell University Press (2003), ISBN 0-8014-3980-9 (cloth), 8014-8919-9 (pbk)

o   The Changing Federal Role in U.S. Health Care, Kronenfeld, Jeannie Jacobs, Praeger Press (1997), ISBN 0-275-95023-9, 0-275-94024-7 (pbk)

o   Hospital Survival Guide, Sherer, David, M.D., Claren

books (2003), ISBN 0-9723736-0-8
o   Rethinking Health Care Policy, Hackey, Robert B., Georgetown University Press (1998), ISBN 0-87840-668-9 (cloth), 0-87840-669-7 (pbk)
o   Betrayal of Trust, Garrett, Laurie, Hyperion Books (2001), ISBN 9780786884407
o   The Long Emergency, Kunstle, James Howard, Atlantic Monthly Press (2005), ISBN 0-87113-888-3
o   108 Days, Lisa Lindell, Lisa, March 5 Press (2005), ISBN 0-97673-0-9
o   License to Steal, Sparrow, Malcolm K., Westview Press (2000), ISBN 0-8133-6810-3
o   Money Driven Medicine, Mahar, Maggie, Collins (2006), ISBN 13-978.0-06-076533-0, 10.0-06-076533-X
o   Internal Bleeding, Wachter, Robert M., M.D. and Shojanin, Kaveh G., M.D., Rugged Land (2004), # 357910864 (the only number, no ISBN)
o   Nursing Against All Odds, Gordon, Suzanne, ILR Press (2005), l.c.d. # 2004028248
o   Rethinking Health Care Policy, The New Politics of State Regulation, Hackey, Robert B., Georgetown University Press
o   Nursing Against the Odds, How Healthcare Cost Cutting, Media Sterotypes, and Medical Hubris Undermine Nurses and Patient Care, Gordon, Suzanne, Cornell University Press
o   License to Steal, How Fraud Bleeds America's Health Care System, Sparrow, Malcolm, Westview Press
o   Internal Bleeding, The Truth Behind America's Terrifying Epidemic of Medical Mistakes, Wachter and Shopjania, Rugged Land Press
o   Wall of Silence, The Untold Story of The Medical Mistakes That Kill and Injure Millions of Americans, Gibson and Singh, Lifeline Press.
o   Money Driven Medicine, The Real Reason Health Care Costs So Much, Mahar, Collins
o   Medical Errors and Medical Narcissism, Jones and Bartlett, Banja
o   A Wrongful Death, One Child's Fatal Encounter with

Public Health and Private Greed, Bing, Leon, Villard

o   The Changing Federal Role in US Health Care Policy, Kronenfeld, Praeger

o   License to Steal, Why Fraud Plagues America's Health Care System, Sparrow Westview.

o   The History of National Medical Enterprises and the Investor-Owned Hospital Industry, Eamer.

o   The Newcomen Society of the United States

o   Reference to Top-Quality, Low-Cost Dental, Cosmetic, Medical Care & Surgery Overseas. Sunrise River Press, (2008)

o   For big surgery, Delhi is dealing, Goering, Laura, The Chicago Tribune, March 28, 2008

o   The Rise of Medical Tourism, Lagace, Martha, Harvard Business School Working Knowledge, December 17, 2007 (retrieved July 1, 2008).

o   Americans look abroad to save on healthcare: Medical tourism could jump tenfold in next decade, Johnson, Linda A, The San Francisco Chronicle, August 3, 2008

o   The Private Cost of Public Queues in 2005, Fraser Institute.

o   Wait times shorter for some medical procedures, Canwest News Service.

o   Medical Tourism growing worldwide, Hutchinson, Becca, UDaily, July 25, 2005 (retrieved September 5, 2006)

o   Medical tourism: Need Surgery, will travel, CBC News Online, June 18, 2004, (retrieved September 5, 2006)

o   Medical tourism and reproductive outsourcing: the dawning of a new paradigm for healthcare, Jones, C.A. and Keith, L.G., Int J. Fertil Womens Med (2006) 51:251-255

o   Ethical and legal conundrums of post-modern procreation, Jones, C., Int. Journal of Gynecology & Obstetrics, Dec 4, 2007

o   Medical Tourism Industry Certifications and Information.

o   Medical Tourism Magazine, Medical Tourism Association, February 2008

o   INDIA: accreditation a must, International Medical Travel Journal

o   World Hospital Monitor.

o   SOFIHA—Welcome to SOFIHA.
o   Healthcare Tourism International
o   United Kingdom Accreditation Form
o   Medical Tourism Association
o   TB Often Misdiagnosed, American Lung Association of Illinois.
o   Incision Care, American Academy of Family Physicians, July, 2005 (retrieved September 18, 2006).
o   World Alliance for Patient Safety.
o   Medical Tourism: Ethical Pitfalls of Seeking Health Care Overseas.
o   Medical Protection Society, MPS UK.
o   IFTF's Future Now: the dark side of medical tourism
o   Organ-transplant black market thrives in India
o   Transplants and ethics in San Francisco, The Epoch Times
o   Indian Journal of Medical Ethics.
o   Medical Tourism Creates Thai Doctor Shortage, NPR.
o   Union Disrupts Plan to Send Airling Workers to India for Cheaper Medical Care, The New York Times.
o   Health Matters: The next wave of medical tourists might include you, McGinley, Laura, The Wall Street Journal, February 16, 2008 (retrieved March 13, 2008).
o   Mini-Meds: Limited benefit plans provide cost-effective compromise, Houston Business Journal.
o   Outsourcing the Patients, Einhorn, Bruce, Business Week, March 13, 2008. `Medical Leave, Lindsay, Greg, Fast Company, May 2008, (retrieved October 15, 2008). Welcoming the world's ills, Haaretz, Feb 8, 2008.
o   Medical Tourism Israel.
o   Jordan tops region as medical tourism hub, Jordan Times, September 7, 2008.
o   Medical Tourism Dubai: Healthcare Tourism in Dubai, Medical Tourism in Dubai—Welcome to Recover Discover—We Facilitate Healthcare.
o   Why opt for the Albert Einstein Jewish Hospital?
o   Joint Commission International (JCI) Accredited Organizations. Surgery in Canada Marketed to U.S. patients, Winnipeg Free Press, Dec 6, 2007.
o   Cubas's Medical Success, BBC News, September 10,

2001 (retrieved July 20, 2007).
o   Commentary: A Novel Tourism Concept, Caribbean Net News, August 18, 2007 (retrieved August 18, 2007).
o   Canadian Firms Offer Cuban Healthcare to U.S., Canadian Patients, Miami Herald, October 7, 2007 (retrieved October 31, 2007).
o   Quality and Low Cost of Medical Care Lure Americans to Mexican Doctors, Hilts, Philip J. New York Times, November 23, 1992 (retrieved October 15, 2008).
o   Discount Dentistry South of the Border, Roig-Franzia, Manuel, Washingtonpost.com, June 18, 2007 (retrieved October 15, 2008).
o   California health costs send patients to Mexico facilities, The Boston Globe.
o   URUHEALTH Medical Tourism in Uruguay.
o   Ministry of Tourism and Sport, Uruguay.
o   Ministry of Public Health, Uruguay.
o   MP Personalized Medicine.
o   SEMM, Mautone Hospital.
    More travel abroad for stem-cell therapy.
o   Americans seek stem-cell treatments in China—Cloning and stem cells, MSNBC.com
o   Trent Accreditation Scheme Newsletter, Iss. 6, 2001.
o   Indian Medical Tourism to Touch Rs 9,500 Crore by 2015, The Economic Times, posted on IndianHealthCare.in.
o   Just what the hospital ordered, Nazir, Zeenat, Indian Express, Sept 18, 2006 (retrieved September 29, 2006).
o   Indian medical care goes global, Aljazeera.Net, June 18, 2006, Nov 11, 2006
o   MoT plans to extend MDA scheme to cover JCI and NABH to boost Medical Tourism, travelbizmonitor.com, February 11, 2009
o   India—The Emerging Global Health Destination, Macguire, Suzanne, EzineArticles, (2007), (retrieved September 12, 2007).
o   Hot Destinations for Medical Tourism, CNN.com.
o   Country Eyes Medical Tourism Boom, IMTJ.
o   Medical Tourism Gets Boost, The Korea Times.
o   Yonsei University Health System.
o   Association of Private Hospitals of Malaysia.

o   One Company With an Eye on U.S. Customers, Washington Post.

o   Globe-trotting to cut down on medical costs.

o   International Travel Information, U.S. Department of State.

o   Medical Tourism to get big push, asianjournal.com.

o   Health system attainment and performance in all Member States,

o   ranked by eight measures, estimates for 1997.

o   Singapore Medicine Website.

o   Medical Tourism: Hidden dimensions, Seth, Rabindar, Express Hospitality, June, 2006 (retrieved September 12, 2006).

o   Vacation, Adventure and Surgery?, CBS News: 60 Minutes, September 4, 2005 (retrieved September 12, 2006)

o   Outsourcing your heart, Kher, Unmesh , time.com (retrieved on September 9, 2008)

o   Ailing MP speaks out: Urges all not to spread rumours about his health, Kantipur Report, July 7, 2006 (retrieved September 12, 2006).

o   World –class Health Care in Thailand, Bumrungrad International Hospital.

o   The World Health Organization's ranking of the world's health systems

o   Travel Alert: Thailand, U.S. Department of State

o   Health Tourism and Medical Tourism—Turkey Offers Rejuvenating Medical Tourism Packages.

o   Academic papers

o   The Realties of Human Organ Trade (Mullen).

o   Keeping an Eye on The Global Traffic in Human Organs, (Hughes).

o   Human Trafficking and Organized Crime, (Thurong).

o   The Biotechnology 'Wheel of Fortune': Who Gets, Who Gives and Who Profits, (Davis).

o   The Dilemma over Live Donor Transplantation, (Garwood)

o   Trillion Dollar Scam: Saul William Seidman, MD, FACS (Universal Publishers)

APPENDIX/REFERENCES

Appendix #1

From: Peter Morley (Dr.) Sent: Monday, February 27, 2006 9:32 PM
To: Jim Goldberg
Cc: RM Nurse - Suthatip Tong-Orn; Apichati Sivayathorn (Dr.); Mack Banner;
Haruetaya Prichasuk (Yai)

Subject: Joshua Goldberg

Greetings Jim,

To clarify we actually have the general toxicology screen still in place the test that was not possible here was for arsenic screening.

Also we do keep the serum and to make sure I called the laboratory manager and instructed then to make sure it is kept aside and stored.

The toxicology result takes about 5-7 days and then will need to be interpreted based upon the medicines Joshua was prescribed and taking and this also included the morphine he had been getting and the methadone he had on the last day but we are hoping the screen will allow some assessment on other possible medicine that might be possible.

*I am very happy to arrange for a meeting with you and **Joshua's attending physician whenever you are ready** and the 8th will be okay.. just call me when you are in Bangkok and I can arrange this for you.*

There is no need to involve Mr. Ted Daley from the American

THE AMERICAN APPENDIX

Citizens Services but that's okay too if you prefer or if it's easier. Really all I need is for you to let me know a time that best suits you on the day and then I need to get the doctor's availability etc. Our Chief Medical officer who is also responsible for assisting in such cases would also be available.

My contact details are in my signature block below you can email me direct anytime.

Regards
Dr. Peter K. Morley
M.B., B.S., Dip. Eng., M.P.H.
Medical Director – International

Appendix #2

From: Peter Morley (Dr.) Sent: Wednesday, March 01, 2006 11:55 PM
To: Jim Goldberg
Cc: Apichati Sivayathorn (Dr.); RM Nurse - Suthatip Tong-Orn; Haruetaya Prichasuk (Yai); Pornpimon (RM) Maneenopphol; Mack Banner
Subject: RE: Joshua Goldberg

Greetings Jim,

Our Chief Medical officer and his team have confirmed the arrangement for a meeting on Wednesday 08 Mar 06. The time of 10.00 still needs confirming and may need to be changed to later in the day to ensure the Doctors are free but we will advise you on this once we know their schedules etc.

Please call to re-confirm closer to the day if possible.

We will meet together at my office on the third floor; at the top of the only set of escalators in the Hospital.

Regards
Dr. Peter K. Morley
M.B., B.S., Dip. Eng., M.P.H.
Medical Director – International

335

Appendix #3

Index of Sentinel Problems Reported
by the Joint Commission

> ➤ Issue 42—December 11, 2008: Safely implementing health information and converging technologies Dec 10, 2008.
> ➤ Issue 41—September 24, 2008: Preventing errors relating to commonly used anticoagulants Sep 23, 2008.
> ➤ Issue 40—July 9, 2008: Behaviors that undermine a culture of safety Jul 02, 2008.
> ➤ Issue 39—April 11, 2008: Preventing pediatric medication errors Apr 09, 2008.
> ➤ Issue 38—February 14, 2008: Preventing accidents and injuries in the MRI suite Feb 13, 2008.
> ➤ Issue 37—September 6, 2006: Preventing adverse events caused by emergency electrical power system failures Sep 05, 2006.
> ➤ Issue 36—April 3, 2006: Tubing misconnections—a persistent and potentially deadly occurrence Mar 27, 2006.
> ➤ Issue 35—January 25, 2006: Using medication reconciliation to prevent errors Jan 25, 2006.

Appendix #4

Here is the chronology of events that took place in early 2006 (dates and times adjusted vs. differences between New York and Bangkok):

January 15: My son, Joshua Goldberg, a 23-year old healthy male, travels to Thailand for his ordination as a Buddhist Monk at Thamkrabok Monastery.

February 1-5: Josh travels to Chang Mai to attend a wedding.

February 6: Josh calls me from the Monastery complaining of an abrasion on his foot, swelling in his left leg and pain (the post-mortem exam reveals fang marks, indicating Josh was likely bitten during his sleep by a cobra or krait-type snake, which would explain all his symptoms).

February 8: His condition is worsening: leg swelling increases, lower back pain and loss of feeling and motion in his left leg develop.

February 12: Pain and immobility are worsening; Josh is taken by a private local driver to Bumrungrad Hospital in Bangkok; he spends the night in the Emergency Room; next morning, Josh is admitted to the hospital by instructions of the attending ER physician.

February 12-13: I call the hospital and speak with the physician on the floor to provide specific instructions not to administer opiates or addictive drugs, given Josh's previous history of substance abuse; Josh, committed to his sobriety and to the sacred vows of monks prohibiting narcotic use, also gives these instructions to his doctors (later, my medical investigative team believes Josh was given massive amounts of intravenous morphine and other highly addictive medications).

February 13-24: Over about 12 days, I have frequent telephone conversations with Josh, sometimes twice a day. Josh sounds fine and says the swelling is going down; his mood in general is upbeat; he never sounds drugged or anything but normal.

February 22-23: Josh tells me he is ready to be discharged on or around February 24.

February 24, around 8:30 PM Eastern Standard Time (the morning of February 25 in Bangkok): I get a call from Dr. Peter Morley, Chief of Administration, Director of Medicine and Head of Quality Control for Bumrungrad. He relates that Josh was found "unresponsive" at 6:00 AM (Bangkok Time) on the morning of February 24; he explains that after Code Blue (Code 3) attempts, Josh was pronounced dead at 6:35 AM, Bangkok time on February 24 (in other words, Morley calls me more than 24-hours after what is claimed to be the time of death).

February 22 or 23, Bangkok Time: An anonymous person phones the Royal Thai Police to inform them of Sentinel Events at Bumrungrad involving the death of Joshua Goldberg.

February 25, Bangkok Time: Police dispatch a government doctor to Bumrungrad around 11:00 AM to inspect and photograph Josh's body, taken from his hospital room to the Bumrungrad morgue; his body is clothed in a shirt and walking shorts.

February 25, Bangkok Time: In the early afternoon, Josh is transported to the Forensic Institute for Post Mortem examination.

February 29, Bangkok Time: Our family arrives in Bangkok; Josh is cremated; a recreation ceremony of his ordination as a Buddhist monk is given for our family's benefit; he is enshrined at the Monastery in Central Thailand.

March 8: I visit Bumrungrad Hospital and meet Dr. Morley; my request to meet with the doctors who attended Josh is denied.
March 8: in the afternoon, I retain legal representation in Thailand.

March 10: A copy of Josh's hospital chart is given to me, along with my son's personal effects.

March 15: I retain a forensic pharmacologist and a forensic medical investigator.

March 16 to May 14: An abbreviated but intense cycle of grieving is coupled with my fierce determination to find answers;

May 15: I return to Bangkok with the forensic medical investigator to meet the Thai Coroner.

From March 8 and onward: Dialog begins with Bumrungrad administration and personnel, who refuse to answer 98 percent of all questions; dialog begins with the Joint Commission, who promise to conduct an investigation, but then refuse to answer specific questions; dialog begins with Ms. Maureen Potter, Joint Commission International (What is her title?), and Howard Bressler, Chief Legal Counsel.

Appendix #5

From: Jim Goldberg Sent: Wednesday, April 12, 2006 2:11 AM
To: 'Maureen Potter'; 'Daley, Daniel N'
Subject: Additional Information Requested Regarding Bumrungrad
Dear Maureen,

As per your website, I formally request the following information regarding Bumrungrad International Hospital in Bangkok, Thailand.

I am also, in my capacity as an American Citizen whose son, Joshua Nathaniel Goldberg, also an American Citizen, who died under suspicious circumstances which is now the subject of a self initiated investigation by the Thai Police, that the American Embassy in Bangkok, Attention Mr. Dan Daley, request that the American Embassy demand the provision of this information.

(Mr. Daley, would you kindly contact Ms. Maureen Potter of the Joint Commission for International Hospital Accreditation, and request that the information listed below, which is information provided on the Joint Commission's website, be released to you at once to aide in the investigation of this Sentinel Event.)

The Joint Commission also provides the following information as appropriate to complainants regarding their complaints:

Any determination that the complaint is not related to Joint Commission standards.
If the complaint is related to standards, the course of action to be taken regarding the complaint.

Whether the Joint Commission has decided to take action regarding an organization's accreditation decision following completion of the complaint investigation. If the Joint Commission has decided to take no action, the complainant is to be so advised.

If the Joint Commission has taken action, the complainant is to be advised in conformance with the guidelines for release of complaint information as set forth above.

Any change in an organization's accreditation decision following completion of the complaint investigation.

The official accreditation decision and any subsequent change in this decision or any designation, such as Accreditation Watch.

Complaint information requested by CMS or state agencies in accordance with deemed status or other recognition requirements, including: action taken on the complaint; the standards area(s) in which requirements for improvement were issued as a result of the complaint evaluation; and the status of the case.

Specific information when an organization is assigned a conditional accreditation, preliminary denial of accreditation or accreditation denied decision.

This includes the following: All final requirements for improvement; a statement, if any, from the organization regarding its views on the validity of Joint Commission survey findings; and a copy of the approved plan of correction and the results of the plan of correction follow-up survey.

Notification of upcoming triennial or focused surveys and retrospective dates of other surveys conducted, such as random unannounced, other announced or unannounced surveys for cause.

A copy of the official Accreditation Decision Report for CMS, upon request respecting deemed status determinations, and for state agencies that have entered into specific information-sharing agreements that permit provider-authorized release of such reports to the state agency.

Given that the event involving Joshua Nathaniel Goldberg on 24 February 2006 is now under police investigation in Bangkok and given that there is sufficient evidence already contained in the chart that gross negligence, mismanagement, poly pharmacy errors, irregular Code 3 procedures, apparent falsification of data supplied to the family of the deceased, we ask now that the Commission exercise its right to publish data as described below.

We Stand ready, at this time to prove, by the evidence so far made available by Bumrungrad, that the accusations of malpractice and negligence are meritorious and that through gross inconsistencies in Bumrungrad's own records, the burden of proof that key events were, other than as recorded in the chart and that this burden is now on the shoulders of Bumrungrad Hospital. I am making this request in my capacity as the father of the deceased and will also ask that this information be requested and released to the FDA and to the U.S. Embassy in Bangkok, Thailand at your earliest opportunity.

It is interesting, Maureen, that the Commission has set up a Sentinel Event program but does not require it's international participants to report such events when they occur.

Either you have a Sentinel Event Alert or you don't. Waiting 45 days for an ex post facto report of a suspicious death and the remedy the hospital intends to take to "fix" that problem, is on its face, absurd. How many other people might die during that 45 day period? If your stated mission is to improve safety, how can you have standards which delay or obfuscate critical reporting?

Further, in the case of Bumrungrad, they did indicate to me that they reported this event to the FDA and to Pfizer . . . .but nowhere can I find any evidence of such a report. Did they report it to the local Thai Health Commission or whatever their credential/supervisory organization is called in Thailand? Did they report it to you . . . .subsequent to my own report to you?

I requested, on several occasions that Bumrungrad provide me with copies of these reports which they represented were made to the FDA and Pfizer. None of these requests ever received a response. Can you tell me why?

Maureen, I have copied you on the entire email stream between myself and Dr. Morley . . the questions I have requested answers for are in no way secret. Nor is it a secret that they have not been answered. If they have answered and supplied answers to you, then please kindly forward these on to me for immediate review.

I have re-read your international standards and protocols. What do you do in a case where specific questions are asked, consistent with the Commissions policy and encouragement to do so, and this information is not forthcoming? Don't you consider that to be a gross violation of your standards? What action have you, the Commission taken in this regard? I hereby supply you with the names of several of the doctors involved in my son's case. Also, Bumrungrad has a sheet in the Chart specifically dedicated to the Code 3. This lists the attendance of, from what I can tell, is 5 doctors and 5 nurses. May I ask that you immediately gather the credentials, histories and employment records of all these individuals at your earliest opportunity?

Also, given the severity of this situation, I strongly urge you to request that Bumrungrad suspend these individuals, as I have done several times since 24 Feb 2006, until the investigation is complete. Bumrungrad has refused to respond to my request for this suspension. Perhaps you will be more persuasive. I think you will be completely in agreement, once you understand the egregious. errors which have been made and which we are, at of this writing, prepared to present to the Commission as we intend to present to Bumrungrad, the Thai Police, The Forensic Investigators in Thailand and to Bumrungrad's lawyers. Please advise me as to your efforts.

The names of these individuals are pasted here below and are attached, as a direct copy/scan of the Code 3 note page from the chart provided by Bumrungrad of the 24th of February, concerning the so called resuscitation procedures performed (or not performed) on my son.

The following are names circled on the Code 3 section of Josh's hospital and appear to constitute, at least from the record, all people in attendance at the time of my son's death. The following individuals have been unilaterally barred by hospital authorities from speaking to me.

Dr. Opas
Dr. R. Visissak Suksa-ard
Dr. Wongsawan Wongprasert
Dr. Sira Sooparb

Dr. Sukitti Panpunnung
Dr. Peter Morley
Dr. Apichati Sivayathorn

Please provide a specific date on which I may expect to receive response. Also, kindly tell me, when you are available for a meeting.

Sincerely,

Jim Goldberg
12/06

Appendix #6

Doctor's Basics in Standards of Care

Standards of Care are the actions a reasonable, competent physician would have taken under similar circumstances:

1.   Accurate, timely, complete history, physical examination, laboratory tests and available records review are required of any competent physician.

2.   Appropriate interpretation of findings and basic knowledge of the significance of test results are required of any competent physician.

3.   Performance of only medically necessary test based on the history, physical, examination and preliminary laboratory evaluation are required of any competent physician.

4.   It is ESSENTIAL to monitor serum electrolytes, Calcium, Magnesium and Phosphorus in a patient receiving toxic potentially lethal combination of medications and are required. There are no known exceptions to this standard.

5.   Appropriate triage and monitoring of the patients admitted in guarded condition, requires a monitored bed at a minimum is a fact known to any competent physician.

6. Immediate discontinuation of all medications in patients with elevated CPK and liver function tests is a known intervention to any competent physician.

7. Appropriate treatment of the acute moderate pain. This does not include intravenous Morphine Sulfate, intravenous Meperidine or any other medications used for chronic pain and neuropathic pain control is a medical fact known to any competent physician.

8. Avoidance of the medications patient reports allergies to is required of any competent physician, pharmacist or nurse.

9. Avoidance of the intravenous pain medications when patient can take oral medications is the medical fact known to any competent physician.

10. Appropriate evaluation of pain level and indications for narcotics in a patient with the history of opiate dependence is a medical fact known to any competent physician.

11. Appropriate evaluation and treatment of the confusion delirium and psychosis in the Hospital setting and polypharmacy is required of any competent physician.

12. Knowledge of the drug to drug interactions, consultations by or with the pharmacist when in doubt, use of medications for known indications is required of any competent physician.

13. Airways protection, intubation and defibrillation are the first actions during a Code 3 procedure during in-Hospital arrest or medical personnel attended arrest. Hospital staff is required to be certified in advanced life support and Code 3 procedures.

14. Use of Adrenaline without defibrillation is not an

acceptable procedure by any authority on resuscitation.

15.   Uninterrupted monitoring during the Code 3 till death is pronounced by a physician is required during in-Hospital arrest.

16.   Complete and accurate notes of the Code 3 procedure are required during in–hospital arrest or any arrest attended by medical professionals.

Dr. Vertkin's List of Bumrungrad's Failures To Follow Standards Of Practice

Failures by Bumrungrad Hospital to meet Standards of Care are action(s) not taken by a reasonable, competent physician under similar circumstances.

1.   Failure to diagnose rhabdomyolysis and to follow this common and lethal medical problem.
2.   Failure to treat rhabdomyolysis.
3.   Failure to prevent early and late complications of rhabdomyolysis, resulting in unnecessary pain, suffering and death.
4.   Failure to exercise prudent caution with known multiple severe drug to drug interactions and direct contraindications resulting in psychosis, unnecessary pain and suffering and ultimately death.
5.   Failure to provide standard evaluation and Intensive Care admission for a patient with guarded prognosis, complex medical history.
6.   Failure to obtain and record medical history, physical examination and diagnosis.
7.   Failure of communications between physicians, pharmacists and nursing staff with concurrent use of multiple directly contraindicated medications, resulting in unnecessary pain, suffering and death.
8.   Failure to consult family and or patient's U.S.- based physician and to obtain family consent.
9.   Indiscriminate medications administration, without medical indications resulting in psychosis, unnecessary pain, suffering and ultimately death.

10. Failure to treat pain and evaluate pain appropriately in a patient with known opiate addiction resulting in psychosis, rapid development of severe dependency, drug to drug interaction and exacerbation of rhabdomyolisis in addition to prolongation of the QT-intervals.
11. Failure to record tests and/or medications administration justification.
12. Failure to prevent administration of the medications patient reported allergies to such as Fentanyl, antipsychotics, Sulfa.
13. Failure to provide appropriate testing including electrolytes, myoglobin blood and urine, liver functions, CBC and CPK till resolution of the symptoms while performing multiple painful tests without medical justification.
14. Failure to discharge patient home as scheduled on February 20, 2006 for unclear reasons. A subsequent discharge date of 24 February was also scheduled.
15. Failure to record medical consultations in appropriate format and failure to dictate the findings.
16. Failure to discuss the intended or actual administration of dangerous medications with the patient and/or his family, in fact administering medications patient specifically refused.
17. Failure to monitor patient with deteriorating vital signs on February 23, 2006.
18. Failure to provide complete and accurate records of the resuscitation efforts.
19. Failure to record death summary.
20. Failure to indicate cause of death, allegedly cardiac arrest due to unspecified cause.
21. Failure to fill out the entire death certificate using known and available information.
22. Hand written corrections of the time of death on the written records.
23. Failure to obtain or provide EKG during entire Code 3, electrolytes, calcium, phosphorus and magnesium levels. The written record exists of EKG showing Asystole (flat line) and of elevated Potassium but the actual results are not in the provided copy of the files.

24.   Failure to administer standard resuscitation procedure for in-hospital arrest: immediate defibrillation and intubations.

Appendix #7

I am familiar with autopsy protocols and investigations of death such as performed by Dr. Kornikiat Wongpirsarnsin, a physician employed by The Thailand Forensic Institute on or about February 24, 2006 on Mr. Joshua Goldberg, in Bangkok, Thailand at the request of the Thai police.

I reviewed the preliminary unofficial translation of the autopsy and personally interviewed Dr. Kornkiat Wongpirsarnsin. I personally reviewed autopsy photographs with the help of Dr. Wongpirsarnsin and obtained written down answers to my questions.

Dr. Wongpirsarnsin answered all the questions voluntarily.

Dr. Wongpirsarnsin in received the Inquest at the Patumwan Police Station at 13:30 hours. Dr. Wongpirsarnsin received the call from Bumrungrad Hospital from Thai police at approximately 10:45 AM and dispatched a resident to evaluate death of Mr. Goldberg.

The resident gained access to the body of the deceased in the holding room of the hospital and obtained photographs of the body. Subsequent to preliminary evaluation, the body of Mr. Joshua Goldberg was transferred to Lumpini Police Station and from there to Forensic Institute of Chulalanghorn University.

Wongpirsarnsin reported that the chain of custody was violated repeatedly and he does not know the whereabouts of the body from the time of alleged death to 11:30 AM, or until the receipt of the body of Joshua Goldberg to his facility. He further reported that very little clinical information was provided by the Bumrungrad Hospital and which should typically accompany the body upon transport for a police autopsy.

I did not receive the exact paperwork provided to the responding police station or information as to who informed the police that they should become involved in investigating the circumstances and death of Mr. Joshua Goldberg. It is my belief that this informant was either someone who worked at the hospital or who occupied one of the three beds in Josh's room.

The initial resident's notes, in unofficial translation, and photographs, revealed that Mr. Joshua Goldberg was lying on a metal stretcher; the body of a foreign male, teenager or young adult, white skin, well built and wearing a T-shirt and red shorts.

The body was lying face up.

The condition of the corpse indicated; there is no wound on the head and no bleeding under the head tissue or evidence of any dark green color that might be due to a lack of air. There are no other wounds evident from the photographs taken by the resident. Rigor Mortis is beginning at the lips. Further review of the resident's photographs revealed; no tubes of any kind, no evidence of an bruises present, no tears or changes of the clothing, an empty and clean suction device in the holding room, and a flat abdomen.

Dr. Kornkiat Wongpirsarnsin indicated that the tubes if any would have been removed AFTER, but not prior to the residents visit. If any such devices were used, they had been removed prior to the arrival of the resident. The location of such tubes, or any other equipment, if any, was not known to the resident or Dr. Kornkiat Wongpirsarnsin.

Dr. Kornkiat Wongpirsarnsin reported that the body arrived dressed in the above-described clothes. The photographic appearance of the naked body, now prepared for autopsy at the Forensic Institute, revealed; massive swelling of the abdomen, swelling of the lower extremities, no evidence of the intravenous tubing wounds, no evidence of defibrillation burns, resolving livido and postmortem skin changes of the face, lips, and skin overall. Dr. Wongpirsarnsin was not aware that Mr. Joshua

Goldberg was thin and never suffered from obesity.

The skin of the leg had blue round lesion on the left lateral malleous compatible with slowly healing insect/ snakebite (a round bleb reported ante mortem) and several small similar brown flat lesions.

Dr. Kornikiat Wongpirsarnsin reported that there was very severe edema in the brain and pons, in particular, as documented by autopsy photographs. He further indicated that, in his opinion, the brain and pons edema was long standing or over several hours. He also indicated that the brain swelled some time prior to death.

Dr. Kornikiat Wongpirsarnsin further confirmed that there was no trauma of the mouth, larynx and trachea what so ever, no hemorrhages or petichiae and that those organs were completely intact. The photograph confirmed this finding. This indicates that no intubation was attempted or accomplished.

Dr. Kornikiat Wongpirsarnsin confirmed that there were no rib fractures, no sternum fractures, no bleeding or contusion of the lungs. Dr. Kornkiat asserted that the heart and the pericardium were intact with no evidence of compression injuries or electrical burns to the chest or pericardium. He further indicated that lung congestion had only occurred because of post-mortem changes. He further indicated that areas of inflammation in the heart and lung muscles consisted of the lymphocytes and neutrophils with some areas of necrosis of the muscle unrelated to blood vessels.

Dr. Kornkiat agreed that such lesions are compatible if not diagnostic of rhabdomyolysis of several days duration. His opinion is that this condition, the inflammation of the muscle, is strongly indicative of rhabdomyolysis.

The kidneys were reported as 100% normal, with no inflammation or casts.

Dr. Kornikiat Wongpirsarnsin specifically indicated that his Institute and he himself are unable to perform toxicology testing. He indicated that the stomach, esophagus and intestine did not contain any drugs.

There was no food or liquid in the esophagus, larynx or lungs. He further indicated that he analyzed food in the stomach and that the type of food found just began digesting and that he timed death to approximately two following dinner.

Dr. Kornikiat Wongpirsarnsin reported that the liver and the spleen did not have any lacerations or tears of the capsule or the organs themselves, no blood collections or any evidence of resuscitation efforts.

Dr. Kornikiat Wongpirsarnsin confirmed that the size of the urinary bladder was considerably increased with 650 ml of the pale urine. He further explained that normal urinary bladder can only hold approximately 150 cc. He agreed that amount of the urine and such severe distention indicated prolonged period of coma prior to death. This also ruled out seizure since involuntary urination would have occurred. He also ruled out that a Foley catheter, pre, peril or post-mortem, had been inserted as would have been consistent in any standard Code 3 procedure. Dr. Kornkiat confirmed that he did not perform any tests for myoglobin. He further indicated that screening tests on the urine were not accurate and were only screens for amphetamines, alcohol and opiates. He informed me that more accurate tests were sent two weeks ago to an external laboratory.

Dr. Kornikiat Wongpirsarnsin specifically indicated that; there was no evidence of heart failure or dilatation of the ventricles, normal heart valves, no fluid retention in the lungs, the liver or other organs. He did agree that it is likely that the heart and the lungs may have stopped due to pons (edema) and generalized edema of the brain.

Dr. Kornikiat Wongpirsarnsin indicated that he does have multiple tissue samples apparently in formalin, not frozen, such as brain, bone, lung, and others and 5 cc of frozen blood. He did confirm that he had sent 5 cc to an external toxicology laboratory for analysis, which, as of this writing, is still pending.

Appendix #8

Some pharmacological details of Dr. Cohen's report have been omitted in this text in the interest of brevity. For those familiar with pharmaceutical interactions, Cohen's entire report is a vital component in this case. His full reports have been posted at www.bumrungraddeath.com, along with all other medical reports and findings.

Dr. Cohen's Report: Possible Causes of Death

> Therapeutic duplication (often 3 and 4 drugs of the same class) was noted with antipsychotics, antidepressants, narcotics, analgesics, sedatives and hypnotics. In most instances the duplications were without indication or justification, and were highly toxic—in essence these combinations are contraindicated.
> A plethora of pharmacodynamic drug-drug interactions were noted. Possible drug-induced causes of death include cardio respiratory depression, torsades-depointes, serotonin syndrome, and Neuroleptic malignant syndrome.
> Drug-Induced Torsade de Pointes (QT prolongation) and Ventricular Tachycardia
> Drug-Induced Respiratory Depression
> Drug-Induced Serotonin Syndrome (Temp 102, tachycardia, elevated CK, rhabdomyolisis)
> Drug-Induced Neuroleptic Malignant Syndrome (NMS) (Temperature 102, tachycardia, elevated CK and LETs, rhabdomyolisis)

Appendix #9

Bumrungrad: Unlicensed Doctors (06 August 2006). This posting was made available in mid 2006 on the www.bumrungraddeath.com website:

After a two-week search of both the electronic and paper files, every doctor listed on the Bumrungrad on their website, has had their license status checked by one of our researchers.

These doctors do not appear anywhere in the record. Their names have been reported to JCAHO, the Joint Commission and we are awaiting response.

- Atima Delaney, General Pediatrics (Children): Pediatric Emergency Medicine
- Chorthip N. Phattanasri, Medicine: Endocrinology (Diabetes)
- Jantra Chennavasin, OB/GYN (Women)
- Laorporn Pawakranond, Radiology
- Pimolruedee Nanawarathorn, Dental: Prosthodontics (Dentures)
- Ranit Suppapipat, Dental: Orthodontics (Braces)
- Siriyaporn Laohakunakorn, General Pediatrics (Children)
- Thanwa SuDoctorsang: Radiology

We provided Bumrungrad with the chance to respond to our research. They remained silent.

These people are not only NOT Board Certified, they were NOT even registered as licensed doctors in Thailand.

Appendix #10

Jerome Walker – AML/CT Enforcement Actions by the OCC in 2006 (Bangkok Bank, New York Branch).

C. In the Matter of Bangkok Bank Public Company Limited, New York, New York, a Federal branch of Bangkok Bank Public Company Limited, Bangkok, Thailand, Consent Order, 2006-29, http://www.occ.treas.gov/FTP/EAs/ea2006-29.pdf (April 20, 2006)

The OCC also issued a cease and desist order against the branch and required:

i.   The branch to stop processing wires, as intermediary or otherwise, unless it sets appropriate, OCC-approved parameters on the branch's GIFTS system to enable the branch to identify potential suspicious activity and monitor transactions by originator and beneficiary. With respect to any wires processed by the branch, even when privacy laws of a jurisdiction outside the United States prevent the sharing or provision of information, the branch must conduct due diligence in order to assess the legitimacy of the transaction.

ii.   *The branch to stop issuing, processing, or honoring demand drafts until its processes can effectively monitor, detect, and report suspicious activities in the issuance, processing, and payment of demand drafts.*

iii.   *Comprehensive enhancements to the bank's AML/CT program, including significant enhancements to internal controls, policies and procedures, audit, training, SAR reporting, recordkeeping, the account opening procedures and other processes and to hire a Risk Manager.*

iv.   *A Look Back. The branch to enhance customer due diligence related to high risk accounts, including politically exposed persons, pouch activity, money service businesses, PUPID accounts, jewelry and precious metals accounts, offshore accounts and import/export company accounts.*

Appendix #11

14 June 06, from our Bangkok Counsel, Alistair Henderson:
Dear Mr. Bressler,

I write in light of your recent email communications with Mr. James Goldberg, father of Joshua Goldberg who died at Bumrungrad Hospital in Bangkok, Thailand in February 2006.

Mr. Goldberg had asked for information regarding JCAHO's investigation of this sentinel event and the consequences regarding Bumrungrad's accreditation. You advised that further communications should be routed through you as JCAHO counsel.

I am therefore writing to reconfirm Mr. Goldberg's information requirements.

1. Please provide a full account of steps being taken to investigate this sentinel event.

Without limitation, please include the following:

a: Has Bumrungrad Hospital made any formal report to JACHO regarding this event? If so, when?

b: If not, has JCAHO attempted to make direct contact with Bumrungrad Hospital regarding this event? If so, when?

c: In either case, what is the nature and extent of contacts between JACHO and Bumrungrad? Are they intensive and ongoing or sporadic and unstructured?

d: Has JCAHO asked for copies of all relevant Bumrungrad records? If so, have those records been provided? For your information, the Royal Thai Police have also demanded copies of relevant records but these requests have so far been unfulfilled, with the Hospital claiming that it needed time to comply.

e: Have JCAHO representatives visited Bumrungrad Hospital since and in connection with this event?
f: When does JCAHO expect to complete its investigation, including (as may be necessary) steps to encourage/compel the Hospital to provide necessary information?

2. What is JCAHO doing to investigate the Hospital's apparent breaches of relevant standards and procedures? Mr. Goldberg has given JCAHO details of many concerns, including for example the apparent involvement of unlicensed personnel in providing medical care to Joshua Goldberg; the fact that medical experts have concluded that cause of death is attributable to the Hospital's (mis)treatment; and the alarming appearance that Hospital staff made a major effort to disguise the time and

*circumstances of death and to create a fictitious record of a Code 3
procedure some 12 hours later.*

*These are very grave matters by any standards and specifically
by JCAHO's own standards, so what specifically is JCAHO doing
to investigate them and to establish the extent to which they
reflect systemic failure in Bumrungrad's procedures and
compliance?*

3. JCAHO's website says:
Initiation of Accreditation Watch
*If the Joint Commission becomes aware that an organization has
experienced a reviewable sentinel event, but the organization
fails to submit or otherwise make available an acceptable root
cause analysis and action plan, or otherwise provide for Joint
Commission evaluation of its response to the sentinel event under
an approved protocol, within 45 days of the event, or of its
becoming aware of the event, a recommendation will be made to
the Accreditation Committee to place the organization on
Accreditation Watch. If the Accreditation Committee places the
organization on Accreditation Watch, the organization will then be
permitted an additional 15 days to submit an acceptable root
cause analysis and action plan, or otherwise provide for Joint
Commission evaluation of its response to the sentinel event under
an approved protocol.*

** The Accreditation Watch status is considered publicly
disclosable information.*

** In all cases of organization refusal to permit review of
information regarding a reviewable sentinel event in accordance
with the Sentinel Event Policy and its approved protocols, the
initial response by the Joint Commission is assignment of
Accreditation Watch. Continued refusal may result in loss of
accreditation.*

*More than 45 days have passed since Joshua Goldberg died. Is
Bumrungrad Hospital therefore now on Accreditation Watch? If
not, why not? - the above-stated policies do not allow for JCAHO
discretion in case of an institution's failure to submit an*

acceptable root cause analysis and action plan within that period, or otherwise to provide for Joint Commission evaluation of the institution's response to the sentinel event under an approved protocol.

4. When and in what circumstances will JCAHO (a body with legal responsibilities regarding promulgation and assessment of the standards of care and competence required for accreditation purposes) revoke or suspend Bumrungrad's accreditation?

Appendix #12

To: David Schwartz, Emilia Di'Santo, United States Senate, Office of The Sub Committee on Healthcare; Senator Charles Grassley (R) Co-Chair, Senator Max Baucus (D), Co-Chair
From: Jim Goldberg
Re: Proposal to the United States Senate, 12.August.2007
Investigative and Legislation Scenario for the Joint Commission and Joint Commission International
17 July 2007

Background
During our many discussions and meetings, I have attempted to keep your committee aware of the discoveries I have made about the American healthcare scene which has arisen from the extensive research I have conducted following the death of my 23 year old son, Joshua, at a foreign Joint Commission International Accredited Hospital.

To memorialize not only the circumstances of his case, but my evolving understanding of how the American medical machine is rapidly positioning itself to boldly move into an international arena transforming the concept of medical Tourism into large scale and systematically planned medical outsourcing, I have created a website repository of various background information at www.bumrungraddeath.com.

My revelation is that the nexus of how this step change is made possible, is through the deliberate planning (read racketeering) of the Joint Commission.

What I briefly wish to propose and which I am prepared to expound upon in detail is summarized in the following scenario which I believe is essential for the Senate and Congress to undertake as the serious business of rescuing the further decline of American Health Care at the expense of the people of the United States and at the greedy and uncaring hands of various major players in the medical machine who have placed profit over the safety and health of the U.S. and now world wide populace.

It is imperative that members of both sides of the house benchmark, realistically, where we are before we can decide where we can go. This investigation, I believe from my up close experience with the Joint Commission convinces me that they are the glue which has permitted, under their watch, for the U.S. to fall to nearly 40th worldwide in healthcare, while, at the same time, spending 2-3 times more per capita than any other country on the face of the earth.

With the Joint Commission's relatively new, bold and I believe illegal activities, they are now rapidly building an international network of healthcare providers which will further increase the profits of THEIR constituents while jeopardizing the health of U.S. Citizens and other peoples of the world, who are being led to believe, with pre-meditated malice, that the U.S. Government is implicitly endorsing foreign medical institutions by Using the mantle of deeming power transferred to them by the Social Security Amendment of 1965.

I have attached a straw man article which describes, in overview, what happened to lead me to this conclusion and incorporates the very words of the people who I believe are responsible for the deliberate and uncaring undoing of one of our last bastions of leadership healthcare.

My Contentions Are:

1. The Joint Commission has broken the law consistently since they received deeming authority in 1965. Specifically, they have ignored their designated role to enforce the standards which they, in conjunction with HEW and now HHS were to have evolved to govern the standards by which various healthcare facilities operate.

2. Since 1965, by the admission of Howard Bressler, the Joint Commission has Accredited over 40,000 institutions for yearly fees, but, though they have had the power to revoke, suspend, sanction or reprimand health Accredited healthcare facilities they have only exercised this power in 1/10th of 1% of all the Accreditations they have ever given. This, essentially means, that Accreditation is for sale and once given is almost never revoked.

In the words of Bressler, when confronted about their required role to enforce, "we're not in the business of enforcing our standards we don't have that kind of infrastructure and resources!" Despite the specific wording of the law, which I have inserted below, the Joint Commission has operated with impunity and defined themselves in any way they have wished despite the very deliberate wording of the Amendment to the Social Security Act of 1965.

3. Because the JC has virtually been without oversight, as prescribed by law, HEW and now, HHS, have become a willing party to allowing the Joint Commission to operate as they wish. Numerous government officials at HHS like Donna Shalala have gone on to very lucrative healthcare industry positions after leaving government. Thus, these government bodies, regardless of party or administration in power, have been allowed to violate the law for nearly 50 years. During those 50 years, astronomical fraud has grown, all time fines in the hundreds of millions and even billions have been assessed and EVEN with that, the organizations whose activities are secretly interwoven with the Joint Commission, have gone without reprimand, investigation, sanction or punishment of any kind.

4. Because the Joint Commission (and its main members with majority voting power to set policy in any fashion they choose) have stretched well beyond the deeming authority given to them. They have expanded into what the GAO has correctly found is a shocking conflict of interest with the establishment of its Joint Commission Resources a euphemism for strong arm consulting which assures hospitals that if they buy what the advice the commission has to sell, that Accreditation is assured.

No hospital, whose very life depends on Accreditation, can chance going with another resource to prepare for Accreditation and their lock on their lock on their consulting clients is growing because it is, in essence, a tied sale.

The commission was never given the right to sell consulting services under the deeming banner, yet, they unashamedly Use this precious bestowed power by the government as if the government has indeed blessed all that the Commission does. This was never the intention of the deeming authority but because the Commission is without oversight, they have learned, over time that they can do pretty much as they wish.

The deeming authority vested in 1965 is inextricably bundled with all else that the Commission does. Your committee, Senators Grassley and Bacchus caught wind of this and rightfully became concerned about the conflict that the GAO report more than adequately reveals.

With respect, however, this is but the tip of the iceberg. The plans of the medical industry are growing and along with that, and to assure that the money flow keeps flowing, the Accreditation game is transforming as I write, into a global phenomena.

As with the audacity imbued in the establishment of the Commission Resources, their foray into the International Accreditation business is an outrageous extension of a very limited role with which their deeming authority actually is based.

5. The value of selling international Accreditation is enormous whether it is legal or not. If it holds importance and credibility in the perception of the public, then it has value. Because the JC has not been overseen, by anyone, they have formulated the Joint Commission International which opens the money flow to foreign providers from the Federal Government supposedly.

The private insurers will follow suit and also reimburse based on the JC Accreditation. This is exactly what they want to do, since these insurers or those for whom they administer insurance, are desperate to lower their payments for procedures the patients be dammed in the event that problems occur. Foreign providers are in jurisdictions which are completely outside of the control of the U.S. and, for the most part, have no medical malpractice laws and therefore, no recourse for those who are hurt, injured or die. Good business, no recourse, no legal exposure, lower costs and NO requirement whatsoever for enforcement of standards.

An ideal world for all except the injured party!

The JCI, a self created entity which is tucked under the arm of the Joint Commission Resources, has developed on its own power, rules for international standards which have no enforcement provisions. Yet to the public, the symbol they use for international Accreditation is virtually the same as for the U.S. and they make NO attempt to separate or distinguish their international Accreditation from that which they sell here in the U.S.

The hospitals make no attempt to say to patients investigating that the Joint Commission International is separate and distinct from that of the U.S. By examining the marketing efforts of U.S. corporations to endorse these offshore programs, they hold up the Joint Commission Accreditation as if it were exactly the same as here at home. Look for an example at www.bumrungrad.com.

So brazen are these people that they even ADVERTISE their Accredited hospitals on the Joint Commission International Website. That's right; ADVERTISE!

To confirm that indeed Medicare is obligated to pay for these offshore services, please consider the actual law passed in 1965. This law is little known and little appreciated except by those who are rapidly positioning themselves to ship patients lock stock and barrel overseas!

6. To make this new directive absolutely clear, please consider the following article regarding what Blue Cross and Blue Shield are doing in the State of South Carolina: While they are forcing PPO's

and others out of business by lowering reimbursement rates they are cutting deals with Bumrungrad and other foreign hospitals

And are even setting up after care treatment centers at home to tend to the patients who have been operated on overseas: (This is taken from a Blue Cross Blue Shield Association Newsletter. Since all the Blue Cross and Blue Shields are interlocked, though separate corporations, for the most part, they share secret information and sell this information concerning patients and doctors to other insurers. Hence, Blue Cross and Shield of South Carolina is packaging this prototype up for the rest of the Blue Shield organizations across the country.)

7. To make it absolutely clear that this is no passing fancy, please note that a company based in Virginia, World Access, a wholly owned division of the largest insurance company in the world, Allianz (Swiss and German) have been contracted by most major health insurers in the U.S. to administer benefits to their members for services overseas.

8. The law which empowered the Joint Commission specifically limits their deeming power to the United States. However, since they operate with impunity, they have taken that deeming authority and stretched it well beyond what congress hand intended.

While the Joint Commission, with its approximately 1100 people breaks even, their 54 person Joint Commission International is making money and they are just getting started. Already offices have been set up in the UAE, France, Singapore etc and they are courting hospital customers with ferocity.

Of course, they will admit to none of this since they admit to nothing claiming confidential privilege but never cite the basis of that privilege. They claim privilege on all matters; foreign and domestic.

9. I contend the following:
A: The Joint Commission has violated the law since 1965, They have been aided and abetted by the HEW and now the HHS. Their

deeming authority should be withdraw by the United States Government for fraud, dereliction of duty and for their participation in cover up crimes, aiding and abetting racketeering, etc.

b: They claim to be a not for profit organization, but go beyond any charter which describes the nature of a not for profit. They talk in their literature about profits and the bottom line this is hardly the talk of a charitable or scientific/educational organization. Their tax exempt status should be removed and they should be held accountable, retroactively for operating as a for profit organization.

c: The internal workings of the Joint Commission should be thoroughly investigated. The commission consists of both for profit and not for profit members or not for profits which are backed by for profit entities such as the principle members of the American Hospital Association. A detailed investigation and audit of all their members should be conducted to see what kinds of money has flowed during their history among their members and how their policy decisions have enriched the private interests of their members.

d: Their Joint Commission Resources activities should be declared to be a conflict of interest and declared a profit making business. Their tax exempt status should be revoked.

e: The Joint Commission International should be sued by the Justice Department for committing fraud by illegally employing the implicit authority of the U.S. Government in drawing business to those entities who pay the Joint Commission International and the Joint Commission Resources for its services.

f: They have also violated truth in advertising laws and should be held accountable in both the U.S. and World Courts for perpetrating a fraud on the American and international public by illegally Using the implied authority of the United States government for their own interests.

g: The HHS should be sued for its failure to set fees and to oversee

the Joint Commission. Please note that the American Nursing Association, during the summer of 2006 sued HHS for its failure to oversee the Joint Commission in assuring that proper staff/patient ratios be maintained.

h: Those individuals found to have participated in accrediting hospitals and in secreting information which could have saved the lives of others had they followed their charter of publicly sharing Sentinel events, should be criminally prosecuted to the full extent of the law. This also goes for HHS officials involved in "looking the other way." They are co-conspirators in these vast rackets.

i. Any company who is found to have participated in any of the crimes committed by HHS and the Joint Commission should be fined and held criminally responsible for their actions. Specific individuals involved, based on whatever statute of limitations applies, should be prosecuted by the justice department to the full extent of the law.

J. A new oversight body should be established to oversee and implement the mission originally designated for the JC in 1965. This new body should be without industry connections and should maintain a completely non partisan position. The composition and function of this body should learn from the terrible mistakes and financial destruction of the American Health Care system while under the watch of the Joint Commission.

This body should most certainly report to a public board and be accountable for their actions.
k. Massive restitution should be made by those parties found to have participated in the various crimes which have been committed.

L. The recent association between the Joint Commission and the World Health Organization should be declared illegal. The Joint Commission has collaborated with the WHO to establish international safety standards.

When considering how dangerous and infected U.S. healthcare institutions have become on the Joint Commission's watch, it is completely ludicrous that the WHO would have teamed with the overseer of the destructions of the once proud and superb healthcare establishment in the U.S.

The implied use of the name of the United States government is being compromised by the activities of the Joint Commission and will continue to diminish the integrity of the United States around the world. This must be brought to an immediate halt by the United States government.

I urge that investigations begin immediately and that a target is established to introduce legislation within the next 18 months. I further ask that all healthcare lobbying interests be banned on the basis that their actions interfere with the 14th Amendment Rights of the Citizens of the United States. The ratio of 4 healthcare lobbyists for every member in Congress and the Senate must cease immediately and the American people given a chance to recover what was once the pinnacle of healthcare in the world to a status which is around 40th in terms of morbidity and mortality statistics.

In addition, I will shortly be submitting, under separate cover, a proposed Bill, The United States Special Patient Protection Act. This act is intended to require that the Joint Commission disgorge all information, since its formation, in its possession regarding their operations, findings, Sentinel Events, financial dealings etc.

Further, this Bill will propose that a Patient Safety Treaty be established in which participating countries, providers and insurers are held responsible by the U.S. Federal Government for malpractice, patient injury and/or death of U.S. citizens who receive medical treatment outside of the United States and its Territories.

I lost my only son half way around the world. I have found out that he died for reasons which are very current and operative here in the United States. The nexus of these activities, I contend, is centered with the Joint Commission who must be completely dismantled in order that the American people enjoy the protection that the Constitution and the Bill of Rights afford them.

The last 50 years, which began with the good intentions of Medicare, have resulted in corruption so vast and so wide spread, that our healthcare system is now in complete shambles. I lay the blame for this at the feet of the HHS and the Joint Commission and they should be held civilly and criminally responsible.

Sincerely,
Jim Goldberg

Appendix #12

Hospital, Insurers and HMOs
(Revenues in Billions of Dollars):

#21 UnitedHealth Group Health Care: Insurance and Managed Care $81,186.0

#77 Aetna Health Care: Insurance and Managed Care $30,951.0

#85 Humana Health Care: Insurance and Managed Care $28,946.0

#88HCA Health Care: Medical Facilities $28,374.0

#132 Cigna Health Care: Insurance and Managed Care $19,101.0

#165 Health Net Health Care: Insurance and Managed Care $15,367.0

#226 Coventry Health Care Health Care: Insurance and Managed Care $11,914.0

#243 Community Health Systems Health Care: Medical Facilities $11,156.0

#381 WellCare Health Plans Health Care: Insurance and Managed Care $6,522.0

#433 DaVita Health Care: Medical Facilities $5,660.0

#467 Universal Health Services Health Care: Medical Facilities $5,081.0

#494 Universal American Health Care: Insurance and Managed Care $4,659.0

#509 Amerigroup Health Care: Insurance and Managed Care

$4,516.0
#511Health Management Associates Health Care: Medical Facilities $4,489.0
#538 Kindred Healthcare Health Care: Medical Facilities $4,194.0
#609 Centene Health Care: Insurance and Managed Care $3,515.0
#673 Molina Healthcare Health Care: Insurance and Managed Care $3,112.0
#719 Vanguard Health Systems Health Care: Medical Facilities $2,789.0
#726 LifePoint Hospitals Health Care: Medical Facilities $2,754.0
#749 Magellan Health Services Health Care: Medical Facilities $2,625.0
#806 Medical Mutual of Ohio Health Care: Insurance and Managed Care $2,387.0
#849 HealthSpring Health Care: Insurance and Managed Care $2,188.0
#861 Select Medical Holdings Health Care: Medical Facilities $2,153.0

Pharmaceuticals:

#29 Johnson & Johnson Pharmaceuticals $63,747.0
#46 Pfizer Pharmaceuticals $48,296.0
#80 Abbott Laboratories Pharmaceuticals $29,528.0
#103 Merck Pharmaceuticals $23,850.0
#110 Wyeth Pharmaceuticals $22,834.0
#120 Bristol-Myers Squibb Pharmaceuticals $21,366.0
#122 Eli Lilly Pharmaceuticals $20,378.0
#138 Schering-Plough Pharmaceuticals $18,502.0
#168 Amgen Pharmaceuticals $15,003.0
#444 Gilead Sciences Pharmaceuticals $5,336.0
#462 Mylan Pharmaceuticals $5,138.0
#502 Genzyme Pharmaceuticals $4,605.0
#517 Allergan Pharmaceuticals $4,403.0
#546 Biogen Idec Pharmaceuticals $4,098.0
#569 Forest Laboratories Pharmaceuticals $3,836.0
#597 Hospira Pharmaceuticals $3,630.0

#769 Watson Pharmaceuticals $2,536.0
#830 Celgene Pharmaceuticals $2,255.0
#852 NBTY Pharmaceuticals $2,180.0
#903 Cephalon Pharmaceuticals $1,975.0
#958 Perrigo Pharmaceuticals $1,822.0

Financial Insurances:

#39 MetLife Insurance: Life, Health (stock) $55,085.0
#84 Prudential Financial Insurance: Life, Health (stock) $29,275.0
#152 AFLAC Insurance: Life, Health (stock) $16,554.0
#270 Unum Group Insurance: Life, Health (stock) $9,982.0
#271 Genworth Financial Insurance: Life, Health (stock) $9,948.0
#273 Principal Financial Insurance: Life, Health (stock) $9,936.0
#274 Lincoln National Insurance: Life, Health (stock) $9,905.0
#537 Conseco Insurance: Life, Health (stock) $4,194.0
#551 Pacific Life Insurance: Life, Health (stock) $4,023.0
#643 Torchmark Insurance: Life, Health (stock) $3,327.0
#729 Securian Financial Group Insurance: Life, Health (stock) $2,746.0
#739 StanCorp Financial Insurance: Life, Health (stock) $2,667.0
#772 American National Insurance: Life, Health (stock) $2,527.0
#776 Protective Life Insurance: Life, Health (stock) $2,506.0
#792 CUNA Mutual Group Insurance: Life, Health (stock) $2,433.0
#863 Phoenix Insurance: Life, Health (stock) $2,151.0

Life, Health Insurance:

#76 New York Life Insurance: Life, Health (mutual) $31,416.0
#82 TIAA-CREF Insurance: Life, Health (mutual) $29,363.0
#118 Northwestern Mutual Insurance: Life, Health (mutual) $21,734.0
#135 Massachusetts Mutual Life Insurance: Life, Health (mutual) $18,745.0
#279 Guardian Life Ins. Co. of America Insurance: Life, Health

(mutual) $9,675.0

#409 Thrivent Financial for Lutherans Insurance: Life, Health (mutual) $6,061.0

#441 Western & Southern Financial Group Insurance: Life, Health (mutual) $5,392.0

#525 Mutual of Omaha Insurance: Life, Health (mutual) $4,312.0

#804 National Life Group Insurance: Life, Health (mutual) $2,400.0

#972 Mutual of America Life Insurance: Life, Health (mutual) $1,773.0

Appendix #13

Clear Channel Communications

Founded in 1972 and headquartered in San Antonio, Texas, Clear Channel Communications (CC Media Holdings, Inc. is the "parent company") is a global leader in the out-of-home advertising industry with radio stations and outdoor displays in various countries around the world. According to its website, Clear Channel "operates over 800 radio stations reaching more than 110 million listeners every week across all 50 states."

Its other major holdings include New York-based Katz Media Group, hailed as "the nation's only full-service media sales and marketing firm." It also owns Clear Channel Total Traffic Network, dominating the space for real-time traffic data via in-car or portable navigation systems, broadcast media, wireless and Internet-based services. Other Clear Channel companies sell scheduling software to radio stations and other broadcast-experience software.

Cox Communications

Cox Enterprises, Inc. has some interesting "political" beginnings. In 1898, founder James M. Cox, a former schoolteacher, became a three-term governor of Ohio. In 1920, the same year he ran for President of the United States as the Democratic nominee, Governor Cox bough the Dayton Evening

News, his first newspaper acquisition. (Cox was defeated by Republican Senator Warren G. Harding, another newspaper publisher from Ohio.)

Fast-forward to Cox 's holdings today and one finds its fingers in many deep-dish pies: newspapers, television stations, radio broadcasting companies and automobile auctions. In 2009, it was the third-largest cable-entertainment and broadband-services provider in the country. It is a privately owned (though previously a public company) and headquartered in Atlanta, Georgia.

Cox Media runs popular networks and programming such as A&E, the Food Network, The Travel Channel, The Learning Channel (TLC) and the Weather Channel. It owns Kudzu, a chain of interactive websites that let consumers use the web to find service providers in their area that are the "right fit for their particular home and personal needs."

Walt Disney Co.

The Walt Disney Company, with revenue of $37.8 billion in 2008, is a large media conglomerate founded on October 16, 1923 by Disney brothers, Walt and Roy Disney. Starting out as a small animation studio, its legendary history has led it to become one of Hollywood's largest studios and a huge media conglomerate.

Disney's vast holdings include several television production companies, cable networks, motion-picture producers and theme parks. Its filmed entertainment brands include Buena Vista, Touchstone, Walt Disney, Hollywood Pictures, Caravan Pictures and Miramax Films.

Disney is an excellent example of immense media expansion. The Disney-ABC Television Group (including ABC Daytime, ABC Entertainment and ABC News divisions) is massive; it also owns ESPN, Inc. Disney also publishes books (Hyperion) and magazines (Disney twenty-three).

Along with its own Internet portals, The Walt Disney Internet Group owns ABC.com, Oscar.com, Mr. Showbiz and sites with Disney-related content such as Family.com, ESPN.com, NBA.com, NASCAR.com and toysmart.com.

Interactive games and music for Disney come through Buena Vista Music Group, Hollywood Records, Lyric Street Records, Mammoth Records and Walt Disney Records.

Disney's most recent acquisition is Marvel Entertainment and its portfolio of more than 5,000 characters.

Gannett Company

Gannett Co., Inc. is one of the largest international news and information companies. Gannet publishes 84 daily newspapers, including the USA Today family of papers and weeklies, as well as nearly 850 non-daily publications in America.

In broadcasting, the company operates 23 U.S. television stations. Its market reach is in excess of 20 million households. In 2008, Gannett obtained a controlling interest in CareerBuilder and ShopLocal as part of its aggressive digital strategy through key business acquisitions.

According to its corporate website in September 2009, Gannett's total online U.S. Internet audience in January 2009 was 27.1 million unique visitors, reaching about 16.1% of the Internet audience, as measured by Nielsen/NetRatings.

General Electric (GE)

It's widely known that when in media holdings, General Electric has a lion's share. It owns NBC Universal after combining two companies—NBC Television and Universal Studios—in 2004.

Inside GE's Media and Entertainment companies are some of the world's most recognizable brands, including CNBC, MSNBC, NBC News, NBC Sports & Olympics, NBC Universal Television, SCI FI, Telemundo, USA Network, Universal Parks & Resorts,

Universal Pictures and iVillage.

In commerce, GE is a leader. It builds aircraft engines, manages finance commercial investments, manufactures countless consumer products and industrial systems, as well as selling insurance, medical systems, plastics, power supplies and transportation-monitoring systems.

News Corporation

Filmed entertainment, television, cable programming, direct broadcast satellite television, magazines and inserts, newspapers and information services, books and "other assets" are the category names of holdings from media mogul Rupert Murdoch's News Corporation.

In television offerings, FOX Broadcasting Company is massive (claiming in 2009 they are "the number one network in the United States), with dozens of stations in the Fox Television Stations group.

News Corporation is also the globe's leading publisher of English-language newspapers. These include The New York Post and The Wall Street Journal and The Sunday Times in the U.K. In publishing, Harper Collins was acquired in 1987, as Harper & Row.

Time Warner Inc.

Time Warner businesses include interactive services, filmed entertainment, television networks and publishing. The household names of their principal companies span the gamut of media and include AOL, Time Inc., Home Box Office, Turner Broadcasting System and Warner Bros. Entertainment.
Time Warner's digital holdings include AOL Video, Music and AIM, MapQuest, Moviefone, HBO on Demand and TMZ.

Time Inc. is one of the world's largest content companies. Its portfolio includes more than 100 titles. Reaching more than 40 million adults with every issue, People magazine is one of their flagship magazines, along with Time, Sports Illustrated, Fortune, InStyle and Money.

NAME INDEX*

A

H

K

L

Las Vegas, 277
Laura, 330–31
Laurie, 329
Lawmakers, 99
The Learning Channel (TLC), 369
Legend, 90
Legislation Scenario, 356
Lehman Brothers, 151
Leon, 328, 330
Leslie June Taylor Randolph, 11
LETs, 351
Levett, Connie, 181, 281
Lewis, 328
Liaoning Province, 256
Library of Congress Cataloging-in-Publication Data Goldberg, 7
Lifeline Press, 328–29
LifePoint Hospitals Health Care, 366
Life Sciences and Health Changes, 328
Lincoln, 292
Lincoln National Insurance, 367
Lincoln's, 292
Linda A, 330
Lindell, Lisa, 329
Lindsay, 331
Lisa, 329
List of Subsidiaries of Tenet Healthcare Corporation, 81, 84
Littell, Bob, 159
Little Help, 157
Little History, 69
Live Donor Transplantation, 333
Liveried, 40
LLC, 114
Locals, 63–75
Locals Five, 8
Lollys, 31
Lone Star State, 165
Long Emergency, 329
Los Angeles, 286
Los Angeles Times, 79, 198
Losing, 8, 114–22
Low Cost, 332
Low-Cost Dental, 330

[Created with TExtract / www.Texyz.com]

Subject INDEX*

50-Year Racket, 8, 123–40

A

338, 347–48, 356, 363
Borders, 277, 284–85, 332
brain, 200, 307, 349–50
branch, 352–53
Britain, 12, 18, 20–21, 71, 76, 91, 327
Buddha, 314–15
Bummers, 8, 63–75
Bumrungrad, 40–42, 46–49, 51–57, 61–75, 81–88, 183–85, 187–93, 195, 201–2, 206–15, 221–32, 238–41, 248–52, 262–71, 294–96, 341–42
  entered, 185, 195
  international Accreditation, 240
  ownership of, 85, 88
Bumrungrad executives, 73, 208
Bumrungrad hospital, 31, 49, 184, 281
  beds, 81
Bumrungrad hospital in Bangkok, 183
Bumrungrad Hospital in Bangkok, 337, 353
Bumrungrad Hospital International, 89–90
Bumrungrad Hospital of Bangkok, 211
Bumrungrad Hospital Public Co, 67
Bumrungrad International, 26, 67, 70
Bumrungrad International Hospital, 19, 48, 52, 55, 59–60, 70, 76, 95, 205, 212, 339
Bumrungrad International Hospital in Bangkok, 28
Bumrungrad management, 47, 88
Bumrungrad Medical Center in Thailand, 81
Bumrungrad Medical Center Limited, 81, 83–84
Bumrungrad morgue, 265, 338
Bumrungrad patient, 197
Bumrungrad's accreditation, 354
Bumrungrad's doctors, 180
Bumrungrad's lawyers, 89, 342
Bumrungrad's rooster of doctors, 70
Bumrungrad to Parkway Holdings of Singapore, 82
bureaucrats, 12
business, 17–18, 72–74, 80, 83, 91, 101–2, 168, 183, 232–34, 254–55, 269–71, 278, 297–98, 300, 357–58, 361–62
business practices, 78

C
capitalism, 93, 95, 257

R

S

UnitedHealth, 163
United Healthcare, 100, 154, 229, 277
UnitedHealthcare, 176, 183, 185, 229, 278–80
UnitedHealth Group, 163
United States, 12–15, 18, 20–22, 24–25, 73, 96–98, 103–5, 116, 130–33, 147–48, 168–70, 200, 275–77, 286–87, 303–4, 364
United States Embassy, 34, 218, 220
United States Government, 24, 28, 33, 44, 97–98, 105, 118, 123, 133–34, 204–5, 297–99
United States of Healthcare Fraud, 8, 141–44
United States Senate, 99, 123, 142, 291, 356
United States Special Patient Protection Act, 299, 364
User's Guide to Medical Tourism, 320–22

V

Vertkin, 51, 53–55, 58, 213–14, 219, 250

W

Washington, 43, 98, 117–18, 122, 139, 141–42, 147, 151–52, 154, 206, 255, 286, 289–90, 293, 301, 303–4
Watson, 161–62, 328
wave, 26–27, 140, 143, 285, 331
website, 45, 61, 68–73, 128–29, 180, 186, 196–97, 211, 219, 324, 327, 339, 351, 368
website www.bumrungraddeath.com, 54
Wellpoint, patient calls, 165
Wongpirsarnsin, 347–48
World Access, 8, 74, 236–47, 249, 263, 274, 361
World Access and Bumrungrad, 241, 264
World Health Organization, 284, 299, 363
Wrongful Deaths, 79, 328–29
www.bumrungraddeath.com, 10, 41, 61, 68–69, 88, 187, 205, 211, 219, 251, 320, 323, 351, 356
www.bumrungraddeath.com website, 196, 351

Z

Zeldox, 46–47, 187–89, 191

[Created with TExtract / www.Texyz.com]

www.ingramcontent.com/pod-product-compliance
Lightning Source LLC
Chambersburg PA
CBHW062151270326
41930CB00009B/1496